Lecture Notes in Computer Science 7686

Commenced Publication in 1973
Founding and Former Series Editors:
Gerhard Goos, Juris Hartmanis, and Jan van Leeuwen

Rainer Keller   David Kramer
Jan-Philipp Weiss (Eds.)

Facing the Multicore-Challenge III

Aspects of New Paradigms and Technologies
in Parallel Computing

 Springer

Volume Editors

Rainer Keller
University of Applied Science
Faculty for Surveying, Computer Science and Mathematics
Schellingstraße 24, 70174 Stuttgart, Germany
E-mail: rainer.keller@hft-stuttgart.de

David Kramer
Karlsruhe Institute of Technology (KIT)
Institute of Computer Science and Engineering
Haid-und-Neu-Straße 7, 76131 Karlsruhe, Germany
E-mail: kramer@kit.edu

Jan-Philipp Weiss
Karlsruhe Institute of Technology (KIT)
Institute for Applied and Numerical Mathematics 4
Fritz-Erler-Straße 23, 76133 Karlsruhe, Germany
E-mail: jan-philipp.weiss@kit.edu

ISSN 0302-9743 ISSN 1611-3349
ISBN 978-3-642-35892-0 ISBN 978-3-642-35893-7 (eBook)
DOI 10.1007/978-3-642-35893-7
Springer Heidelberg Dordrecht London New York

Library of Congress Control Number: 2010935359

CR Subject Classification (1998): C.1.4, C.1.3, C.4, D.1.3, D.3.4, I.3.1, B.2.1, B.2.4,
B.3.2, D.4.2, D.4.8, F.2.2

LNCS Sublibrary: SL 1 – Theoretical Computer Science and General Issues

Typesetting: Camera-ready by author, data conversion by Scientific Publishing Services, Chennai, India

Printed on acid-free paper

Springer is part of Springer Science+Business Media (www.springer.com)

Preface

Welcome to the proceedings of the third conference "Facing the Multicore-Challenge," which was held in Stuttgart, Germany, during September 19–21, 2012. Recent hardware developments have again presented the Multicore-Challenge to software developers: this applies to the development of software with regard to scientific computing, system-level software, as well as compilers. The introduction of highly parallel architectures based on commodity processors, such as the Intel Xeon® Phi™, or the highly threaded Kepler GPGPUs by NVIDIA, requires programmers even more to identify sections of code amenable to parallelization on various levels, identify load imbalance, reorder inefficient data structure accesses, and finally analyze and optimize data transfers.

By "Facing the Multicore-Challenge" we initiated a series of conferences that allow young scientists to present high-quality, relevant, and up-to-date research on scalable applications, middleware, and compilers on these architectures. These proceedings, together with the previous two, attest to the importance of this series' approach. The first conference was organized in 2010 at the Heidelberg Academy of Science, the second conference in the following year was held at the Karlsruhe Institute of Technology (KIT). This year's conference was held at the Hochschule für Technik Stuttgart, University of Applied Science, in the city center of Stuttgart, Germany.

In all we received 21 full papers out of which ten were selected by the Program Committee – each paper was reviewed by at least three independent experts with a short rebuttal period to balance differing opinions. Apart from the full-paper presentations, the conference featured a poster session with 12 selected contributions. Another feature of the conference is a set of short talks showing the latest results that are not yet ready for publication but allow the speakers to present their first data, to receive feedback, and to discuss novel ideas. In a similar vein, the conference features invited talks: this year they comprised a keynote on the technology obstacles to be tackled for the exascale with reality checks, a talk presenting the status of MPI-3, one presentation on the Extoll network interconnect, and last but not least a talk on the exascale preparations at sandia national labs. To dig into detail to overcome roadblocks to scalability, we hosted three tutorials: the first was provided by Cray on large-scale computing, another tutorial from Roguewave focused on single-node performance using Threadspotter, and the last tutorial by Intel introduced the programming for Intel Xeon® Phi™.

Thanks to the German Gauß-Allianz for Supercomputing, the conference was able to offer best paper, best poster, and best presentation awards. The best paper awards were selected by the Program Committee; the best paper in the application category was awarded to the group of authors represented by Christoph Altmann, Institute of Aerodynamics and Gas Dynamics of the

University of Stuttgart, with their paper "An Efficient High-Performance Parallelization of a Discontinuous Galerkin Spectral Element Method." The best paper with regard to theory was awarded to Marek Pałkowski from the West Pomeranian University of Technology for his paper "Impact of Variable Privatization on Extracting Synchronization-Free Slices." The best poster and best talk awards were selected by the 55 participants. Both awards were granted to participants from the Technical University of Denmark. The best poster award went to Peter E. Aackermann, Peter J. Dinesen Pedersen, and co-authors for their contribution "Development of a GPU-Accelerated MIKE 21 Solver for Water Wave Dynamics," while the best presentation was awarded to Allan S. Nielsen for his presentation "The Parareal Algorithm for Multi-layered Parallelism."

The conference organizers and editors would like to thank the paper and poster authors for submitting their novel material, making this event an interesting conference. We would especially like to thank all the members of the Program Committee for their experience, guidance, and great effort in the review process, not only for selecting the material, but also for providing authors with valuable feedback on improvements and comments for future work. In the name of all participants and invited speakers, we would especially like to thank the Gauß-Allianz for Supercomputing in Germany for sponsorship, which allowed the conference to provide awards and travel grants.

September 2012

Rainer Keller
David Kramer
Jan-Philipp Weiss

Organization

General Chair

Rainer Keller   University of Applied Sciences Stuttgart,
                             Germany
David Kramer   Karlsruhe Institute of Technology, Germany
Jan-Philipp Weiss   Karlsruhe Institute of Technology, Germany

Program Committee

Michael Bader   University of Stuttgart, Germany
Richard Barrett   Oak Ridge National Labs, Oak Ridge, USA
Carlo Bertolli   Imperial College London, UK
Christian Bischof   RWTH Aachen, Germany
Arndt Bode   TU Munich, Germany
George Bosilca   University of Tennessee Knoxville, USA
Rainer Buchty   TU Braunschweig, Germany
Mark Bull   EPCC, Edinburgh, UK
Hans-Joachim Bungartz   TU Munich, Germany
Franck Capello   LRI, Université Paris Sud, France
Jack Dongarra   University of Tennessee, USA
David Ediger   Georgia Tech, USA
Claudia Fohry   Kassel University, Germany
Dominik Göddeke   TU Dortmund, Germany
Georg Hager   University of Erlangen-Nuremberg, Germany
Thomas Herault   Université Paris Sud, France
Hans J. Herrmann   ETH, Zürich, Switzerland
Peter Heusch   HfT Stuttgart, Germany
Vincent Heuveline   Karlsruhe Institute of Technology, Germany
Lee Howes   AMD, UK
Wolfgang Karl   Karlsruhe Institute of Technology, Germany
David Kramer   Karlsruhe Institute of Technology, Germany
Rainer Keller   HfT Stuttgart, Germany
Michael Klemm   Intel, Germany
Hiroaki Kobayashi   Tohoku University, Japan
Dimitar Lukarski   Uppsala University, Sweden
Norihiro Nakajima   JAEA and CCSE, Tokyo, Japan
Dieter an Mey   RWTH Aachen, Germany
Claus-Dieter Munz   Stuttgart University, Germany
Fabian Oboril   Karlsruhe Institute of Technology, Germany
Christian Perez   INRIA, France

Table of Contents

Full Papers

Poster Abstracts

Invasive Computing on High Performance Shared Memory Systems

Michael Bader, Hans-Joachim Bungartz, and Martin Schreiber

Department of Informatics,
Boltzmannstrasse 3, 85748 Garching, Germany
{bader,bungartz,martin.schreiber}@in.tum.de
http://www5.in.tum.de/

Abstract. In this work, we tackle several important issues to improve the throughput of runtime-adaptive applications on state-of-the-art HPC systems. A first issue is the, in general, missing information about the actual impact of unforeseeable workload by adaptivity and of the unknown number of time steps or iterations on the runtime of adaptive applications. Another issue is that resource scheduling on HPC systems is currently done before an application is started and remains unchanged afterwards, even in case of varying requirements. Furthermore, an application cannot be started after another running application allocated all resources. We combine addressing these issues with the design of algorithms that adapt their use of resources during runtime, by releasing or requesting compute cores, for example. If concurrent applications compete for resources, this requires the implementation of an appropriate resource management.

We show a solution for these issues by using *invasive paradigms* to start applications and schedule resources during runtime. The scheduling of the distribution of cores to the applications is achieved by a global resource manager. We introduce scalability graphs to improve load balancing of multiple applications. For adaptive simulations, several scalability graphs exist to consider different phases of scalability due to changing workload.

For a proof-of-concept, we show runtime/throughput results for a fully adaptive shallow-water simulation.

Keywords: Invasive computing, resource awareness, shared-memory, runtime adaptive applications, OpenMP, TBB.

1 Introduction

The current trend to many-core systems was forced to still fulfill Moore's Law for performance and energy efficiency reasons [1]. The parallel efficiency of applications on such many-core systems is usually represented by the scalability of a parallel application [2]. To overcome scalability problems of applications (e. g. due to a small workload), the execution of multiple programs in parallel is one of the main approaches in HPC (among others [3,4]). So far, those scheduling

R. Keller et al. (Eds.): Facing the Multicore-Challenge III 2012, LNCS 7686, pp. 1–12, 2013.
© Springer-Verlag Berlin Heidelberg 2013

algorithms in HPC assume knowledge about fixed resources to run computations and well-known or well-estimated run-time.

1.1   Our Approach for Dynamically Changing Applications

In this work we show a solution for the above mentioned issues, focussing on shared-memory platforms. We build on the already existing functionality of *OpenMP* (driven by the OpenMP Architecture Review Board), where parallelization is obtained via pragma compiler directives, and *Intel TBB*, which provides thread-and task-features offered via C++ language features such as class derivation and is directly developed by Intel [5] with an open-source version. Related approaches, for example, would be *OmpSs*, an extension of OpenMP providing input and output dependencies among tasks [6].

The following issues are so far not considered in the threading libraries mentioned above:

- An application should not be started when *all resources are used by other applications*. Otherwise the simulation run-time immediately gets worse since the caches are shared among both running applications [7]. This also plays a crucial role for urgent computing (see e. g. [8]): starting an application – probably with a higher priority – while another is already running.
- Highly dynamic algorithms have *several phases of scalability* which cannot be considered in a-priori resource allocation. When running multiple applications in parallel, those phases are also not considered so far. E. g. an algorithm using parallel adaptive mesh refinements during run-time leads to a varying workload over simulation time and, thus, to changing scalability behavior. An example for a changing workload for a shallow-water simulation is given in Figure 3. Also multi-grid algorithms have a strongly varying difference in workload during run-time. This workload decreases due to restriction- and increases due to propagation-operations.
- Applications should be able *to extend or shrink their currently* allocated cores in a way that the throughput is maximized considering all concurrently running applications: this would lead to an improvement of overall throughput e. g. by giving applications more cores when they have better scalability. By taking cores away from an application, this allows starting an application even when all cores are already assigned to other applications.

These problems and the introduced flexibility of applications leads to a dynamically changing efficiency value for the resource-utilization. This requires a global scheduling which overthrows previous decisions to replace them with improved ones. In this work we show our approach using *invasive paradigms* (Sec. 2) to schedule applications using a resource manager (Sec. 3) with changing number of resources for applications during run-time and without any estimation of the overall run-time of the application. Our test applications have to provide scalability graphs which represent a local view of the application only for determining global optimum throughput (Sec. 3.3). A fully adaptive shallow-water simulation (Sec. 4) is used to show results (Sec. 5) for applying the invasive paradigms.

2   Invasive Paradigms

Resource-aware programming using invasive paradigm was originally developed for embedded systems [9] with a distributed memory (DM) architecture using the following constructs:

- *invade(constraints)*: request resources that satisfy certain constraints (e. g. min/max number of cores which are requested by the application).
- *infect(iLet)*: execute *iLet*-code (kernel-code for the invasive commands) on previously invaded resources.
- *retreat()*: release reserved resources (allocated by invade).

In this work we use a subset of this paradigm to tackle the previously mentioned problems on shared-memory settings and extend this paradigm with appropriate functionality and enhancements for the HPC area. Considering that the *iLet*-code is implicitly given by the application code that follows after the invade and infect API calls, *invade()* and *infect()* are represented by an *invade()*. Changing the number of used resources is then implicitly done during execution of *invade()*. However we like to emphasize that the *infect()* is expected to be necessary for an extension of this work e. g. to a distributed memory system to start the execution of a specific piece of code on another node.

In this work we implemented the following extensions for efficiency reasons:

- *invade-nonblocking(constraints)*: non-blocking version of invade to overcome message latency overhead to/from the resource manager.
- *reinvade()*: A reinvade executes a retreat and an invade atomically. No constraints are used by this invade to avoid packing and forwarding of constraints into a message in order to send it to the resource manager. This is done by assuming that the same constraints are already stored in the resource manager by a previously executed *invade(...)*.
- *reinvade-nonblocking()*: Nonblocking version of *reinvade()* to overcome message latency overhead.
- *constraints*: We distinguish between hard- (e. g. max/min number of cores) and soft-constraints (e. g. scalability graph provided for each phase of the application, see Sec. 3.3 for the utilization of this graphs).

3   Implementation of a Resource Manager

Our assumption is that multiple clients (applications) are running on the same shared memory (SM) architecture leading to two aspects which have to be considered: (1) Two clients sharing one core typically results into a severe slowdown due to L1 cache-sharing by context switches; (2) those clients compete for core resources. Therefore a resource manager (RM) and a collision-free protocol have to be determined which never allow two non-idling clients to be scheduled by the OS to run on the same core. Resources are further considered to be cores of equal computational performance.

In contrast to resource managers for distributed memory systems (e. g. [10]), our approach is based on shared-memory systems only. Therefore we can use IPC *System V message queues* for the communication of a client with the RM. This involves a successive message handling in the RM which implicitly avoids any race-conditions. Due to the non-blocking extensions (see Sec. 2), we distinguish between two different kinds of communications: The first communication mechanism are *blocking calls* which are *waiting for an ACK* from the communication partner. The second is a *non-blocking* communication *without an explicit wait* for an ACK from the RM. Messages from the RM are therefore handled by testing at specific points in the application whether there is a message available in the queue or not, including an appropriate handling of the message.

3.1   Data Structures for Managing Clients in the RM

The following data structures are used for each client in the RM: *Constraints* (min/max number of cores, scalability graphs) are stored in the RM for each client to allow determination of a global best-throughput which can be achieved only with constraint information of all other clients. Therefore storing these constraints in the RM is a crucial point. A list of *reserved cores* is also necessary to improve releasing cores and assigning them to other clients.

The RM utilizes the following data-structures to manage and re-schedule the available cores: A vector $V(i)$ stores the number of cores which have to be assigned to each client i to get the global maximum throughput. Vector $C(n)$ with an entry for the client i associated to the core n is used to search for free cores. Note that this search operation has linear runtime which can be improved by using a list of free cores. However, for the number of cores we use in our results, we do not expect a huge impact on the overall runtime for the search operation.

3.2   Invasive Command Space

The following paragraphs describe the utilized invasive command space and the implementation in more detail.

Setup (blocking): Client: Each client initially registers itself at the RM to get at least one core for the serial program execution. *Server*: If at lease one core is free, an ACK is send to the client. Otherwise the client is blocked until at least one core is available. Once a client releases some resources, *delayed ACKs* are sent to clients with each client setting an affinity for its process.

Invade (blocking): Client: The client sends an invade message including the constraints to the RM to release or invade resources. *Server*: The RM updates the client data structures and runs the search for the global maximum throughput (see Sec. 3.3) which is stored in V. If the client is executing an *invade(...)* that has to *release* some resources, an appropriate number of cores are released from the list with currently assigned cores by updating the core allocation vector C. These cores are idling until another client for which the resources were freed executes an invade or sends an ACK for a non-blocking update message which releases cores. If the client has to *invade* some resources, free cores are searched by iterating over the global core allocation array C and by setting appropriate reservation information. Finally an ACK message with the new number of cores and the corresponding affinity settings are sent back to the client.

Reinvade (blocking): Client: A reinvade is similar to the *invade(...)*, but without sending constraint information to overcome the message-packaging overhead of the parameters since the constraints are already stored in the RM. A reinvade as well as an invade can also lead to a loss of cores.

Non-blocking protocol: Using a non-blocking protocol, the RM sends asynchronous messages to clients in order to update the currently used number of cores and affinities. An important aspect is a collision-free protocol which is necessary to avoid resource conflicts. E. g. for cores, this would lead to sharing the L1 cache and thus a severe slowdown of both applications sharing the same core.

invade_nonblocking(...) and *reinvade_nonblocking()* are equal to the blocking versions except two differences: First, there is no wait for the ACK send from the RM to the client. Thus the clients can immediately continue their computations. Second, a non-blocking receive-message call is used which handles the asynchronously sent messages. In case of a resource update request sent from the RM, the new number of cores and the new thread affinities are set, and updated information about the recently assigned cores is sent back to the RM.

The *restriction* of the RM of sending only one asynchronous message to the client for the *non-blocking* communication described above is motivated by the following example situation of a resource conflict: Assume that the current core assignment of a client is $(2, 3)$ and the RM sends the following successive messages to the client: $m_1 = (2, 3, 4)$ (add core #4), $m_2 = (2, 3, 4, 5)$ (add core #5). After sending the last message, also core 5 is assigned to the client. Since the client has to send back its currently reserved cores, the message $(2, 3, 4)$ is send to the RM which updates the client assigned cores to $(2, 3, 4)$. Right now the RM is allowed to reschedule core #5 to another client with the message m_2 still not handled and allowing the client to take core #5. This would lead to one core being assigned to two different applications which leads to a severe slowdown of the computations due to cache sharing. Results regarding reduced overhead for this non-blocking protocol are given in Sec. 5.

Setting Client-Side Thread Affinities: Once specific cores were assigned to a client, the maximum number of utilized cores and their affinities are set according to the different threading which is used. For OpenMP, the number of threads has to be set outside a parallel region (see [11]). The thread-affinities are then set via a *parallel-for* with *static(1)* scheduling and the affinities set in the parallel-for scope. This parallel-for is only executed for setting the thread affinities, not for the computations itself. Using TBB, the number of threads is modified by reallocating the task scheduler with the appropriate number of threads. Then, tasks are executed with appropriate thread-affinities which set the core-affinities of the thread inside each task. Work-stealing is avoided by using a semaphore-like mechanism prohibiting task to be finished until all tasks set the affinities.

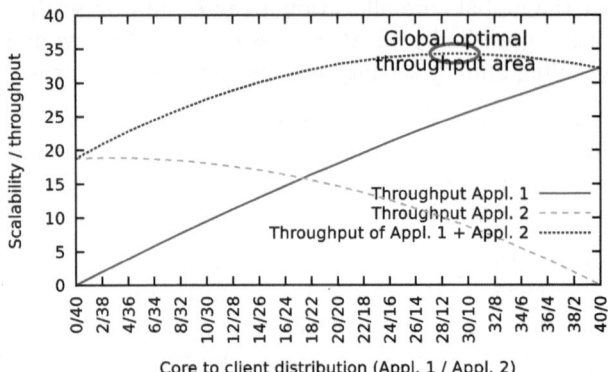

Fig. 1. Graphs representing the scalability behavior of two different applications on a 40-core workstation. The scalability graph for the 2nd application is drawn mirrored starting from the right side with no core assigned (dashes plot).

3.3 Scheduling to Maximize Global Throughput

By considering only the minimum and maximum number of requested cores, an a-priori decision which computes the global maximum throughput is not feasible for adaptive applications. Therefore clients have to promise more information about their efficiency.

Providing scalability graphs: With clients providing scalability graphs, the main idea is to give clients more cores when they provide a better scalability. These graphs also represent the normalized throughput with the global throughput to be maximized with the side-constraints of several concurrently running clients. An example of two applications with a scalability graph for each application is given in Fig. 1. These scalability graphs represent a normalized throughput value and have to be forwarded to the RM by the applications. Then, the RM is responsible for scheduling resources in a way to optimize the global overall throughput. This global overall throughput depends on the core-to-application assignment with the overall throughput determined by the sum of the samples of the scalability graphs with the number of cores assigned to an application representing the sampling point.

Greedy algorithm: In order to optimize the throughput of multiple applications with respect to their scalability behavior, decisions need to consider more information than only the number of running applications. We use a greedy search algorithm to compute the global optimum for arbitrary number of applications based on scalability graphs provided by the application as a soft-constraint.

Let N be the number of available cores and A the number of clients running in parallel. Each client i has to provide a scalability graph f_i which is strictly monotonously increasing ($f_i'(x_i) > 0$) and strictly concave ($f_i''(x_i) < 0$). Thus no super-linear speedups (see e.g. [12]) are considered, which allows an efficient search for the maximum overall throughput. The overall throughput $F(\boldsymbol{x}) = \sum_i f_i(x_i)$ assigns x_i cores to each client. Applications have to provide

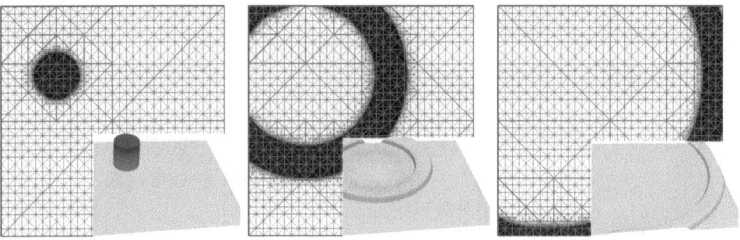

Fig. 2. Radial breaking-dam simulation scenario with initial depth of 6 and maximum refinement depth of 12. Sub-partitions are split when the number of grid-cells exceeds 512. Top images: Fine grid-cells in black and sub-partitions in red.

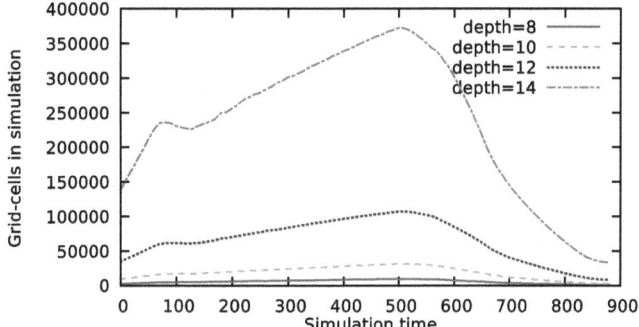

Fig. 3. Changing workload for the simulation

fixed scalability graphs in case their graph does not fit these requirements. Another greedy search algorithm presented in [10] also uses parametrized scalability graphs which are inherently monotonic.

Searching for the maximum overall throughput $F_{max}(\boldsymbol{x})$ leads to a multivariate concave optimization problem with the side-constraint $F_{max}(\boldsymbol{x}) = \sum_i x_i \leq N$. Due to the monotonicity, and since there are no local extrema, a steepest descend method [13] can be used to solve the problem. Our greedy algorithm searches locally in orthogonal directions (one for each client) for the largest throughput gain, testing for one step in each client-core-increasing direction. Since one step in this search space represents adding one core, the number of iterations is limited to the number of cores with a direction search over all applications, resulting in a runtime of $O(\#cores \times \#apps)$ for the greedy algorithm.

4   Application

To use the invasive interface presented in the previous section, the applications have to provide the necessary information to the RM and have to be able to adapt their resources. By providing hard and soft constraints, the RM then optimizes the number of cores assigned to each application successively.

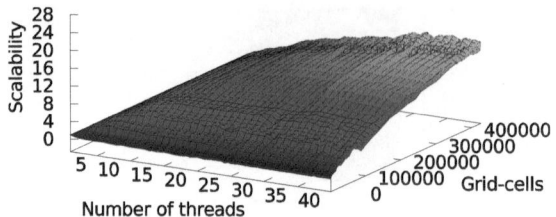

Fig. 4. Scalability graph for different phases of simulation

To give a proof-of-concept we implemented a fully adaptive simulation [14] (`http://www5.in.tum.de/sierpi/`) based on the shallow-water equations. Fig. 2 gives a screenshot of a running adaptive simulation with changing workload.

In this simulation, grid-cells are represented by triangles with the cell-data being stored on an inherently cache-optimized data-structure (see [15,16]). For the implementation used in this work, a refinement of triangle cells is done when the water surface exceeds a specific level; cells are coarsened when the water height is below a specific limit. Parallelization is achieved by using a massive splitting approach that creates a large number of clusters (see red triangles in Fig. 2). Computations on such clusters can then be executed in parallel using typical task constructs provided by TBB or OpenMP.

During such a fully-adaptive simulation the workload changes substantially during simulation. The number of triangle cells over the simulation is plotted in Fig. 3 which directly represents the workload for each time-step. While the scalability typically approaches asymptotically the linear speedup, we consider smaller problem sizes to have scalability patterns expected to be closer to applications executed on larger HPC systems.

Since the workload is changing, also the scalability changes during the simulation, as shown in Fig. 4 for a smaller workload. As a demand on the application to use the invasive scalability soft-constraint, the application forwards those new scalability information using *invade()* or *invade-nonblocking()* to the RM once a new 'phase' in the simulation is reached – e. g. for a sufficient change of workload. Otherwise a *reinvade()* is executed to optimize the currently assigned resources. These commands are executed between each time-step which fulfills the requirements of being out of a parallel region scope (see Sec. 3.2).

5   Results

Non-blocking Invasions: A two-socket workstation with Intel Xeon CPUs (X5690, 3.47GHz, 6 cores per socket) was used for this benchmark. To determine the overhead for using invasive commands, a shallow-water simulation with a very small problem size was started using different threading libraries. With the small problem size, only 1814 time-steps were executed for the overall simulation with invasive calls executed between each time-step. The runtime of the simulation is given in Fig. 5. Compared to the non-invasive OMP and TBB

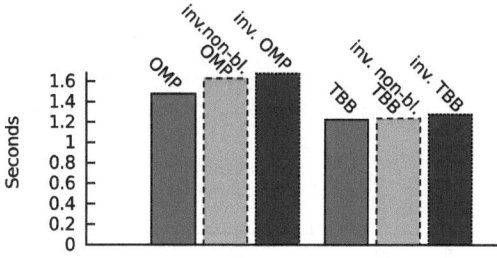

Fig. 5. Overhead of blocking and non-blocking invades compared by OpenMP and TBB implementations without invasive overhead. Results are averaged over 10 simulation runs. The maximum deviation from the mean value is below 0.01 for each single simulation run.

implementations and running only one application utilizing the RM, communication time is saved by using non-blocking communication. Many applications accessing the RM concurrently would automatically lead to some idling of applications when another message is currently handled by the RM. Also the greedy search algorithm takes linearly more computation time depending on the number of applications.

Multiple Simulations in Parallel with Uniform Assignment of Cores to Applications: Next, we show results for starting multiple identical simulations in parallel without changing any scalability graphs. This benchmark and the following were executed on a workstation with 4 Intel Xeon CPUs (E7-4850@2.00GHz, 10 cores per CPU / 20 threads per CPUs). Identical scalability graphs are forwarded to the RM leading to an equal distribution of the cores among all applications. E. g. executing 5 applications would lead to an assignment of 8 cores per application. The invasive paradigms are used in a blocking way with a non-changing scalability graph being handed over to the RM in each simulation time-step. The results are given in Fig. 6 (number of applications started in parallel vs. triangle-cell throughput of all simulations executed in parallel). A saturation of the maximum achievable throughput is reached when executing about 6 applications in parallel.

We like to emphasize, that this uniform benchmark-setting can also be efficiently executed using traditional OMP/TBB mechanism by setting appropriate affinities: starting the simulations with appropriate affinities and without any invasive paradigms results in a slightly reduced execution time due to the invasive overhead shown in Sec. 5.

Invasive Allocation of Cores to Applications: The next benchmark consists of four applications with the same scenario-setups and thus equal problem sizes which are started with a small delay of a few seconds. Fig. 7 shows the corresponding core distribution of this setting. Scalability graphs were handed over to the RM with respect to the different phases of the simulation. The scalability was limited to the maximum scalability of a core plus some additional overhead to account for measurement inaccuracy during determination of the scalability

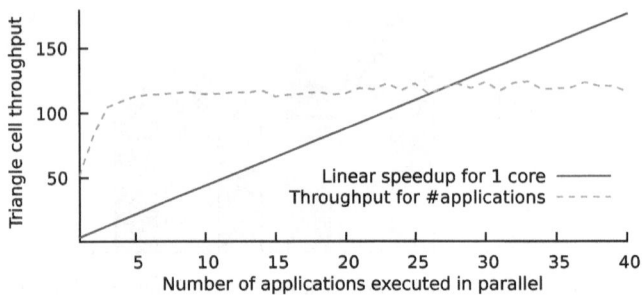

Fig. 6. The green dashed line shows the overall triangle cell throughput for the shallow-water simulation depending on the number of applications executed in parallel. The red line shows the linear speedup which is the extrapolated throughput based on running one application on only one core.

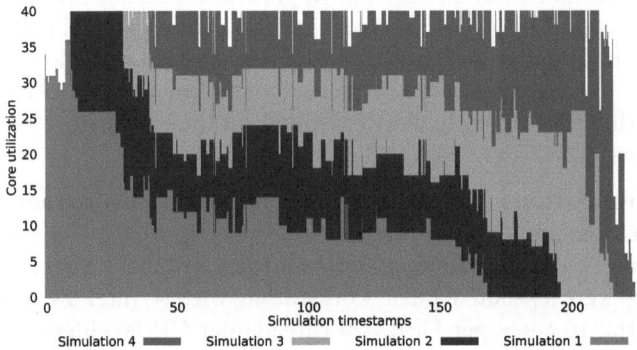

Fig. 7. Scheduling of 4 applications which are started with a short delay using non-blocking invasive commands

graphs. During the starting phase of the first application, many cores are idling since there is no scalability gain by using cores. Thus fewer cores are assigned to the first application even when no other applications are running. During execution of the second application, less cores are initially assigned to the 2nd application compared to the 1st application since the problem size is smaller compared to the 1st application. Thus also the scalability is worse leading to an assignment of more cores to the 1st application. During the simulation time, some cores are idling (see Sec. 3.2). This occurs during the assignment of a core to another application by the RM or by releasing the core until other application executes a invade or reinvade.

This solved our two main issues (see Sec. 1): We are now able to start applications at any time even when all other applications are currently using all cores. Furthermore, we also avoid considering the overall run-time of applications by immediately starting an application and distributing the resources using the scalability graphs.

6   Related Work

A conceptual presentation of invasive paradigms in HPC was presented in [17]. Requesting only a range of number of cores for each application was proposed to optimize the local applications view. Since a local view is insufficient when executing several applications in parallel, we introduced the scalability graphs to run a global optimization. Also scheduling algorithms for applications with dynamically changing scalability on distributed systems have been considered in [10]. Compared to these approaches, we are using a centralized resource manager, non-blocking communication and provide scalability graphs which accounts for the current simulation phase of a dynamically changing application. Handling load imbalances and data mis-placement on software distributed shared memory systems for a single application by loop-repartitioning and page migration is presented in [18]. Overcoming workload imbalance in an MPI+OpenMP parallelized program is also presented in [19]. Synchronous communication barriers among MPI-nodes and scheduling of resources depending on the amount of imbalance was used to overcome these issue. In our work we focus on several applications executed in parallel assuming that the application itself is responsible for work-balancing and maximizing for global throughput among concurrently executed applications by using dynamically changed scalability graphs.

7   Conclusions, Outlook and Acknowledgement

In this work we demonstrated a proof-of-concept of using invasive paradigms in HPC. Scalability graphs are used to search for a global optimum of throughput. The responsibility of applications is to provide a resource awareness by means of providing scalability graphs and being able to handle the resources which are allocated for the application. Latency and thus idle time for many cores is reduced by non-blocking communication. Using invasive paradigms allows us to efficiently start applications even when other applications have already reserved all resources. To give an outlook of our ongoing work, invasive computing can be applied to urgent computing by giving applications with higher priorities more resources. Another improvement is expected by smoothing the frequently changing scalability hints. This could lead to a reduction of frequently changing resource distributions. For larger systems, the greedy algorithm to determine the global maximum throughput has to be replaced by an improved one – e. g. using some heuristics to search for the global optimum throughput. Energy efficiency is expected to be improved by immediately shutting down cores when they are not used (see Fig. 7). The determination of scalability graphs by using monitoring data or performance counters during runtime and further soft-constraints using auto-tuning features is also part of our ongoing research.

This work was supported by the German Research Foundation (DFG) as part of the Transreg. Collab. Res. Centre "Invasive Computing" (SFB/TR 89).

References

1. Borkar, S., Chien, A.A.: The future of microprocessors. Commun. ACM 54 (2011)
2. Kumar, V., Gupta, A.: Analysis of scalability of parallel algorithms and architectures: a survey. In: Proc. of the 5th Int. Conf. on Supercomp. (1991)
3. Isard, M., Prabhakaran, V., Currey, J., Wieder, U., Talwar, K., Goldberg, A.: Quincy: fair scheduling for distributed computing clusters. In: Proc. of the ACM SIGOPS 22nd Symp. on Operating System Principles (2009)
4. Armstrong, T., Zhang, Z., Katz, D., Wilde, M., Foster, I.: Scheduling many-task workloads on supercomputers: Dealing with trailing tasks. In: 2010 IEEE Workshop on Many-Task Computing on Grids and Supercomputers, MTAGS (2010)
5. Reinders, J.: Intel Threading Building Blocks: Outfitting C++ for Multi-Core Processor Parallelism. O'Reilly Media (2007)
6. Duran, A., Perez, J.M., Ayguadé, E., Badia, R.M., Labarta, J.: Extending the OpenMP Tasking Model to Allow Dependent Tasks. In: Eigenmann, R., de Supinski, B.R. (eds.) IWOMP 2008. LNCS, vol. 5004, pp. 111–122. Springer, Heidelberg (2008)
7. Kim, S., Chandra, D., Solihin, Y.: Fair cache sharing and partitioning in a chip multiprocessor architecture. In: Proc. of the 13th Int. Conf. on Par. Arch. and Compilation Techniques (2004)
8. Beckman, P., Nadella, S., Trebon, N., Beschastnikh, I.: SPRUCE: A System for Supporting Urgent High-Performance Computing. In: Gaffney, P.W., Pool, J.C.T. (eds.) Grid-Based Problem Solving Environments. IFIP, vol. 239, pp. 295–311. Springer, Boston (2007)
9. Teich, J., Henkel, J., Herkersdorf, A., Schmitt-Landsiedel, D., Schröder-Preikschat, W., Snelting, G.: Invasive computing: An overview. In: Multiprocessor System-on-Chip – Hardware Design and Tool Integration. Springer (2011)
10. Kobbe, S., Bauer, L., Lohmann, D., Schröder-Preikschat, W., Henkel, J.: Distrm: distr. rm for on-chip many-core systems. In: Proc. of the 7th IEEE/ACM/IFIP int. conf. on Hardware/Software Codesign and Syst. Synth. (2011)
11. OpenMP Arch. Review Board: OpenMP Appl. Progr. Interf. Version 3.0 (2008)
12. Alba, E.: Parallel evolutionary algorithms can achieve super-linear performance. Information Processing Letters 82(1) (2002)
13. Fletcher, R., Powell, M.J.D.: A rapidly convergent descent method for minimization. The Computer Journal 6(2), 163–168 (1963)
14. Schreiber, M., Bungartz, H.J., Bader, M.: Shared Memory Parallelization of Fully-Adaptive Simulations Using a Dynamic Tree-Split and -Join Approach. In: 19th Annual International Conference on High Performance Computing (2012)
15. Bader, M., Schraufstetter, S., Vigh, C., Behrens, J.: Memory Efficient Adaptive Mesh Generation and Implementation of Multigrid Algorithms Using Sierpinski Curves. Int. J. of Computat. Science and Engineering 4(1) (2008)
16. Bader, M., Böck, C., Schwaiger, J., Vigh, C.A.: Dynamically Adaptive Simulations with Minimal Memory Requirement - Solving the Shallow Water Equations Using Sierpinski Curves. SIAM Journal of Scientific Computing 32(1) (2010)
17. Bader, M., Bungartz, H.J., Gerndt, M., Hollmann, A., Weidendorfer, J.: Invasive programming as a concept for HPC. In: Proc. of the 10h IASTED Int. Conf. on Parallel and Distr. Comp. and Netw, PDCN (2011)
18. Sakae, Y., Sato, M., Matsuoka, S., Harada, H.: Preliminary Evaluation of Dynamic Load Balancing Using Loop Re-partitioning on Omni/SCASH. In: Proc. of the 3rd Int. Symp. on Cluster Computing and the Grid (2003)
19. Corbaln, J., Duran, A., Labarta, J.: Dynamic Load Balancing of MPI+OpenMP Applications. In: ICPP (2004)

A Similarity-Based Analysis Tool for Porting OpenMP Applications*

Wei Ding, Oscar Hernandez, and Barbara Chapman

Dept. of Computer Science, University of Houston
Oak Ridge National Laboratory
{wding3,chapman}@cs.uh.edu,
{oscar}@ornl.gov

Abstract. Exascale computers are expected to exhibit an unprecedented level of complexity, thereby posing significant challenges for porting applications to these new systems. One of the ways to support this transition is to create tools that allow their users to benefit from prior successful porting experiences. The key to such an approach is the manner in which we define source code similarity, and whether similar codes can be ported in the same way to a given system. In this paper, we propose a novel approach based on the notion of similarity that uses static and dynamic code features to check if two serial subroutines can be ported with the same OpenMP strategy. Our approach creates an annotated family distance tree based on the syntactic structure of subroutines, where subroutines that belong to the same syntactic family and share the similar code features have a greater potential to be optimized in the same way. We describe the design and implementation of a tool, based upon a compiler and performance tool, that is used to gather the data to build this porting planning tree. We then validate our approach by analyzing the similarity in subroutines of the serial version of the NAS benchmarks and comparing how they were ported in the OpenMP version of the suite.

1 Introduction

The High Performance Computing (HPC) community is heading toward the era of exascale computing. An exascale machine and the programming models deployed on the machine are expected to exhibit a hitherto unprecedented level of complexity. New tools will be needed to help the application scientist restructure programs in order to exploit these emerging architectures, improve the quality of their code and enhance its modularization to facilitate maintenance. As scientists port their application codes to new systems, they must restructure their applications to exploit the multi-cores available in each node. OpenMP [13], a de-facto standard for shared memory programming, is widely used due to its

---

* This work was funded by the ORAU/ORNL HPC grant and NSF grant CCF-0917285. This research used resources of the Leadership Computing Facility at Oak Ridge National Laboratory and NICS Nautilus supercomputer for the data analysis.

R. Keller et al. (Eds.): Facing the Multicore-Challenge III 2012, LNCS 7686, pp. 13–24, 2013.

simplicity, incremental parallelism, and wide availability. However this simplicity comes at a performance cost. For example, programmers need to take care of false sharing issues and apply aggressive data privatization to achieve good performance.

During the porting process of parallelizing serial codes with OpenMP, we observed that, in some applications, many of the porting strategies are highly repetitive, although not necessarily easily detected. For example, many similar computational kernels that need to be parallelized with OpenMP may appear in different parts of the application, where code is slightly modified to meet specific computational needs. Locating and porting these code regions is a time-consuming and error prone process that needs to be systematically addressed.

One way to improve the productivity and reduce the potential problems is to create tools that allow users to benefit from prior successful porting experiences that can be applied to multiple code regions in an application. In this paper, we explore different code characteristics similarities and make a lot of improvement based on a tool called KLONOS [6] that can better assist user to accurately port their applications by combining the notion of syntactic code similarity. An adaptation strategy that is successful for one code region could then also be applied to similar regions. We use this tool to demonstrate how the concept of similarity can be used to parallelize serial codes with OpenMP more easily and productively. With this goal in mind, we have developed a tool that is able to classify subroutines in similar families of codes that may follow the same optimization strategy. Our tool uses the concept of code syntactic distance and a k-means clustering approach to classify codes based on their static and dynamic features (such as parallelization and hardware counters profiling information). Our hypothesis is that we can classify the subroutines of an application with a family distance tree, where subroutines that share similar syntactic structure and program features will have a high likelihood to be ported in the same way. In this paper we focus specifically on finding similar codes that can be ported to the shared memory systems using OpenMP with the same strategy.

This paper is organized as follows: Section 2 helps further explain the motivation of our work. Section 3 summarizes the related work on similarity research and current practice for the software porting. Section 4 describes the functionality and design of the tool we build to detect similar fragments of code. The implementation, including the compiler infrastructure that it is based upon, is then introduced in section 5. Section 6 describes our evaluation of the KLONOS tool using the serial and OpenMP version of the NAS benchmarks. Finally, Section 7 briefly discusses our conclusions and future work.

2   A Motivating Example

A byproduct of the efforts to enhance and port applications, particularly as a result of incremental improvements, is an increasing likelihood of code similarity in an application. Developers may implement similar versions of an algorithm, redevelop parts of it, copy and paste code multiple times and adapt it for specific

```
y_solve_ : EZTTNBYEZZZ-----TGYZZZTJYMM-ZTTBGYEZZZTJY--------MZTTGGYEZZZTG
       ...||||||||||  |||||||| ||| |||||||||||| |        ||||||||||||...
x_solve_ : EZTTNBYEZZZYMZZZTGYZZZTGYMMSZTTBGYEZZZTGYZZZTBYDSMZTTGGYEZZZTJ
```

Length of alignment = 3003

Fig. 1. NAS BT OpenMP benchmark x_sove, y_sove sequences alignment

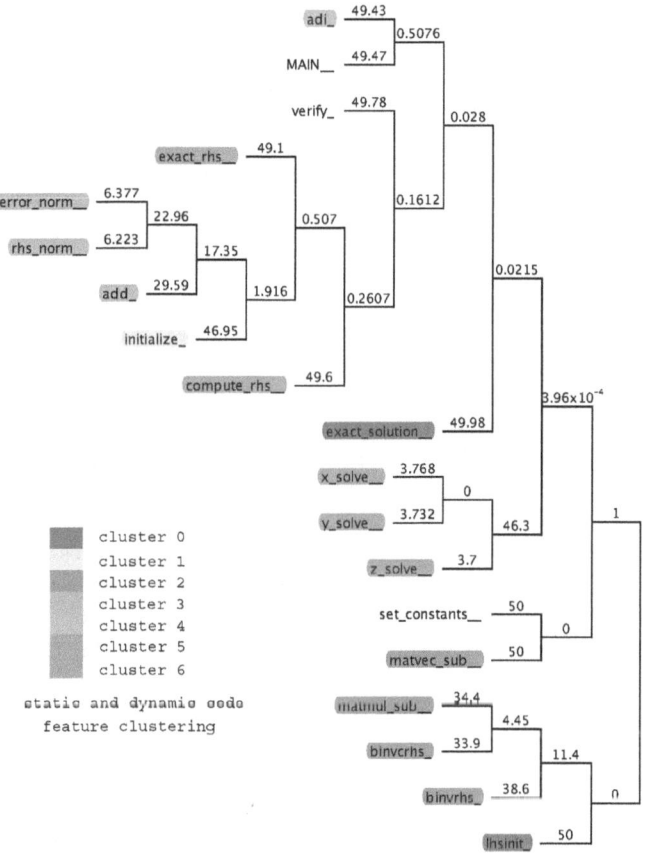

Fig. 2. NAS BT benchmark porting planning tree

needs, or use a code transformation tool that creates many instances of similar code. Therefore, there is a possibility that we may be able to reuse given porting strategies on similar codes and benefit from prior porting experiences. To illustrate our motivation, we use the BT serial NAS benchmark to demonstrate how our notion of similarity can be used to help the user parallelize this code with OpenMP. BT belongs to a family of CFD code that uses a multi-partiton scheme to solve three sets of uncouple systems of equations in a block triagonal of 5x5 blocks. The direction of the solvers are in the x, y and z dimensions over several disjoint sub-blocks of the grid. The solvers use the same algorithm along the different directions before the results are exchanged among the different blocks.

Because of this algorithmic property, BT is a good candidate to illustrate how our notion of similarity can help to analyze and parallelize this code.

One way to quantify the source code similarity is to convert the intermediate representations of subroutines of a program into sequences of characters that can be aligned using a global sequence alignment algorithm. The result can then be used to calculate their pair-wise syntactic distance based on their percent of identity. Figure 1 shows one portion of the pair-wise sequences alignment of subroutines x_solve and y_solve. The length of the alignment is of 3003 characters. The vertical lines indicate the portions of the sequences that are identical and the portions of the subroutines that have identical operators.

We can then use the Neighbor-Joining algorithm to create a family distance tree based on the pair-wise distance of the subroutines. Figure 2 shows the family distance tree for the BT serial benchmark. Each edge of the tree is annotated with a distance score, which represents the degree of their syntactic code differences. The distance between two subroutines can be calculated by adding the distance value of the edges between them.

By looking at the tree, we find that *x_solve, y_solve* and *z_solve* are siblings in the tree. *x_solve, y_solve* are grouped into one subtree, and their parent node is grouped with *z_solve* into another subtree. By calculating the distance among these three subroutines, we get *x_solve* $\sim$ *y_solve*=7.5, *x_solve* $\sim$ *z_solve*=7.468, *y_solve* $\sim$ *z_solve*=7.432. These subroutines have small distances among them because they have a high degree of similarity in their source code which is consistent with the algorithm of BT. Although the source code of the subroutines: *x_solve, y_solve* and *z_solver* look very similar, their data accesses are different. The subroutine *x_solve* has contiguous memory accesses but *y_solve* and *z_solve* have discontinuous memory accesses. This may impact the optimization strategy for these subroutines on a cache based system. For example, the OpenUH [14] compiler optimizes the serial version of *x_solve, y_solve* similarly (when inspecting their intermediate representations after optimizations) but uses a different strategy for *z_solve*.

Based on this information, if we want to parallelize these subroutines, using OpenMP, we cannot rely on the syntactic similarity analysis because other code features need to be taken into consideration (for example, the number of parallel loops in the subroutine, the values of hardware counters that characterize the data access and the amount of work done for each subroutine). We can define a set of program features (analyses) that are relevant to OpenMP optimizations and cluster the them to further classify the subroutines. For the BT Benchmark, we clustered its subrotuines based on the number of parallel loops, data cache accesses and misses, total number of cycles, TLB misses and total number of instructions. The subroutines were classified into seven clusters (the number of families in level three of the distance tree), using the K nearest neighbor (K-NN). The k-means method is favored when the number of data points is small. The result of the cluster is shown in Table 1. The dynamic code features were calculated by running the BT serial benchmark with class B on a hex-core Opteron 2435 processor. Each cluster consists of a set of subroutines

Table 1. Subroutine clusters for the serial BT benchmark based on the code features

Cluster 0	Cluster 1	Cluster 2	Cluster 3	Cluster 4	Cluster 5	Cluster 6
lhsinit	initialize	matvec_sub	add	adi	exact_rhs	z_solve
exact_solution		matmul_sub	error_norm		compute_rhs	
		binvcrhs	rhs_norm		x_solve	
		binvrhs			y_solve	

Table 2. Cluster center point for the serial BT benchmark based on the code features

Attributes	Cluster 0	Cluster 1	Cluster 2	Cluster 3	Cluster 4	Cluster 5	Cluster 6
DC accesses	0.0004	452.5	0.0007	84.058	0	1747.5666	1629.2438
DC misses	0.0004	25.5	0	10.2338	0.005	420.6692	858.1244
DTLB L1M L2M	0	0.5	0	0.6202	0	4.5561	37.9751
CPU clocks	0.0008	623.5	0.0012	194.0514	0.005	2718.1974	2913.2836
Ret branch	0.0001	113.5	0.0001	9.2769	0	210.1474	139.8806
Ret inst	0.0005	1227	0.0015	125.8657	0	3485.2936	3125.7264
# parallel loops	1.5	21	0	3.3333	0	22.5	15

with the closest Euclidean distance among their feature vectors. Table 2 shows the list of code features of each subroutine that is used for the clustering. It also shows the average values of the code features per cluster. In our experiment, we use the Instruction Based Sampling(IBS) events, since those events are the key factors which can summarize the memory access pattern (or internal application behavior) of each subroutine. Besides, those memory events have direct link with the optimization which contributes to the final performance. For the AMD Family 10h processors, although IBS is a statistical method, the sampling technique delivers precise event information and eliminates inaccuracies due to skid [2]. Using the clustering results we can annotate families of codes that share important code features for OpenMP optimizations. Figure 2 shows the resulting annotated serial BT benchmark porting planning tree we get based on the collected static and dynamic information of the syntactic similarity of the code and its features. The subroutines marked with the same color have a greater potential to be optimized similarly if they are syntactically close enough to each other in the same subtree with small syntactic distance. Our sampling performance tool was not able to collect hardware counter information for the subroutines *MAIN*, *verify* and *set_constants*, because their execution time was too short. We excluded these subroutines from further similarity analysis.

After collecting this information, the next step is porting planning. We notice that *x_solve*, *y_solve*, and *z_solve* fall into two different code features clusters although their syntactic distance is small, with *x_solve*, *y_solve* in the same code feature cluster. So we can predict that *x_solve* and *y_solve* can be optimized using the same OpenMP strategy, while *z_solve* might need a different one since it falls into cluster 6 based on the code feature clustering. This result suggests that the user should first attempt to parallelize *x_solve* with OpenMP, then based on this experience develop a porting strategy that can be applied to *y_solve*. For the

```
!$omp parallel default(shared)
!$omp& private(i,j,k,m,...,u_exact,rms_local)
!$omp&        shared(rms)
  do m = 1, 5
     rms_local(m) = 0.0d0
  enddo
!$omp do
  do k = 0,grid_points(3)-1
     zeta=dble(k)*dnzm1
     do j=0,grid_points(2)-1
        eta=dble(j)*dnym1
        do i=0,grid_points(1)-1
           xi=dble(i)*dnxm1
           call exact_solution(xi,...u_exact)

           do m = 1, 5
              add=u(m,i,j,k)-u_exact(m)
              rms_local(m)=rms_local(m)+add*add
           enddo
        enddo
     enddo
  enddo
!$omp end do nowait
  do m = 1, 5
!$omp atomic
     rms(m)=rms(m)+rms_local(m)
  enddo
!$omp end parallel
```

```
          . . .

!$omp parallel default(shared) private(i,...)
!$omp&           shared(rms)
  do m = 1, 5
     rms_local(m) = 0.0d0
  enddo
!$omp do
  do k=1,grid_points(3)-2
     do j=1,grid_points(2)-2
        do i=1,grid_points(1)-2
           do m=1,5
              add=rhs(m,i,j,k)
              rms_local(m)=rms_local(m)+add*add
           enddo
        enddo
     enddo
  enddo
!$omp end do nowait
  do m = 1, 5
!$omp atomic
     rms(m)=rms(m)+rms_local(m)
  enddo
!$omp end parallel
```

(a) error_norm

(b) rhs_norm

Fig. 3. subroutine rhs_norm and error_norm code snippet of the NAS BT benchmark

case of *z_solve*, a different porting strategy is needed. When we inspected the corresponding OpenMP version of these solvers, we noticed that the user inserted an OpenMP *do* directive at the same loop level of the main computation loop. The user also used the same privatization and data scoping strategy for the data. The user chose not to optimize the data access of *z_solve* and left this job to the compiler. This is perfectly captured by the planning scheme supplied by our tool. The user used the same parallelization strategy applies for the subroutines *error_norm* and *rhs_norm* that fall under the same syntactic distance family and the code feature clusters. Our tool predicted that these two subroutines may be parallelized by using a similar OpenMP strategy. Figure 3 shows a partial code listing of those two subroutines after being parallelized with OpenMP (from the OpenMP version of the benchmark). We observed that the programmer used exactly the same OpenMP strategy as suggested by our similarity tool.

Based on these findings, we believe that the experiences gained when porting a subroutine using OpenMP can be used for similar subroutines and benefit from previous optimizations/transformation strategies. This paper includes a new approach to define the code similarity based on syntactic structure of the codes and code features that are relevant for the OpenMP parallelization. If two codes are similar, there is a high probability that these codes can be ported with the same OpenMP strategy.

3 Related Work

Similarity analysis is one of the techniques that is used to identify the code regions that are similar in a given program. One early use was to identify students who copied code from others in a programming assignment; later some researchers applied this technique in the software engineering to detect the redundant code for the code maintenance. This technique proved very effective detecting code clones, especially for a large legacy application developed by a team of people over a long period, which makes the code maintenance very difficulty. Besides code maintenance, TSF [4] and other work [10] also developed a notion of similarity in order to detect related code regions for the purpose of applying transformations. Such analysis typically examined loop nests, their nesting depth and certain details of the data usage patterns they contained. There is no *precise* definition of similarity between programs [19], in part because the appropriateness of any given metric depends on the context in which it is being used [18]. In addition to syntactic approaches based upon the source text, graph-based approaches that use data flow and control flow information have been employed to detect sections of code that are similar. Duplix [11] is a tool that identified "similar" code regions in programs, the idea is based on finding subgraphs that are similar stemming from duplicated code in fine-grained program dependency graphs. In this work, identified subgraphs could be directly mapped back onto the program code and presented to the user. Walenstein et al. [19] considered *representational* similarity and *behaviorial* similarity. Roy et al. [16] proposed four categories of clones to differentiate the level of code clones. I [9] presented a scalable clone detection algorithm that helped in reducing a complex graph similarity problem to a simpler tree similarity problem.

Although some of these prior efforts have focused on helping to restructure applications by detecting code clones at the syntactic level, few have attempted to detect similar code regions that can potentially be optimized in the same way for a given architecture. Given a code portion that has benefited from a specific optimization strategy, our goal is to determine other parts of the code that exhibit, not just a certain level of syntactic similarity, but also similarity with respect to the code optimization characteristics. We ultimately need to develop effective porting strategies to automate the task of restructuring codes to exploit the capabilities of emerging architectures. We note that the cost of adapting these strategies to a new environment strategies should be less than the cost of re-development. The Milepost/Collective tuning project [8] proposed 56 metrics for each subroutine. It used probabilistic and transductive machine learning models to search for similar compiling flags from similar subroutines based on previous experience on which flags yield good performance. Their proposed method is able to predict the performance, and normally the suggested flags are good for contributing good performance. However, their approach does not consider syntactic similarity and code features that are relevant for a specific optimization or porting goal (i.e. OpenMP parallelization, etc.). In their automated framework, the user has little input on what optimizations, and the exact code transformations / optimizations that lead to good performance, other than compiler passes and flags, are not clear.

4   Design of Our System

In order to automate the application porting analysis, we designed a porting planning system. Figure 4 shows the overall design of "KLONOS", our system. We have adapted an existing compiler, OpenUH, to create a tool that is capable of detecting similar codes based on static and dynamic information. The user submits a code to the modified compiler for the code pattern extraction, then KLONOS extracts "sequence patterns" at a very high level just after the internal WHIRL tree structure has been generated by the compiler. The compiler then produces an executable which is run, and performance metrics are collected. The generated sequences are subsequently input to an alignment engine, which returns the a syntactic similarity score that is used to construct a family distance. Then the user extracts other code features such as the number of parallel loops in the subroutines and hardware counter information which is fed into the "code feature similarity matching engine" to cluster the subroutines based on these code features. As a last step, the system analyzes and processes the family distance tree together with the code feature clustering, and outputs an annotated distance tree that can be used to develop a porting plan to incrementally add OpenMP in an application. In the pattern extraction phase, we perform this operation by analyzing the code at this first level of representation, which is closely related to the source program form called the Abstract Syntax Tree (AST). The AST is then "lowered" into a representation that is language independent and may be used to optimize codes written in multiple languages. Once the extraction is completed, our sequence pattern representation is input to a sequence alignment program called EMBOSS [1] to calculate the similarity score which is used to evaluate the degree of syntactic similarity.

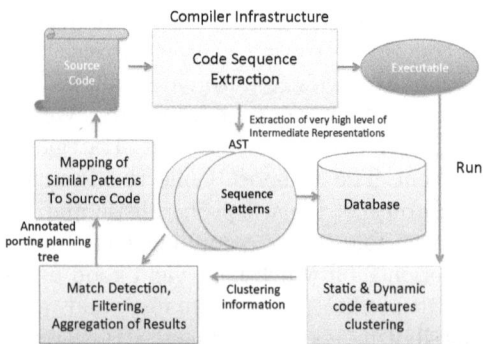

Fig. 4. The KLONOS Porting Planning System

In the design of our system we leverage the bioinformatic techniques for multiple sequence alignments. Compared with other approaches that generate program graphs for graph comparison, this gives us the freedom to compare large code without being constrained by graph size and graph complexity.

5   Implementation

Our implementation is based on OpenUH, an open source research compiler suite for C, C++ and Fortran 95, OpenMP 3.0 and the IA-64 Linux ABI and API standards. The compiler first translates different languages to a high level intermediate format (IR), called WHIRL [5]. For each subroutine, we summarize the intermediate representation (IR) into character sequences by traversing the IR in post-order. The characters in the sequences represent operators and operands based on a "node-map" described in [7].

Building the Distance Matrix: After extracting the sequences, we perform a pair-wise global alignment to compare the degree of syntactic similarity between the subroutines. For this, we used the Needleman-Wunsch algorithm [12] using the identity substitution matrix. A score is generated for each pair-wise alignment using the value for their percent of identity. A percent of identity of 100% means the sequences are identical. We used the pair-wise comparison similarity score for each pair of sequences to calculate a distance matrix by substracting the percent of identity with 1 and then times 100.

Constructing the Family Distance Tree: There are several algorithms [15,17,20] that can be used to classify sequences into distance trees. In our case, we used the Neighbor-joining [17] to build our syntactic distance tree for its simplicity and because it is distance matrix based. This algorithm aims to minimize the sum of all branch lengths. It starts by generating the distance matrix from the input of multiple sequence. Then, it contiguously selects two nodes which have the least distance, and replaces them with another new node until all nodes have been consumed.

Building the Optimization Planning Tree: According to the generated family distance tree, sequences with less distance have been clustered into groups. In other words, similar subroutines have been grouped together based on their syntactic similarity. The generated family distance tree can precisely give us the overall code structure relationship over the all subroutines. However relying solely on the syntactic code structure does not enable capture of the similar code optimization similarity. More metrics are needed to determine if two codes can be applied for a given optimization strategy (in our case OpenMP parallelization).

Since loop parallelization information and data accesses are important factors for codes with OpenMP, we extract this information from the compiler and gather hardware counter data when we execute the serial version of the code on the processor. As our experiments were conducted in a hex-core Opteron processor, so we gathered the following hardware counters using AMD CodeAnalyst: "DC accesses", "DC misses", "DTLB L1M L2M", "CPU clocks","Ret branch" and "Ret inst". Once we get those metrics, we use Weka [3] to help us cluster the subroutines based on these code features, using the K-means algorithm based on the calculation of the Euclidean distance for each pair of subroutine. After that, we append the Euclidean distance clustering back to the family syntactic distance tree, which serves as the optimization guidance. KLONOS predicts that if two subroutines fall in the same subtree which are also in the same performance cluster, then there is a high probability that those two subroutines should be optimized the same way.

Verification of Optimization Strategy: In order to further verify this hypothesis, we use a similar concept for extracting the code sequence. To generate the optimization distance, we first trace the functions in charge of the OpenMP transformation. We used an unique letter to denote each function called during the OpenMP translation phase. Those functions are responsible for translating a given OpenMP construct. So, the optimization process has been converted to a flattened sequence for a comparison. Similarly, we can derive the optimization distance from the OpenMP version of NAS based on the optimization similarity score as the steps described above. The generated optimization distance is then used to check if two codes were lowered and optimized in the same way.

6   Experiments

NAS Benchmark-3.3 has nine benchmarks. We focused on the BT, CG, FT, MG and SP, UA because they are written in Fortran. KLONOS is able to support codes C/C++ and Fortran, but we have only verified it with Fortran at this stage in our experiment. As described in Section 5, we first extract all the subroutine sequence patterns and collect the static and dynamic program features which include hardware counter information. We then use this information to build the annotated distance tree for optimization planning support.

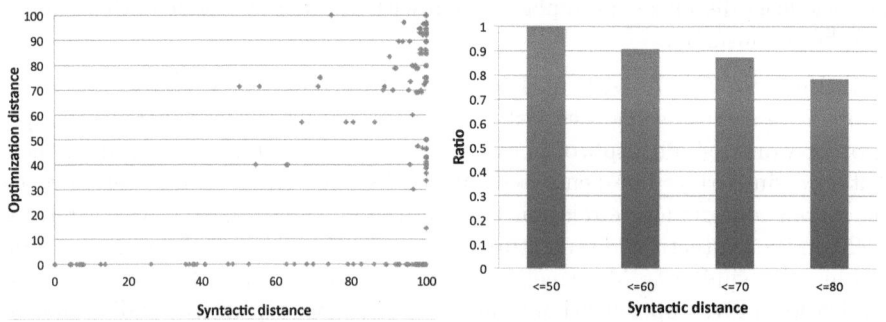

(a) Syntactic and optimization distance for a pair of subroutines

(b) Percentage diagram for the syntactic distance

Fig. 5. NAS Benchmark-3.3 Experimental result

In Section 2, we explained how we used the similarity technique to find the similar porting strategy which could can be applied to the similar subroutines inside the BT benchmark. Due to the space limitations, we are not able to the list all the family distance trees and code feature clusters for the rest of the five benchmarks. However, in Figure 5, all the pair-wise subroutines' comparison from the six benchmarks including the BT are shown. Each dot inside this diagram refers to a pair of subroutines with respect to their syntactic and optimization distance. The x axis is the syntactic distance which shows the syntatic distance between a pair of subroutines, and the y-axis is the optimization distance used to represent the optimization similarity of the comparison of two subroutines.

According to Figure 5(a), we observe that a syntactic distance of 50 is an appropriate threshold for the NAS benchmark. For the subroutine pairs with a syntactic distance less than 50, they are more likely to have an identical OpenMP optimization strategy. Figure 5(b) shows the percentage of subroutine pair with their optimization distance equals to zero when their syntactic distance are less than 50, 60, 70 and 80 respectively. When the subroutine pairs have syntactic distance less than 50 (or a percent of similarity score is greater than 50), we found that they all optimized in the same way with OpenMP. However only 90 percent of the subroutine pairs are optimized in the same way when their syntactic distance is less than 60. The optimization strategy starts to change when the syntactic distance goes beyond 50. And this trend continues, as the code structure further diverges, the optimization similarity keeps decreasing. This is generally true that different subroutines are optimized differently. Back to the generated family distance tree, we verified that all the subroutine pairs, which classified into the same syntactic and code feature clusters, used the same optimization strategy with OpenMP as long as their syntactic distance is less than 50. We also observe that for some cases they use the same optimization strategies although they diverges dramatically from each other.

7   Conclusions and Future Work

We have further expanded the notion of code similarity by exploring different dynamic code metrics for similarity in the context of accurately helping users port their codes to a multicore system using OpenMP. We use the concept of syntactic distance to check codes for the degree of similarity in their syntactic structure. We then extract static and dynamic program features to describe the parallelism and data accesses of the codes. Finally, we cluster the codes based on these code features, and annotate the family distance tree, where codes that belong to the same family and cluster can be ported in the same way with OpenMP. We validate our results with the NAS parallel benchmarks.

Future work will include exploring whether two similar codes maintain their syntactic similarity during critical compilation phases inside a compiler. If this new measure is utilized, we can guarantee that two similar codes can be optimized in the same way by the user or compiler on a target platform. We will also explore the use of code feature sets that are relevant to a given optimization goal (i.e. porting by using OpenMP or GPU directives.).

References

1. Emboss: The european molecular biology open software suite (2000)
2. Codeanalyst user's manual (2010)
3. Machine Learning Group at University of Waikato. Weka 3: Data mining software in java, http://www.cs.waikato.ac.nz/ml/weka/
4. Bodin, F., Mével, Y., Quiniou, R.: A user level program transformation tool. In: International Conference on Supercomputing (July 1998)
5. Open64 Compiler. Open64 compileri, whirl intermediate representation, http://www.mcs.anl.gov/OpenAD/open64A.pdf
6. Ding, W., Hsu, C.-H., Hernandez, O., Chapman, B., Graham, R.: Klonos: Similarity-based planning tool support for porting scientific applications. Concurrency and Computation: Practice and Experience (2012)
7. Ding, W., Hsu, C.-H., Hernandez, O., Graham, R., Chapman, B.M.: Bioinspired similarity-based planning support for the porting of scientific applications. In: 4th Workshop on Parallel Architectures and Bioinspired Algorithms, Galveston Island, Texas, USA (2011)
8. Fursin, G., Temam, O.: Collective optimization: A practical collaborative approach. ACM Transactions on Architecture and Code Optimization
9. Gabel, M., Jiang, L., Su, Z.: Scalable detection of semantic clones. In: Proceedings of the 30th International Conference on Software Engineering, pp. 321–330. ACM (2008)
10. Kessler, C.: Parallelize automatically by pattern matching (2000)
11. Krinke, J.: Identifying similar code with program dependence graphs. In: WCRE, p. 301. IEEE Computer Society (2001)
12. Needleman, S.B., Wunsch, C.D.: A general method applicable to the search for similarities in the amino acid sequence of two proteins. Journal of Molecular Biology 48(3), 443–453 (1970)
13. OpenMP: Simple, portable, scalable SMP programming (2006), http://www.openmp.org
14. The OpenUH compiler project (2005), http://www.cs.uh.edu/~openuh
15. Sokal, R., Michener, C.: A statistical method for evaluating systematic relationships. University of Kansas Science Bulletin 38, 1409–1438 (1958)
16. Roy, C.K., Cordy, J.R.: An empirical study of function clones in open source software. In: Proceedings of the 2008 15th Working Conference on Reverse Engineering, Washington, DC, USA, pp. 81–90 (2008)
17. Saitou, N., Nei, M.: The neighbor-joining method: a new method for reconstructing phylogenetic trees. Molecular Biology and Evolution 4(4), 406–425 (1987)
18. Smith, R., Horwitz, S.: Detecting and measuring similarity in code clones. In: International Workshop on Software Clones (March 2009)
19. Walenstein, A., El-Ramly, M., et al.: Similarity in programs. In: Duplication, Redundancy, and Similarity in Software. Dagstuhl Seminar Proceedings (April 2007)
20. Fitch, W.M., Margoliash, E.: Construction of phylogenetic trees. Science 155(3760), 279–284 (1967)

Array-Based Reduction Operations for a Parallel Adaptive FEM

Martina Balg[1], Jens Lang[2], Arnd Meyer[1], and Gudula Rünger[1]

[1] Department of Mathematics, Chemnitz University of Technology, Germany
{martina.balg,arnd.meyer}@mathematik.tu-chemnitz.de
[2] Department of Computer Science, Chemnitz University of Technology, Germany
{jens.lang,gudula.ruenger}@cs.tu-chemnitz.de

Abstract. For many applications of scientific computing, reduction operations may cause a performance bottleneck. In this article, the performance of different coarse- and fine-grained methods for implementing the reduction is investigated. Fine-grained reductions using atomic operations or fine-grained explicit locks are compared to the coarse-grained reduction operations supplied by OpenMP and MPI.

The reduction operations investigated are used for an adaptive FEM. The performance results show that applications can gain a speedup by using fine-grained reduction since this implementation enables to hide the reduction between calculation while minimising the time waiting for synchronisation.

1 Introduction

For applications of parallel scientific computing, reduction operations play an important role. In many cases, the performance of reduction operations, which aggregate data located on different processors to a common result datum using a specified operation, is crucial to the overall performance of the application. One example is the adaptive Finite Element Method (FEM) [1] applied to deformation problems (1) which is considered in this article.

$$\mathrm{div}(\sigma(u)) + \rho\, f = 0 \quad \textit{with appropriate boundary conditions.} \tag{1}$$

In the adaptive FEM, the created mesh is refined stronger around critical points which allows, compared to total refinement, more exact results within the same execution time. In order to being able to process large problems, a fast reduction operation is needed. The basic concept of this FEM is the discretisation of the domain Ω with hexahedral elements el and the approximation of all functions as a linear combination of linear or quadratic ansatz functions Ψ_k:

$$u(X) \approx u_h(X) = \sum_{k=1}^{N_X} u^{(k)} \Psi_k(X) \quad . \tag{2}$$

Hence, every element el consists of 6 faces, 12 edges and 8, 20 or 27 element nodes $X^{(k)}$ and all $\Psi_k(X)$ are defined by the degrees of freedom of each element, i.e. by their function value in each element node. Applying this discrete ansatz to (1) leads to a discrete linear system of equations:

$$A\underline{u} = \underline{b} \tag{3}$$

R. Keller et al. (Eds.): Facing the Multicore-Challenge III 2012, LNCS 7686, pp. 25–36, 2013.

where the vector $\underline{u}$ consists of all $u^{(k)}$ and represents the solution u. A denotes the system matrix, called stiffness matrix, and $\underline{b}$ the right-hand side, called load vector. Using the restriction of the ansatz for each element, the given problem decomposes into a sum of element-wise contributions:

$$A = \sum_{el} L_{el}^t A_{el} L_{el} \quad \text{and} \quad \underline{b} = \sum_{el} L_{el}^t \underline{b}_{el} \tag{4}$$

with appropriate projections L_{el} and L_{el}^t. So, it is convenient to just compute all A_{el} and $\underline{b}_{el}$ instead of assembling the whole stiffness matrix and load vector.

The adaptive FEM investigated executes the following steps consecutively until a given accuracy is reached: (I) adaptive, instead of total, mesh refinement, (II) assembly of the stiffness matrices, (III) solution of a linear system of equations with the conjugate gradient method which involves a reduction operation, and (IV) error estimation for next refinement. Steps (II) and (III) are available in a parallel implementation. Step (III) is investigated in this article.

The main goal of this article is to optimise the execution time of the FEM. The contribution of this article is the optimisation in the reduction phase of step (III) by introducing fine-grained reduction. Several implementations of the reduction are investigated in isolation, as well as in the context of the adaptive FEM. Examining the background shall enable to generalise the findings for transfer to related problems. Section 2 describes the parallel solution of linear systems of equations. Section 3 proposes variants of the fine-grained reduction. Their implementations in OpenMP are given in Sect. 4. Section 5 shows experimental results. Section 6 discusses related work and Sect. 7 concludes the article.

2   Solution of Linear Systems of Equations

Step (III) of the adaptive FEM is performed as follows [1]: The conjugate gradient method [9] is used for solving the linear system of equations (3). This iterative method minimises the residuum $\underline{r}^{[n]} := A\underline{u}^{[n]} - \underline{b}$ along a corresponding search direction in each step starting from an initial solution $\underline{u}^{[0]}$. Each iteration produces a correction term which generates an improved approximated solution $\underline{u}^{[n]}$.

According to Formula (4), the matrix A is composed of the element stiffness matrices A_{el}. This leads to a sparse structure that is exploited to compute products of the type

$$\underline{y}^{[n]} = A\underline{u}^{[n]} \quad . \tag{5}$$

The projector L_{el} converts $\underline{u}^{[n]}$ into a vector $\underline{u}_{el}$ containing only those entries that belong to the nodes of el, i.e.:

$$\underline{u}_{el} = L_{el}\underline{u}^{[n]} \quad . \tag{6}$$

A_{el} is applied to $\underline{u}_{el}$ in order to create the element solution vector $\underline{y}_{el}$:

$$\underline{y}_{el} = A_{el}\underline{u}_{el} \quad . \tag{7}$$

The vector $\underline{y}_{el}$ is then interpolated to the whole length of $\underline{y}$ by applying the transposed projector L_{el}^t and added to the overall solution vector $\underline{y}^{[n]}$:

$$\underline{y}^{[n]} = \sum_{el} L_{el}^t \underline{y}_{el} \quad . \tag{8}$$

2.1 Data Structures

Each element stiffness matrix A_{el} is symmetric and is stored column-wise as a packed upper triangular matrix (BLAS format TP [2]). The values for the nodes are stored consecutively. Each node needs n_{dof} values if there are n_{dof} degrees of freedom (dof). When considering three-dimensional deformation problems with 3 degrees of freedom in 27 element nodes, the element stiffness matrix has a size of 81 × 81. Correspondingly, the size of the vectors $\underline{x}_{el}$ and $\underline{y}_{el}$ is 81. While the size of the element-related data structures A_{el}, $\underline{x}_{el}$ and $\underline{y}_{el}$ is constant over the whole runtime of the FEM, the size of the overall data structures $\underline{u}$, $\underline{b}$ and $\underline{y}$ increases with each refinement step as the number of elements increases. The size of the overall data structures is proportional to the number of elements and can be up to some hundreds of thousands.

The element solution vectors $\underline{y}_{el}$ are added to the overall solution vector $\underline{y}$ according to Formula (8) where the projector L_{el}^t defines to which entry of $\underline{y}$ an entry of $\underline{y}_{el}$ is added. For memory efficiency, the implementation does not store the projector as a large matrix but uses a separate array for each element el for this assignment. In Fig. 1, which illustrates this principle, this array is represented by the arrows from the source entry in $\underline{y}_{el}$ to the target entry in $\underline{y}$. The figure also illustrates that each node, represented by a square, consists of 3 degrees of freedom. When calculating Formula (8), the corresponding location in $\underline{y}$ is looked up in the array for each entry of $\underline{y}_{el}$. To each entry of $\underline{y}$, entries from two $\underline{y}_{el}$ are added if and only if this node is part of these two elements.

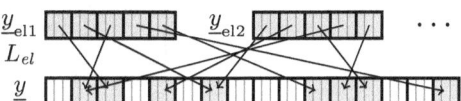

Fig. 1. Summation of element solution vectors $\underline{y}_{el}$ to the overall solution vector $\underline{y}$ using the projection of L_{el}

2.2 Parallelisation

The parallelisation of the FEM method described exploits that the calculations of Formula (7) are independent of each other. Each element is assigned to one processor p of the set of processors P which calculates (6) and (7). For the result summation in (8), a local solution vector $\underline{y}^\circ$, which has the same size as $\underline{y}$, is used on each processor. The part of non-null entries in $\underline{y}^\circ$ is greater than $\frac{1}{p}$ and they need much less memory than the element stiffness matrices so that they can be stored in a dense format. After Formula (8) has been calculated on all processors $p \in P$, the local solution vectors $\underline{y}^\circ$ are added to the overall solution vector $\underline{y}$, i.e.

$$\underline{y} = \sum_{p \in P} \underline{y}^{\circ,p} \quad , \tag{9}$$

where $\underline{y}^{\circ,p}$ denotes the local solution vector of processor p in this summation. Formula (9) is the reduction being optimised in this work.

The SPMD-style parallel algorithm calculating Formula (5), i.e. one iteration of approximating the solution of (3), is shown in Alg. 1. The algorithm receives the element stiffness matrices A_{el} and the projectors L_{el} for all elements el as well as the approximation $\underline{u}$ for the solution of the linear system of equations (3) as input and returns the vector $\underline{y}$ as output. In this algorithm, $\underline{y}$ is a shared variable; all other variables are private, i.e. only accessible by the processor owning them. After setting $\underline{y}$ to zero (Line 1), the calculation of Formulas (6) to (8) is executed for each element (Lines 4 to 7) in a parallel section. The reduction operation at the end of the parallel section (Lines 8 to 10) adds the local solution vectors $\underline{y}^\circ$ to the overall solution vector according to (9). In order to avoid conflicts when accessing $\underline{y}$, this addition is performed within a critical section. The absence of conflicts could also be ensured by other methods, for example by a global barrier in Line 8, followed by an arbitrary reduction algorithm. In any case, after the barrier operation, only reduction, and no computation, is performed.

Input: A_{el}, L_{el} for all el, $\underline{u}$
Output: $\underline{y}$
1 $\underline{y} := \mathcal{O}$ // shared vector $\underline{y}$
2 **begin parallel**
3      $\underline{y}^\circ := \mathcal{O}$
4   **foreach** *element el* **do**
5          $\underline{x}_{el} := L_{el}\underline{u}$
6          $\underline{y}_{el} := A_{el}\underline{x}_{el}$
7          $\underline{y}^\circ := \underline{y}^\circ + L_{el}^t \underline{y}_{el}$
8   **begin critical section**
9          $\underline{y} := \underline{y} + \underline{y}^\circ$
10   **end critical section**
11 **end parallel**

Algorithm 1. Parallel calculation of (5)

Input: A_{el}, L_{el} for all el, $\underline{u}$
Output: $\underline{y}$
1 $\underline{y} := \mathcal{O}$ // shared vector $\underline{y}$
2 **begin parallel**
3   **foreach** *element el* **do**
4          $\underline{x}_{el} := L_{el}\underline{u}$
5          $\underline{y}_{el} := A_{el}\underline{x}_{el}$
6          $\underline{y}^\circ := L_{el}^T \underline{y}_{el}$
7   **foreach** *entry i of* $\underline{y}^\circ$ *with* $\underline{y}^\circ[i] \neq 0$ **do**
8   atomic_add($\&\underline{y}[i]$, $\underline{y}^\circ[i]$)
9 **end parallel**

Algorithm 2. Parallel calculation of (5) with atomic addition of $\underline{y}$

3   Fine-Grained Reduction

In contrast to the coarse-grained reduction in Alg. 1, which locks the whole vector $\underline{y}$, the reduction can also be implemented in a fine-grained way. Fine-grained reduction means that each update of a vector entry is synchronised separately. This method allows to interleave reduction with computation and enables multiple threads to access $\underline{y}$ concurrently if they are processing different entries. Blockings due to concurrent write accesses to an entry of $\underline{y}$ may only occur for nodes shared by elements stored on different processors. This is true only for a small part of the nodes. Furthermore, the implementation does not need to store $\underline{y}^\circ$ explicitly. In contrast to a sequential implementation, the order of writes to $\underline{y}$ is not defined. However, the addition is commutative and $\underline{y}$ is only read after finishing the reduction. Hence, the order in which the elements are processed is irrelevant.

Two methods for the fine-grained synchronisation of updates of the overall solution vector $\underline{y}$ are investigated: *atomic operations* and *fine-grained locks*.

3.1   Atomic Operations

Atomic operations, which combine several semantic instructions in one non-preemptible function, can be implemented in hardware or in software. Hardware-supported atomic operations are generally more efficient than operations implemented in software as the thread synchronisation of the software implementation is very complex.

Use of Atomic Operations. Let the function `atomic_add`(*double* a, double b*) be a function which adds the value of b to the value which a points to in a non-preemptible way. Algorithm 2 uses this function for an alternative implementation of Alg. 1: Instead of reducing the local solution vectors $\underline{y}^{\circ}$ to the overall solution vector $\underline{y}$ globally at the end of the parallel execution (Lines 8 to 10 in Alg. 1), each vector entry of $\underline{y}^{\circ}$ is now added individually to the corresponding entry of $\underline{y}$. Each update of an entry is synchronised by using an atomic addition operation (Line 8 in Alg. 2).

Atomic Operations Using Compare & Swap. For many operations, such as addition, subtraction or logical operations, there exist atomic hardware instructions on most common platforms. If, however, no such atomic hardware instruction exists for the operation required, it has to be emulated in software. For this emulation, the atomic *compare & swap instruction* (`CAS`), which is available on most platforms, can be used.

```
1  bool CAS(T *location, T oldVal, T
      newVal)
2  begin
3  |    begin atomic
4  |    |   if *location == oldVal
   |    |   then
5  |    |   |  *location = newVal;
6  |    |   return (*location ==
   |    |   oldVal);
7  |    end atomic
8  end
```

Algorithm 3. Compare & swap according to [6]

```
1  void atomic_add(double *sum,
      double a)
2  begin
3  |    repeat
4  |    |   double oldSum = *sum;
5  |    |   double newSum = oldSum
   |    |   + a;
6  |    until CAS(sum, oldSum,
   |    newSum) ;
7  end
```

Algorithm 4. Emulation of an atomic addition using compare & swap

In this article, the compare & swap instruction as defined in Alg. 3 is used: First, the value of the variable *oldVal* is compared to the value of *location*. If these values are equal, the value of *newVal* is written to the memory location which *location* points to. The return value of `CAS` is the result of the comparison.

Algorithm 4 shows how any binary operation can be emulated using the atomic `CAS` operation taking the addition as an example [4]: The old value of the result, *sum*, is stored in the variable *oldSum*. This variable is used to calculate the new value *newSum*. If the memory location which *sum* points to has not been altered by another processor intermediately, *newSum* is written to this location. Otherwise, the operation is repeated with the current value of *sum*.

```
1  int* locks[N_LOCKS]; // initialise with 0
2  void lock(int i)                    12  void unlock(int i)
3  begin                               13  begin
4  |   while (true) do                 14  |   atomic_add(
5  |   |   int lock_status = atomic_add(  15  |   |   &locks[i % N_LOCKS], -1);
6  |   |   &locks[i % N_LOCKS], 1);    16  end
7  |   |   if (lock_status == 0) then
8  |   |   |   break;
9  |   |   unlock(i);
10 |   |   usleep(1);
11 end
```

Algorithm 5. Implementation of the functions `lock()` and `unlock()`

3.2   Fine-Grained Locks

Optimising the granularity of locks for given conditions has been investigated for a long time [10]. In this subsection, a fine-grained locking technique is presented which uses a separate locking variable for a small number of entries of the solution vector y instead of always locking the whole vector y as in Alg. 1. Before each access to an entry i of y, the corresponding lock is acquired by calling `lock(i)`; after the access it is released by calling `unlock(i)`. Line 8 in Alg. 2 is replaced by the instruction $y[i] := y[i] + y^\circ[i]$, surrounded by the lock and unlock statements.

The implementation of the functions `lock()` and `unlock()` is shown in Alg. 5. N_LOCKS lock variables are stored in the array *locks*. The parameter of `lock()` and `unlock()` is the index of the data array entry to be accessed. The current thread attempts to acquire the lock corresponding to the given index by incrementing the lock variable. If this is successful, *lock_status* is equal to zero. Otherwise, the attempt is undone by calling `unlock()` and another attempt to acquire the lock is made. The function `unlock()` releases the lock by atomically decrementing the value of the lock variable by 1. Section 5.2 investigates which values should be chosen for N_LOCKS. The instruction `usleep(1)` in Line 9 avoids livelocks by suspending the current thread for one microsecond if acquiring the lock fails.

4   Implementation

Solving the linear system of equations (3) is implemented in the function *ppcgm* in the FEM investigated. The parallel section of the OpenMP implementation is shown in Listings 1 and 2. In Listing 1, the reduction of the private array Y is performed by OpenMP when leaving the parallel section. In contrast, in Listing 2 each access to the shared array Y is performed in an atomic way so that the reduction operation at the end of the parallel section can be avoided.

The loop in Line 6 of the source code of the Listings 1 and 2 runs over all elements which have been assigned to the current processor. The calculation of x_{el}

```
1 real*8 Y(N),U(N),El(N,Nnod*Ndof)
2 real*8 Uel(Nnod*Ndof),Yel(Nnod*Ndof)
3 integer L(N),i,j,k,Kn,N,Ndof,Nel,
      Nnod
4 Y = 0d0
5 !$omp parallel reduction(+:Y)
6   do k=1,Nel
7     call UtoUel(Ne0,Ndof,Uel,U)
8     call DSPMV('l',Nnod*Ndof,1.0d+0,
          El(k),Uel,1,0D+0,Yel,1)
9     do i=1,Nnod
10      Kn = L(i)*Ndof
11      do j=1,Ndof
12
13        Y(Kn+j) = Y(Kn+j) + Yel(Ndof
              *(i-1)+j)
14      end do
15    end do
16  end do
17 !$omp end parallel
```

Listing 1. Implementation of *ppcgm* in OpenMP using coarse-grained reduction

```
1 real*8 Y(N),U(N),El(N,Nnod*Ndof)
2 real*8 Uel(Nnod*Ndof),Yel(Nnod*Ndof)
3 integer L(N),i,j,k,Kn,N,Ndof,Nel,
      Nnod
4 Y = 0d0
5 !$omp parallel
6   do k=1,Nel
7     call UtoUel(Ne0,Ndof,Uel,U)
8     call DSPMV('l',Nnod*Ndof,1.0d+0,
          El(K),Uel,1,0D+0,Yel,1)
9     do i=1,Nnod
10      Kn = L(i)*Ndof
11      do j=1,Ndof
12 !$omp atomic
13        Y(Kn+j) = Y(Kn+j) + Yel(Ndof
              *(i-1)+j)
14      end do
15    end do
16  end do
17 !$omp end parallel
```

Listing 2. Implementation of *ppcgm* in OpenMP using fine-grained reduction with atomic addition

(Line 5 in Alg. 1) is shown in Line 7 in the source code. The following matrix-vector multiplication is performed by the BLAS routine DSPMV. The addition of the $\underline{y}_{el}$ to y° (Line 7 in Alg. 1) is performed in lines 9 to 15 of the source code. The variable $\overline{Kn}$ (Line 10) contains the index of Y to which the current node of Yel is added. This assignment, which is defined by L_{el} in Alg. 1, is stored in the array L in the source code. The private arrays Y of all threads, that contain the intermediate results, are added to the shared array by OpenMP at the end of the parallel section in Line 17. This section corresponds to the lines 8 to 10 in Alg. 1.

In contrast, Y is a shared variable in Listing 2. In Line 13, each thread writes its results directly to the shared array Y without using an intermediate array. The write operation is synchronised by the atomic OpenMP statement in Line 12 which corresponds to Line 8 in Alg. 2.

5 Experiments

In synthetic tests, the execution time of the different implementation variants of the reduction operation have been investigated. Also, the actual implementation of the FEM was investigated using an example object as input to explore which speedup can be achieved if the reduction performed by the different implementation variants and in order to find a suitable number of locks for the implementation variant presented in Sect. 3.2.

For the experiments a 24-core shared-memory *Intel machine* with 4 × Intel Xeon X5650 CPUs @ 2.67 GHz and 12 GB of RAM and a 24-core *AMD machine* with 4 × AMD Opteron 8425 HE CPUs @ 2.1 GHz and 32 GB of RAM have been used. For the tests with the actual FEM implementation, the example object *bohrung*, which represents a cuboid with a drill hole, has been used, see Fig. 2. The object initially consist of 8 elements and hence of 32 nodes.

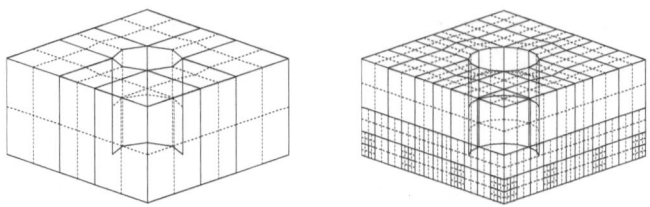

Fig. 2. Example object *bohrung* in initial state and after 3 refinement steps

5.1 Synthetic Tests

A first test investigated how many CPU clock cycles the AMD machine needs for performing an integer addition $a := a + b$ in the following scenarios: (i) a is a private variable for each thread, (ii) a is a shared variable updated without synchronisation, possibly leading to a wrong result, (iii) a is a shared variable with updates synchronised by (iii-a) an atomic hardware operation, (iii-b) an atomic operation emulated using compare & swap, or (iii-c) explicit locks. A loop performing 100 000 additions was used for the measurement. This loop was executed once by a single thread and once by 24 threads in parallel. The execution time of the loop was measured using hardware performance counters accessed via the PAPI library [3].

The results of this test are shown in Fig. 3a. The value for using a single thread shows how many clock cycles are needed in any case for performing the addition and, if applicable, the synchronisation operation. The value for using 24 threads shows the behaviour of the execution time when there are concurring accesses. If private memory is used, the execution time decreases to $\frac{1}{24}$ of the original value as the addition can be performed in parallel without any conflicts. If shared memory is used without synchronisation, the execution time increases as the updated value of the variable has to be propagated to the caches of all processors, i.e. they have to be kept coherent. If the atomic add hardware instruction is used, the execution time increases as all writes to the result have to be serialised. The increase of the execution time for the emulated atomic instruction using the compare & swap operation is even larger as in the case of conflicts, one thread has to wait using busy waiting for the other threads to finish their write operations. If explicit locks are used, only short waiting times occur, resulting in an execution time decrease to approximately $\frac{1}{15}$.

In a second test on the same AMD machine, a certain amount of computation was performed between two addition operations. The duration of this additional computation was varied. The results for the scenarios (i)–(iii-c) as defined above are shown in Fig. 3b. The curves show the execution time needed by 24 threads for 15 million addition operations on one variable including the time for the additional computation. The time for the additional computations is shown in

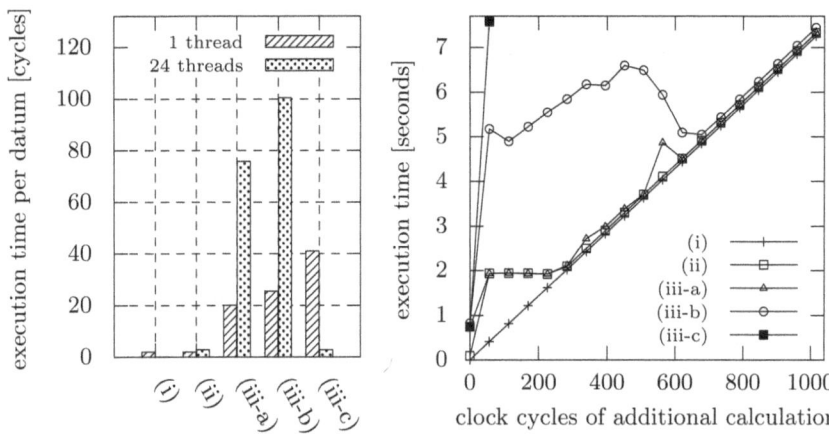

(a) Number of clock cycles needed by the addition for different implementation variants

(b) Execution time for addition operations with additional computation between two operations

Fig. 3. Execution times for addition operations on a single memory location: (i) using private memory, (ii) with unsynchronised access, (iii) with synchronised access using (iii-a) an atomic add machine instruction, (iii-b) compare & swap, (iii-c) locks

the abscissa. The use of private memory, i.e. without synchronisation, results in a straight line. Compared to that, the synchronised or unsynchronised access to a shared variable causes extra costs. The results indicate that no substantial extra costs are introduced if the atomic hardware operation is used with an additional computation of at least 300 clock cycles or, if the atomic operation using compare & swap is used, with an additional computation of at least 700 clock cycles between two operations. In contrast, the execution time increases rapidly when using the explicit lock.

5.2   Fine-Grained Explicit Locks

The method of using fine-grained explicit locks presented in Sect. 3.2 has been investigated concerning the execution time of the function *ppcgm* when varying the number of lock variables with the example object *bohrung*. Figure 4 shows the execution times for three refinement levels of the FEM consisting of 28 152, 58 736 and 84 720 nodes with data array sizes of 84 456, 176 208 and 254 160, respectively: For all array sizes, the execution time decreases rapidly with an increasing number of lock variables until a value of approximately 240 is reached, whereas it remains nearly constant afterwards. In order to minimise memory consumption, it seems reasonable not to provide more than 240 lock variables.

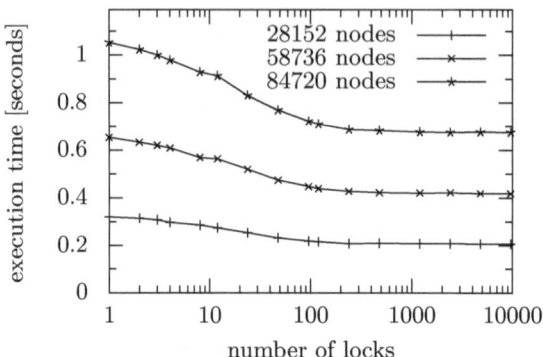

Fig. 4. Execution time of the function *ppcgm* depending on the number of lock variables used for different array sizes

5.3 Reduction Operations in the FEM Implementation

The reduction operation for solving the linear system of equations (3) has been implemented in the function *ppcgm* FEM investigated in the following variants:

(a) coarse-grained reduction according to Alg. 1
  – using a distributed memory model in MPI (MVAPICH2 1.5.1),
  – using a shared memory model in OpenMP (GNU Fortran 4.4.7),
(b) fine-grained reduction
  – with atomic addition operation using compare & swap according to Alg. 2,
  – with explicit locks,
  – without synchronisation (potentially producing wrong results).

As there is no hardware instruction for adding double precision floating point numbers atomically on the available hardware, that variant could not be used. The results obtained with the example object *bohrung* for the Intel and the AMD machines are shown in Fig. 5. The execution times of the OpenMP variant obtained with GNU Fortran did not differ significantly from results obtained using the commercial Intel Fortran compiler.

For the parallel implementation of the function *ppcgm*, which does contain both, sequential and parallel parts, a speedup between 4 and 6 is achieved for the variants with coarse-grained reduction, independent of the memory model used. For the variants with the fine-grained implementation of the reduction using compare & swap or explicit locks, a speedup of approximately 8 is achieved. This speedup is equal to the speedup of the variant with an unsynchronised addition of the results. The results for the variants with fine-grained reduction show that no additional execution time is required for avoiding memory access conflicts. As it appears, the time intervals between two write accesses to an element are large enough to hide the reduction operation between calculations as shown in Sect. 5.1. The waiting time which occurs when using the coarse-grained reduction can be eliminated nearly completely by using fine-grained reduction operations.

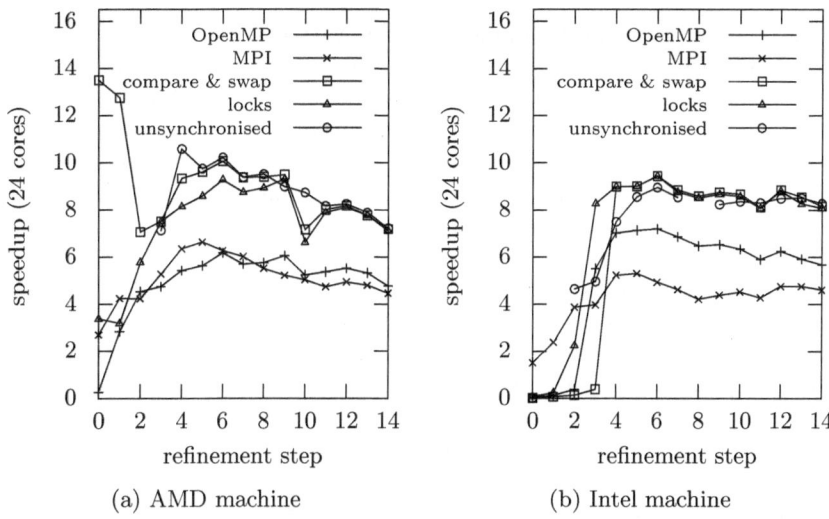

(a) AMD machine   (b) Intel machine

Fig. 5. Speedup of the function *ppcgm* when using the different implementation variants of the reduction operation

6 Related Work

Recent works which deal with reductions investigate the reduction of scalars in most cases. They often achieve a runtime benefit by combining operations for implementing the barrier needed by the reduction with the calculation of the reduction result [11,12]. [12] performs a tree-like reduction which synchronises sibling nodes in the tree using busy waiting. Yet, it does not need atomic read-modify-write or compare & swap instructions. [11] introduces a novel concept of *phaser accumulators* which achieves a runtime benefit by separating phases of the reduction in order to enable overlap between communication and computation.

A molecular dynamics particle simulation, which calculates forces between a number of atoms, is investigated in [8]. The forces are stored in an array and each processor calculates a part of each force acting on a particle. The partial forces are added to the total force acting on the respective particle using a reduction. Among the investigated implementation variants, the variant utilising the OpenMP statement *atomic* performs worst. The variant using the OpenMP statement *reduction* performs better, but still worse than two other variants, one using a private array and one using the BLAS routine `DGEMV`. The results of [8] are contrary to the results of this article, where the application benefits from atomic add instructions to shared arrays. One can assume that this is due to the memory access pattern of the particle simulation which has more frequent write operations to the same memory location than the reduction in the FEM. Similar results where array privatisation yields a performance benefit are, e.g., presented in [5] and [7].

7   Conclusion

This article investigated several implementation variants of a reduction of arrays on shared-memory machines. A fine-grained reduction has been compared to existing implementations of coarse-grained reductions in OpenMP and MPI.

A result of this work is that the operations needed for synchronising write accesses to a shared vector can be hidden between computations if there is enough time between the write accesses. In the parallel routine investigated in detail, the vector being reduced has non-null values for each entry only on a small number of processors and the write operations to the result vector can be interleaved with computations. Thus, the condition mentioned above is fulfilled, and using fine-grained reduction improves the runtime of the adaptive FEM. The results of Sect. 5.3 show that, in contrast to other works which commonly suggest array privatisation, also writing directly to shared arrays can be efficient if fine-grained reduction operations are used.

Acknowledgement. This work is supported by the cluster of excellence *Energy-Efficient Product and Process Innovation in Production Engineering (eniPROD)* funded by the European Union (European Regional Development Fund) and the Free State of Saxony. This work is also part of a project cooperation granted by the German Research Foundation DFG-PAK 97 (ME1224/6-2 and RU591/10-2).

References

1. Beuchler, S., Meyer, A., Pester, M.: SPC-Pm3AdH v1.0 Programmers manual. Preprint SFB393 01-08, TU Chemnitz (2001) (revised 2003)
2. Basic linear algebra subprograms technical (BLAST) forum standard (2001)
3. Browne, S., Dongarra, J., Garner, N., Ho, G., Mucci, P.: A portable programming interface for performance evaluation on modern processors. Int. J. High Perform. Comput. Appl. 14(3), 189–204 (2000)
4. Case, R., Padegs, A.: Architecture of the IBM System/370. Commun. ACM 21(1), 73–96 (1987)
5. Gao, D., Schwartzentruber, T.: Optimizations and OpenMP implementation for the direct simulation monte carlo method. Comput. Fluids 42(1), 73–81 (2011)
6. Greenwald, M.: Non-blocking synchronization and system design. Ph.D. thesis, Stanford University, Stanford, CA, USA (1999)
7. Liu, Z., Chapman, B.M., Wen, Y., Huang, L., Hernandez, O.: Analyses for the Translation of OpenMP Codes into SPMD Style with Array Privatization. In: Voss, M.J. (ed.) WOMPAT 2003. LNCS, vol. 2716, pp. 26–41. Springer, Heidelberg (2003)
8. Meloni, S., Federico, A., Rosati, M.: Reduction on arrays: comparison of performances between different algorithms. In: Proc. EWOMP 2003 (2003)
9. Meyer, A.: A parallel preconditioned conjugate gradient method using domain decomposition and inexact solvers on each subdomain. Comput. 45, 217–234 (1990)
10. Ries, D., Stonebraker, M.: Effects of locking granularity in a database management system. ACM Trans. Database Syst. 2(3), 233–246 (1977)
11. Shirako, J., Peixotto, D., Sarkar, V., Scherer, W.: Phaser accumulators: A new reduction construct for dynamic parallelism. In: Proc. IPDPS (2009)
12. Speziale, E., di Biagio, A., Agosta, G.: An optimized reduction design to minimize atomic operations in shared memory multiprocessors. In: Proc. IPDPS, Workshops and PhD Forum (2011)

An Efficient High Performance Parallelization of a Discontinuous Galerkin Spectral Element Method

Christoph Altmann, Andrea D. Beck, Florian Hindenlang, Marc Staudenmaier,
Gregor J. Gassner, and Claus-Dieter Munz

Institute of Aerodynamics and Gas Dynamics
Universität Stuttgart, Pfaffenwaldring 21, 70569 Stuttgart, Germany
{christoph.altmann,andrea.beck,florian.hindenlang,marc.staudenmaier,
gregor.gassner,claus-dieter.munz}@iag.uni-stuttgart.de
http://www.iag.uni-stuttgart.de/nrg

Abstract. We describe an efficient parallelization strategy for the discontinuous Galerkin spectral element method, illustrated by a structured grid framework. Target applications are large scale DNS and LES calculations on massively parallel systems. Due to the simple and efficient formulation of the method, a parallelization aiming at one-element-per-processor calculations is feasible; a highly desired feature for emerging multi- and many-core architectures. We show scale-up tests on up to 131,000 processors.

Keywords: Discontinuous Galerkin, Spectral Element, MPI, Parallel, HPC.

1 Introduction

For nowadays modern computations, the trend goes towards large scale computations of turbulent phenomena. When trying to perform large eddy simulations (LES) or even direct numerical simulations (DNS), efficient numerical codes are the key requirement. Since todays processor hardware already makes a transition from multi- to many-core CPUs, efficient parallelization for very large numbers of processor cores is necessary. Still, schemes that can take on this challenge are rare. A potentially promising candidate is the explicit discontinuous Galerkin spectral element method (DGSEM). DGSEM schemes are used in a wide range of applications such as compressible flows [2], electromagnetics and optics [8], aeroacoustics [11], meteorology [12], and geophysics [4]. Very easy to code, its accuracy is very high, especially when being compared to the computational costs. In general, the locality of a DG scheme makes it an ideal candidate for parallelization, since only direct von Neumann communication has to be established, in other words, the scheme relies only on communication of face neighbors. The simple step-by-step design of the DGSEM method allows for an highly efficient latency hiding by overlapping communication and computation. This is

R. Keller et al. (Eds.): Facing the Multicore-Challenge III 2012, LNCS 7686, pp. 37–47, 2013.

the main ingredient for a successful and competitive scheme. In the following, we will describe the parallelization of the DGSEM method.

2   Description of the Method

In this section, we briefly describe the discontinuous Galerkin spectral element method (DGSEM). The key features of the method are:

- Computational domain consists of hexahedral elements
- Equations are mapped to reference element space
- Each element is mapped onto the reference cube element $E = [-1, 1]^3$
- Solution and fluxes are approximated by a tensor-product basis of 1D Lagrange interpolating polynomials
- Volume and surface integrals are replaced by Gauss-Legendre or Gauss-Legendre-Lobatto quadrature
- Collocation of integration and interpolation points

Consider a system of nonlinear PDEs of the form

$$U_t + \nabla \cdot \boldsymbol{F}(U) = 0, \tag{1}$$

where U denotes the vector of conservative variables and $\boldsymbol{F}(U)$ the advection flux matrix. We now define a transformation $\boldsymbol{X}(\boldsymbol{\xi})$ of Equation (1) into a reference space $\boldsymbol{\xi} = (\xi_1, \xi_2, \xi_3)^T$. Equation (1) in reference space reads

$$J(\boldsymbol{\xi})U_t(\boldsymbol{\xi}) + \tilde{\nabla} \cdot \tilde{\boldsymbol{F}}(U(\boldsymbol{\xi})) = 0, \tag{2}$$

where $J(\xi)$ is the Jacobian of the transformation and $\tilde{\boldsymbol{F}}$ being the fluxes, transformed into reference space. We now start our usual DG formulation by multiplying Equation (2) with a test function $\Phi = \Phi(\boldsymbol{\xi})$ and integrating over a reference element E

$$\int_E JU_t\Phi d\boldsymbol{\xi} + \int_E \tilde{\nabla} \cdot \tilde{\boldsymbol{F}}(U)\Phi d\boldsymbol{\xi} = 0. \tag{3}$$

To obtain the weak formulation, we integrate by parts the second term as usual

$$\frac{\partial}{\partial t} \int_E JU\Phi d\boldsymbol{\xi} + \int_{\partial E} \tilde{G}\Phi ds - \int_E \tilde{\boldsymbol{F}}(U) \cdot \tilde{\nabla}\Phi d\boldsymbol{\xi} = 0, \tag{4}$$

where $\tilde{G}$ represents a Riemann solution of $\tilde{\boldsymbol{F}} \cdot \boldsymbol{n}$ at the reference element boundary since we have two values here, due to our discontinuous ansatz. The solution in our cells is now approximated as a DG polynomial in tensor-product form as

$$U(\boldsymbol{x}_i) = \sum_{i,j,k=0}^{N} \hat{U}_{i,j,k}\Psi_{i,j,k}(\boldsymbol{x}_i), \text{ with } \Psi_{i,j,k}(\boldsymbol{x}_i) = l_i(\xi_1)l_j(\xi_2)l_k(\xi_3), \tag{5}$$

with $l_x(\xi_y)$ being one-dimensional Lagrange interpolating polynomials, defined by a nodal set $\{\xi_i\}_{i=0}^N$. For these nodal points, either Gauss or Gauss-Lobatto nodes can be chosen. We refer the reader to [5] for more information on which points to choose. The transformed fluxes $\tilde{F}$ are approximated by an interpolation onto the same nodal points that are used for integration. This interpolation can be seen as a discrete projection and is exact up to the polynomial degree of the integration. Because we have nonlinear fluxes and probably a nonlinear transformation, we will introduce errors, known as aliasing [3]. For more information on the DGSEM scheme, the interested reader is referred to [10,9]. Since the scheme is of tensor product nature, the calculation of the integrals in (5) can be simplified. This becomes significant in the implementation, overall operation count as well as in the parallelization capabilities, especially when it comes to latency hiding.

In two dimensions, Figure 1 shows the location of Gauss points for the approximation of the numerical flux f^* for a single element in reference space $\boldsymbol{\xi} = (\xi^1, \xi^2)^T$. Once can clearly see the tensor product behavior of the operation.

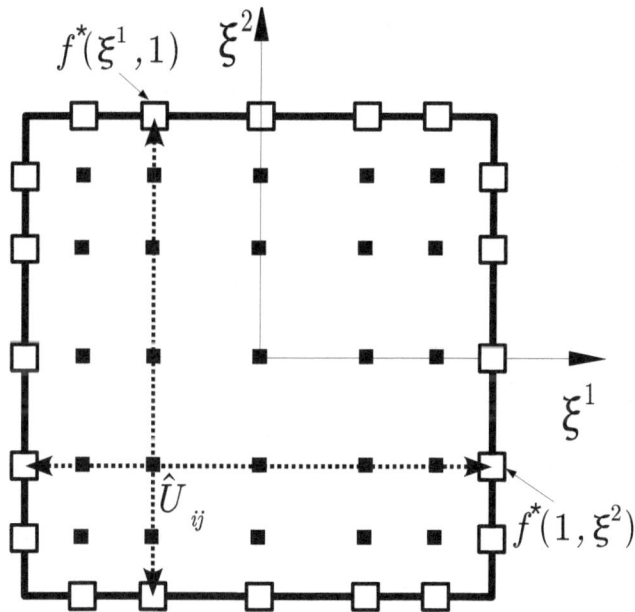

Fig. 1. Location of Gauss points ■ and boundary fluxes □ in 2D

For a detailed specification of the operations count as well as the a memory footprint estimation of the DGSEM scheme, the reader is referred to [7].

Using the DGSEM method described above, we solve the compressible Navier-Stokes equations on a structured curvilinear hexahedral mesh and use a standard explicit low-storage Runge-Kutta time integration. Choosing a structured mesh simplifies greatly the analysis, parallelization and data structure. However, geometric flexibility is limited and we are currently developing the data structure and parallelization to apply DGSEM on unstructured hexahedral meshes, in combination with a time-accurate local time stepping as e.g. described in [6].

3   Parallelization Concept

Since the focus is on one-element-per-processor calculations, a very efficient way for parallelization has to be found. We do not want to spend more time on communication than really necessary. The computational load should also be minimized when continuing processing the transferred data. We therefore implemented a ping-pong strategy, that minimizes necessary computations as well as communication. To be able to overlap computation and communication, non-blocking send and receive operations are used. The described tensor-product nature of the DGSEM method will hereby help us to do this efficiently, since its operations can be split dim-by-dim in a very fine-grained manner. This way, we can use all parts of the DG operator as buffer elements to hide communication latency.

The communication pattern for a discontinuous Galerkin scheme are limited to direct-neighbor communication of boundary values for the calculation of the numerical flux. For the Navier-Stokes equations, the Riemann solvers at the cell boundaries need left and right values of the state U as well as its gradient ∇U. Once the neighbor's values of U and ∇U are obtained, the numerical flux can be calculated. This part can of course be split into an advective operation (only requiring U) and a diffusive operation (additionally requiring ∇U). One can describe this as ping-pong style communication pattern. That pattern minimizes the operations on each MPI side which is an important aspect in one-element-per-processor calculations. Since we are having a structured hexahedral grid, we can use the following communication strategy: Each cell communicates U and ∇U to its right neighbor dim-by-dim in positive spatial direction. This neighbor then calculates the flux, once the necessary data was received and immediately starts sending the data back to the left neighbor. This strategy, shown in Figure 2 for a pure advection flux, is then repeated for the other dimensions.

Non-blocking send and receives are used to provide an overlap of communication and computation. This will only have an effect if the send-receive operations are buffered by computations in between. We therefor split all operator-parts dim-by-dim into fine-grained packages to provide a well-matching buffer. For the first communication direction, we need to use buffer-routines that do not depend on any of the data that has to be transferred. The other dimensions can then utilize routines depending on previous completed send-receive operations as buffers.

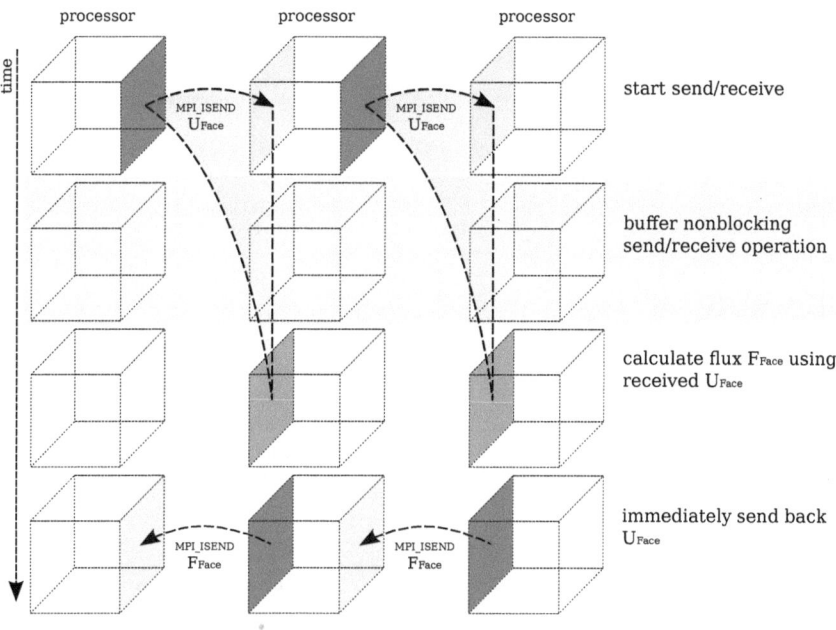

Fig. 2. Buffered ping-pong communication strategy for the calculation of the advection flux

4 DGSEM Parallelization in Detail

We will now provide a detailed look into the DGSEM parallelization. To keep things as simple as possible, all diagrams are being cut after having processed the first (ξ) direction, since the other directions are more or less straight forward. To be able to perform a time update within the DGSEM method, we need to go through two blocks in sequence. We first have to build the gradients of our solution via lifting, using a standard BR1 scheme as shown in [1]. After this block is completed, we move on with the DG time update by evaluating volume and surface integrals. For the lifting part, we only need to communicate the state at the domain boundaries to be able to calculate the necessary inter-processor flux. For the DG time update, also the gradients of the state have to be communicated, since we need them for the viscous flux of the Navier-Stokes equations. In the following, we will present the calculation-communication pattern of the lifting operator. Figure 3 shows the detailed communication pattern for the BR1 lifting operator.

With the additional send-receive of the gradients, the DG operator is shown in Figure 4. Since more communication is involved, we use a finer-grained send-receive buffering as for the BR1 lifting operator. We are not longer separating buffering dim-by-dim but are instead interweaving the DGSEM operations. For example, gradients in η-direction are already sent while the numerical flux in ξ-direction is yet to be calculated. This is important since all send-receive operations have to be buffered.

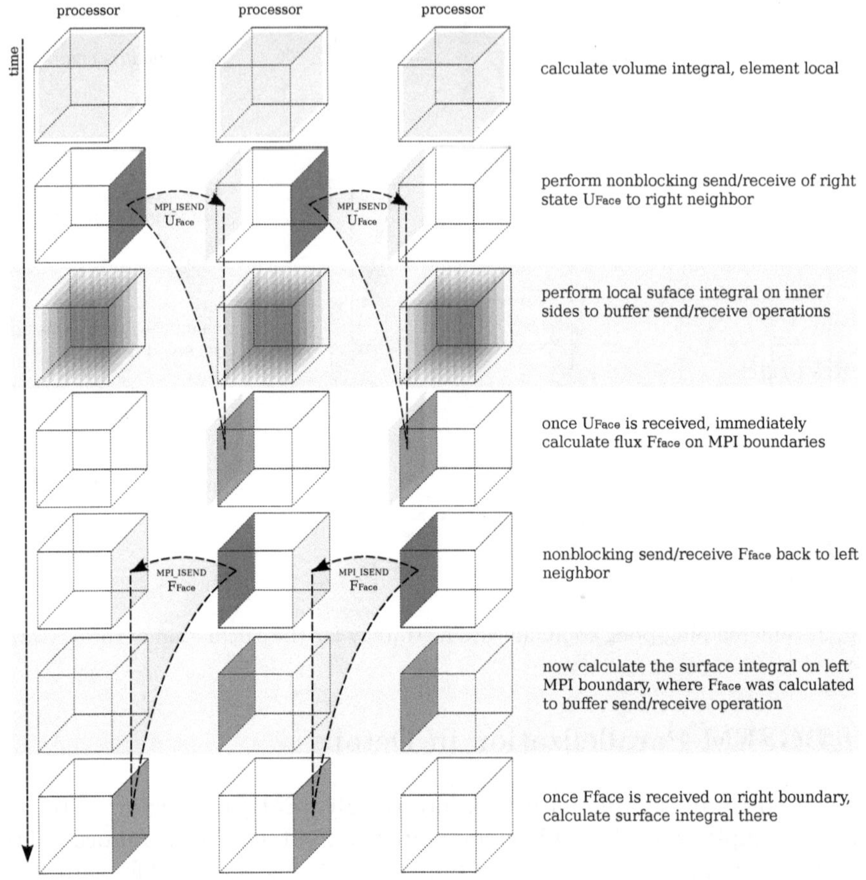

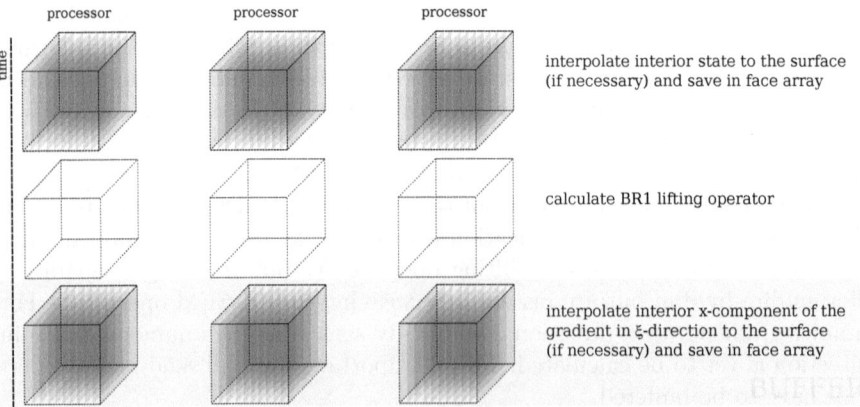

processor   processor   processor

time

calculate volume integral, element local

MPI_ISEND U_Face   MPI_ISEND U_Face

perform nonblocking send/receive of right state U_Face to right neighbor

perform local suface integral on inner sides to buffer send/receive operations

once U_Face is received, immediately calculate flux F_face on MPI boundaries

MPI_ISEND F_Face   MPI_ISEND F_Face

nonblocking send/receive F_face back to left neighbor

now calculate the surface integral on left MPI boundary, where F_face was calculated to buffer send/receive operation

once Fface is received on right boundary, calculate surface integral there

Fig. 3. Buffered ping-pong communication strategy for the calculation of BR1 lifting in ξ-direction

processor   processor   processor

time

interpolate interior state to the surface (if necessary) and save in face array

calculate BR1 lifting operator

interpolate interior x-component of the gradient in ξ-direction to the surface (if necessary) and save in face array

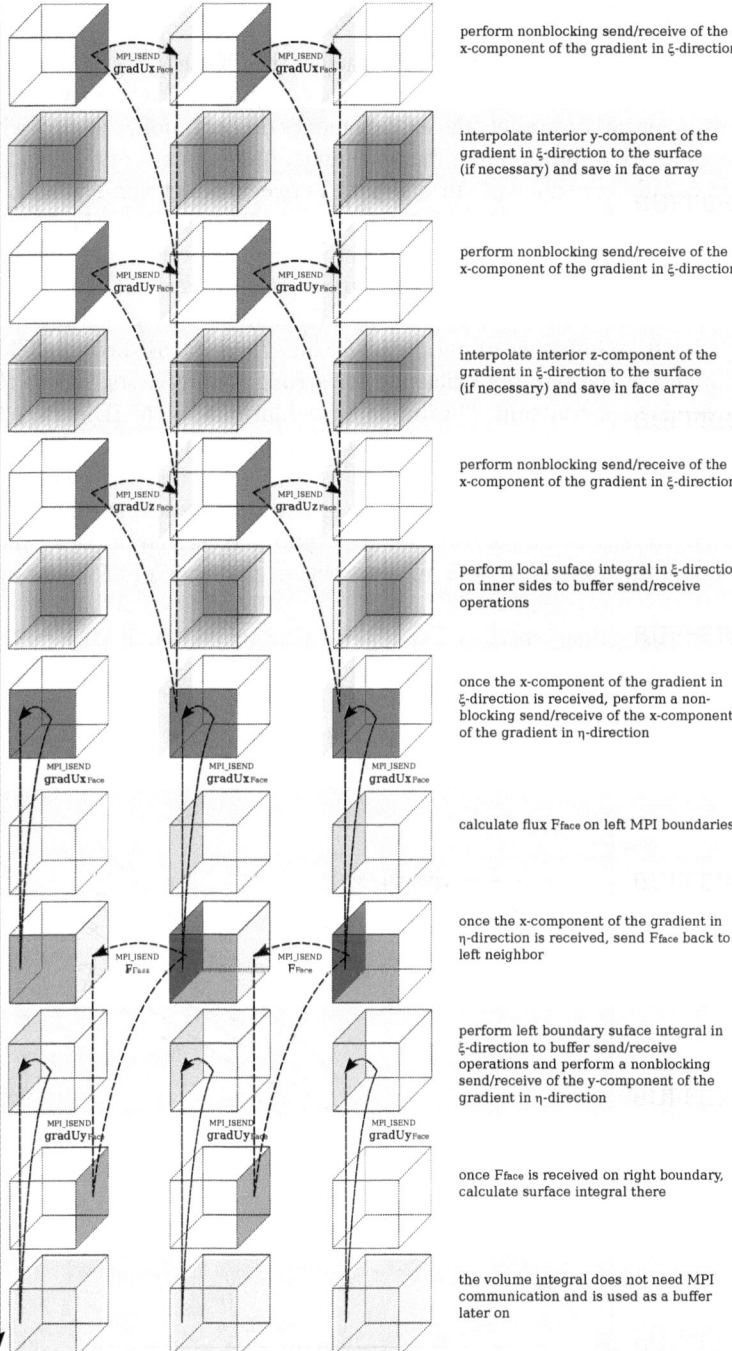

Fig. 4. Buffered ping-pong communication strategy for the calculation of the DG operator

5   Scale-Up Efficiency

Besides the promising fundamental efficiency of the DGSEM method, its main advantages are based on its "high performance computing" capability. The DG algorithm is inherently parallel, since all elements do communicate only with their direct neighbors via solution and flux exchange. Independent of the local polynomial degree, only exchange of surface data between direct von Neumann neighbors is necessary. Note that the DG operator can be split into the two building blocks, namely the volume integral – solely depending on element local DOF – and the surface integral, where neighbor information is needed. This fact helps to hide communication latency by exploiting local element operations and further reduces the negative influence of data transfer on efficiency, as shown in Chapter 3.

Table 3 shows the parallel efficiency for strong scaling tests, where the total problem size is kept constant, obtained by calculations on the IBM Blue Gene/P Cluster "JUGENE" at the Jülich Supercomputing Centre (JSC). The specialty here is the fact that 4096 elements were used in total and the calculation was distributed up to its maximum onto 4096 processors (reaching one element per processor!). We reach almost 70% for a polynomial degree of 5. By increasing the polynomial degree to $N = 7$, an even better efficiency of 88% was achieved.

Table 1. Strong scaling efficiency [%] of the DGSEM code on JUGENE (IBM Blue Gene/P), 4096 elements

Nb. of processors	1	8	64	512	2048	4096
$N=5$, 0.9 mio. DOF	-	100.0	96.5	89.1	80.3	73.9
$N=7$, 2.1 mio. DOF	-	100.0	98.3	94.8	88.9	88.2

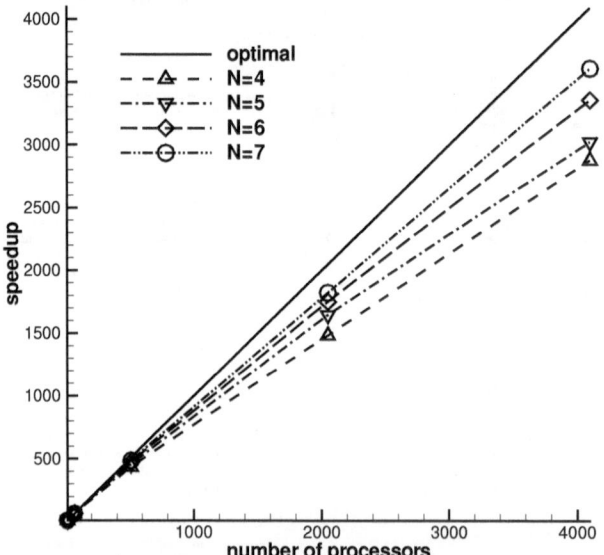

Fig. 5. DGSEM strong scaling, polynomial degrees 4 to 7

Table 2. Weak scaling of the DGSEM code on JUGENE (IBM Blue Gene/P) $N=8$, $91,125$ DOF per processor

Nb. of processors	1	8	64	512	2048	4096
Efficiency [%]	-	100.0	99.8	99.3	99.2	99.2

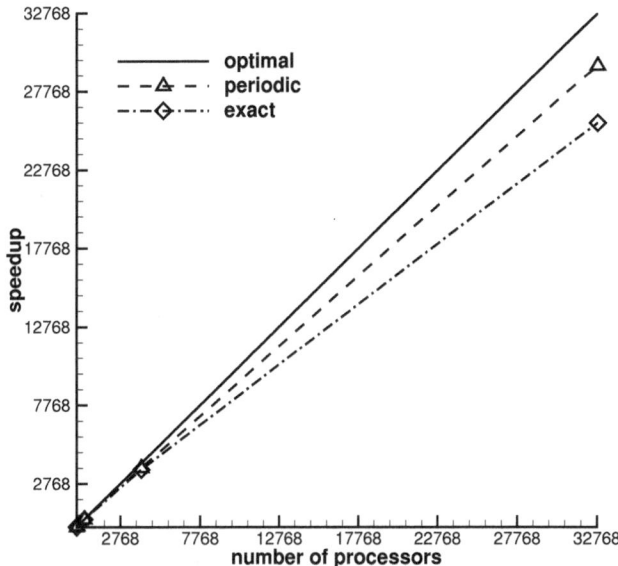

Fig. 6. DGSEM strong scaling using periodic and exact boundary conditions

Figure 5 shows the speedup plot of strong scaling for polynomial degrees from 4 to 7. As expected, the scaling efficiency increases with increasing polynomial degree, since the workload per DG element rises. In that case, computation takes more time and thus communication is hidden more efficiently.

Next, Table 2 lists weak scaling results, also obtained on "JUGENE". Here, the load per processor is kept constant. As expected, the scaling of such problem is almost perfect.

To determine the code's ability for real-life extreme scale computations, additional studies were made. Especially the influence of boundary conditions had to be investigated, since the examples above were all set up using periodic boundaries, which clearly is no real-life setting. If boundaries are not periodic, no MPI communication takes place here, so this boundary is cheaper in terms of CPU time. We were therefore using exact boundaries in the following computations and compared the outcome with a pure periodic run. This time, we were using up to $32,786$ processors on "JUGENE". Because of the limited memory of the system, a single core run was not feasible any more. We thus started with an 8 core computation. Again, we are finally reaching a one-element-per-processor calculation. Figure 6 shows the results for this $N = 7$, 32^3 elements run.

Table 3. Strong scaling efficiency [%] of the DGSEM code on JUGENE (IBM Blue Gene/P), 150^3 elements, exact boundaries

Nb. of processors	864	2048	6912	16,348	55,296	131,072
$N = 7$, 1.728 billion DOF	-	100.1	97.3	96.7	92.8	87.3

We are reaching 89,8% scaling efficiency for the one-element-per-processor case with periodic boundaries and still 78.6% with exact boundaries. When looking at the calculation with 4096 DOF per processor, the differences between these boundary types almost vanish: We then discover 96.9% for the periodic and 95.1% for the exact case.

To target extreme scale computations, a large strong scaling test up to $131,072$ processors with exact boundaries was set up. The final configuration had $13,824$ DOF per processor, which is a desirable value for real-life computations with the DGSEM code on JUGENE.

We reach a very good 87.3% strong scaling efficiency for the $131,072$ processor run and consider the code ready to tackle very large real-life problems.

6   Conclusions and Outlook

We have shown an efficient parallelization of a DGSEM scheme that utilizes the tensor-product structure of the method to overlap computation and communication and therefore provides a latency-hiding mechanism. Since we can evaluate the DG operator dimension by dimension, we can split it into several small parts that can be evaluated during a pending non-blocking send-receive operation. With the good parallel results shown in this paper, the DGSEM code is ready to tackle large scale turbulent problems. To exploit the full potential of the code, we will focus on LES+acoustics for turbulent jets. Since structured grids imply limited geometric flexibility, necessary modifications to the parallelization strategy for large scale DGSEM computations on unstructured hexahedral meshes are currently being developed.

The research presented in this paper was supported by the Deutsche Forschungsgemeinschaft (DFG), amongst others within the Schwerpunktprogramm 1276: MetStroem and the cluster of excellence Simulation Technology (SimTech), Universität Stuttgart.

References

1. Bassi, F., Rebay, S.: A high-order accurate discontinuous finite element method for the numerical solution of the compressible Navier-Stokes equations. J. Comput. Phys. 131, 267–279 (1997)
2. Black, K.: A conservative spectral element method for the approximation of compressible fluid flow. Kybernetika 35(1), 133–146 (1999)
3. Canuto, C., Hussaini, M., Quarteroni, A., Zang, T.: Spectral Methods: Fundamentals in Single Domains. Springer (2006)

4. Fagherazzi, S., Furbish, D., Rasetarinera, P., Hussaini, M.Y.: Application of the discontinuous spectral Galerkin method to groundwater flow. Advances in Water Resourses 27, 129–140 (2004)
5. Gassner, G., Kopriva, D.: A comparison of the dispersion and dissipation errors of gauss and gauss lobatto discontinuous galerkin spectral element methods. SIAM Journal on Scientific Computing 33(5), 2560–2579 (2011)
6. Gassner, G.J., Hindenlang, F., Munz, C.-D.: A Runge-Kutta based Discontinuous Galerkin Method with Time Accurate Local Time Stepping. In: Advances in Computational Fluid Dynamics, vol. 2, pp. 95–118. World Scientific (2011)
7. Hindenlang, F., Gassner, G., Altmann, C., Beck, A., Staudenmaier, M., Munz, C.D.: Explicit discontinuous galerkin methods for unsteady problems. Computers & Fluids 61, 86–93 (2012)
8. Kopriva, D., Woodruff, S., Hussaini, M.: Computation of electromagnetic scattering with a non-conforming discontinuous spectral element method. International Journal for Numerical Methods in Engineering 53 (2002)
9. Kopriva, D.: Metric identities and the discontinuous spectral element method on curvilinear meshes. Journal of Scientific Computing 26(3), 301–327 (2006), http://dx.doi.org/10.1007/s10915-005-9070-8
10. Kopriva, D.A.: Implementing Spectral Methods for Partial Differential Equations. Springer (2009), http://dx.doi.org/10.1007/978-90-481-2261-5_8
11. Rasetarinera, P., Kopriva, D., Hussaini, M.: Discontinuous spectral element solution of acoustic radiation from thin airfoils. AIAA Journal 39(11), 2070–2075 (2001)
12. Restelli, M., Giraldo, F.: A conservative discontinuous Galerkin semi-implicit formulation for the navier-stokes equations in nonhydrostatic mesoscale modeling. SIAM J. Sci. Comp. 31(3), 2231–2257 (2009)

Reducing the Memory Footprint
of Parallel Applications with KSM

Nathalie Rauschmayr[1] and Achim Streit[2]

[1] CERN - European Organization for Nuclear Research, Switzerland
[2] Steinbuch Centre for Computing, Karlsruhe Institute of Technology, Germany
nathalie.rauschmayr@cern.ch

Abstract. In the era of multicore and manycore programming, memory represents a restrictive resource and it is therefore necessary to share as much as possible between processes. But in many cases, in which a parallel execution of an application has never been foreseen, it is difficult to apply a shared memory model afterwards. The KSM-tool (Kernel Same Page Merging) provides an easy ad-hoc-solution to reduce the overall memory footprint. This paper shows that in the applications of the LHCb experiment at CERN between 8% and 48 % of memory can be gained. In addition it will be discussed how to adjust KSM in order to balance the gain in memory and the additional CPU consumption.

1 Introduction

LHCb is one of the LHC experiments at CERN [14]. The data produced by the detector is approximately 1.5 PB per year, which has to be processed using the LHCb applications. According to the size of data this cannot be performed by using one computing center. Consequently the Computing Grid, provided by WLCG [2], is used as a platform for data processing, which provides 11 Tier-1 sites, about 150 Tier-2 sites and many Tier-3 sites. Each of those layers provides a certain set of services, as an example the Tier-1 sites provide not only computing power but also storage facilities. LHCb runs its applications on 6 Tier-1 sites and about 75 Tier-2 sites. These applications are based on a complex software framework and the memory consumption plays an important role as it is very often the reason why grid jobs fail. Worse, it appears that especially the memory bounded applications of LHCb cannot run efficiently on today's hardware of the WLCG, which typically provides 2 GB per core. Consequently only a subset can be used instead of running on all cores. In order to get a better efficiency, it would be necessary to share most of the common datasets between the processes in order to keep the overall memory consumption low. In fact the software of the LHCb experiment could save a lot of memory, because most of the preallocated datasets are used in read only mode after initialization and can be potentially shared between several processes. However the experiment applications are integrated in a complex software framework, as described in [11]. It is not trivial to apply a shared memory model without major changes to

R. Keller et al. (Eds.): Facing the Multicore-Challenge III 2012, LNCS 7686, pp. 48–59, 2013.

the framework. Here we evaluate the Kernel Same Page Merging (KSM) as an automatic tool for memory deduplication [4].

The paper is structured as follows. Section 2 gives an overview about KSM. Section 3 describes how KSM is used and adapted to the test cases. Section 4 introduces the test applications and shows the results. An evaluation of those is given in section 5, followed by a discussion of possible problems in section 6. Section 7 gives an overview about related work and section 8 concludes the paper.

2   Overview about KSM

KSM is a Linux kernel module that has been developed for the KVM hypervisor in order to share system libraries between virtual machines, which are running similar distributions, as described in [4]. KSM is based on the Linux Copy-On-Write principle, which means that datasets remain in shared memory as long as no process writes to them and it works with standard sized 4 kB pages. All pages are regularly scanned, if the content is equal only one copy is kept in memory. The scanning can be computing intensive and it is important to tune KSM to the current workload, which can be done via 2 parameters. The parameters *pages_to_scan* and *sleep_millisecs* define how many pages must be scanned after a certain period of time and they represent in fact the maximum merging rate. The standard values are 100 pages and 20 ms which is equal to a maximum merging rate of $(100 \cdot \frac{4}{1024}$ MB $\cdot \frac{1}{0.02}$ s $) = 19.5$ MB/s.

2.1   Basic Principle

In a first step allocated memory must be registered for being potentially shared by KSM. Afterwards KSM builds two internal data structures, the *stable* and *unstable tree* [4]. Those are implemented as a red-black tree, which is a binary search tree and allows modifications with a complexity $\mathcal{O}(\log_2 n)$, where n is the cardinality of the dataset [5]. The stable tree contains all pages, that are shared by KSM and thus they are write protected. The unstable tree contains pages whose contents did not change for a certain period and which are therefore registered as potential candidates for sharing. When a new page is scanned, a checksum is calculated in order to estimate in the next scan whether a page was modified. If not, the content will be bytewise compared with pages from the stable and unstable tree.

2.2   Monitoring KSM

Since Linux kernel version 2.6.32 KSM is based on the *madvise* kernel interface [12], a tool for memory handling. A new parameter was introduced, that indicates whether a page is mergeable and must be scanned by KSM. The page can then be registered as:

- pages_sharing: amount of memory saving
- pages_unshared: content is not equal to any of the already registered pages

- pages_shared: already shared
- pages_volatile: content changes too often

A quick example shall illustrate how the pages are handled. Assuming that 2 processes allocate two separate arrays with a size of 10^7 zeros, then KSM will scan about $(10^7 \cdot \frac{\text{sizeof } (int)}{1024} \text{ kB }) \cdot \frac{1}{4} = 19531$ pages. As all have the same content, only one of them is kept and the rest is removed. *pages_sharing* shows a value of 19530 pages and *pages_shared* a value of 1, because only one page is kept in shared memory. Consequently a high ratio between *pages_sharing* to *pages_shared* indicates a good efficiency of KSM.

3   Setting Up KSM

In order to use KSM from inside an application, the kernel function *madvise* must be called, which can be either done in the software itself for certain objects or as a malloc-hook. The disadvantage of the latter approach is that KSM has to scan every page, which has been allocated by the application. Therefore the merging rate has been adapted to the worst case scenario. The LHCb applications consist of three software packages which have different system requirements. Analysis jobs are usually heavily memory bounded. Their processes usually reach 1.7 GB during the initialization and increase during the processing loop. Therefore the worst case scenario on an 8-core machine is caused by a parallel analysis job running with 8 worker processes and allocating memory with a rate of 40 MB/s per process. This concludes that a merging rate of $8 \cdot 40MB/s = 320MB/s$ must be already sufficient. For the tests the value has been set a bit higher to 20 ms and 3000 pages which is equal to a merging rate of 585 MB/s. In order to compare the results a second scenario has been used in which the values have been set to 20 ms and 10^6 pages which presents a rate of 190 GB/s. All 4 different types of pages, as listed in section 2.2, have been monitored during the execution of the tests.

4   Execution of Test Applications

The LHCb experiment uses different kinds of data intensive processing applications, which are described in [11]. The following three ones have been used for testing KSM:

- *Gauss:* It represents the simulation software of the LHCb experiment. In a first step random seeds and numbers are generated which are used for producing randomized particles. After that the response of the detector is simulated. This software is normally CPU bounded; the physical memory consumption is only 1.1 GB and does not increase during event processing [6].
- *Brunel:* The application reconstructs particles and calculates their decays via pattern recognition and clustering algorithms. The physical memory

consumption starts with 1.2 GB and usually increases depending on the processed datasets. Histograms and counters for each type of particle are calculated and written out.

- *DaVinci:* This application provides analysis tools which are used for descriptive statistics on the physics data, which are then written into file buffers. As that software has to handle several input and output buffers, it is memory bounded and those kind of jobs run very often out of memory. Without writing output files the physical memory consumption starts at about 1.7 GB and increases during event processing.

The test environment consist of two nodes, where each node is an Intel Xeon processor (L5520) with 2.26 GHz. Thus the system provides 16 logical and 8 physical cores in total. As hyperthreading is switched off the maximum number of processes for the tests has been limited to 8. Furthermore the system provides 24 GB RAM, two 32 kB L1 caches per core, one 256 kB L2 cache per core and one 8192 kB L3 cache per node. The machine has been running the current CERN Scientific Linux 6 [1]. Furthermore the parallel prototype of the LHCb framework has been used with different number of worker processes, namely 2, 4 and 8. In the beginning of this section results reached within the simulation application are shown, after that the results of parallel analysis job and in the end different merging rates are compared. And as KSM does not only reduce memory of parallel processes but also inside a single instance, the applications have also been executed in serial mode. KSM influences in fact the Proportional Set Size (PSS) of processes. This value indicates the real physical memory consumption as it accounts the memory in such a way that shared pages are only accounted partly. It means when a 4 kB page is shared by 4 processes then the PSS value would be 1 kB and the Resident Set Size (RSS) would be 4 kB for each process.

Figure 1 shows the monitoring results of KSM for a parallel execution of a Gauss job with 2 worker processes. It is obvious that after the phase of initialization, a stable value of *pages_sharing* is reached. That concludes that most of the allocated memory is not modified during the main loop of the application. Indeed for simulating collisions most of the datasets are read only, such as the magnetic field map and the geometric description of the detector. These datasets are usually big and can be shared between parallel processes. Furthermore it appears that the accounting of *pages_volatile* and *pages_unshared* influences each other, as a positive peak on the one side causes a negative peak on the other side. These fluctuations are seen in the memory regions to which the processes write quite often and which cannot be merged, because the content changes too often. It is likely that a single peak represents a preallocated file buffer, which is listed as *pages_volatile* as soon as a process writes to it and it is then registered as *pages_unshared* after that. Neither *pages_volatile* nor *pages_unshared* reduce the memory footprint, so these fluctuations do not influence the overall memory gain caused by KSM. Using 8 worker processes, KSM needs more time to reach the stable value for *pages_sharing*, as shown in figure 2. In contrast to the 2 worker case, it is now reached after 200 seconds. Furthermore it is obvious that *pages_volatile* increases quite a lot during the phase of initialization and a peak

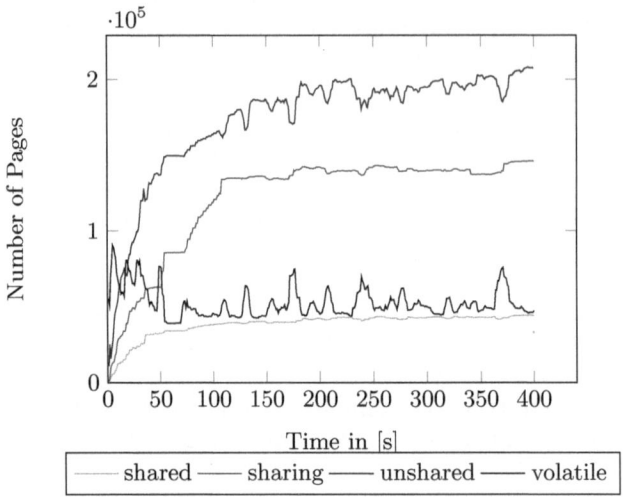

Fig. 1. KSM monitoring results within 2 worker processes (Gauss application)

occurs in the beginning which is slightly decreasing afterwards as then the pages
are accounted as unshared. It appears that KSM has a problem to register and
scan all the pages in the beginning, as there are many processes allocating a lot
of memory at the same time. It might be a reason why KSM needs nearly 100
seconds more for reaching a stable value. Increasing the merging rate does not
improve the situation, which will be shown at the end of this section. That the
problem is directly connected to the data rate at which memory is allocated is
likely due to the fact that this problem gets even worse in the memory bounded
applications of LHCb. Figure 3 shows an analysis job and it appears that the
problem is even worse. A significant peak occurs for *pages_volatile* when 8 memory bounded worker processes are executed. Its maximum is even higher than
the stable value reached by *pages_sharing* after 450 seconds. It appears again
that the more processes are running the later the stable value is reached. In
serial mode this happens after 80 seconds, with 4 worker processes after 200 and
with 8 after 450 seconds. As explained in the previous section it is important to
tune the maximum merging rate in order to keep the CPU consumption low. In
figure 4 the results reached by KSM have been compared with different merging
rates. A very high merging rate with 190 GB/s has been compared to 585 MB/s.
It appears that the maximum value of *pages_sharing* do not differ much. On the
other side, the peak of *pages_volatile* cannot be removed and even the stable
value cannot be reached earlier with a higher rate. This suggests that setting
the KSM parameter to a higher value than the rate at with which memory is allocated by the processes, is not reasonable as no additional gain can be achieved
by that. Regarding the CPU consumption it appears that the KSM-thread consumes only 20-30 % in parallel simulation jobs and 30-50% in parallel analysis
jobs compared to full CPU consumption with a rate of 190 GB/s.

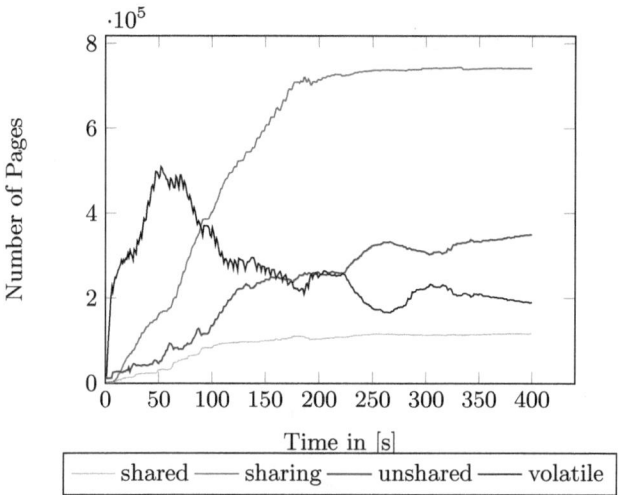

Fig. 2. KSM-monitoring results within 8 worker processes (Gauss application)

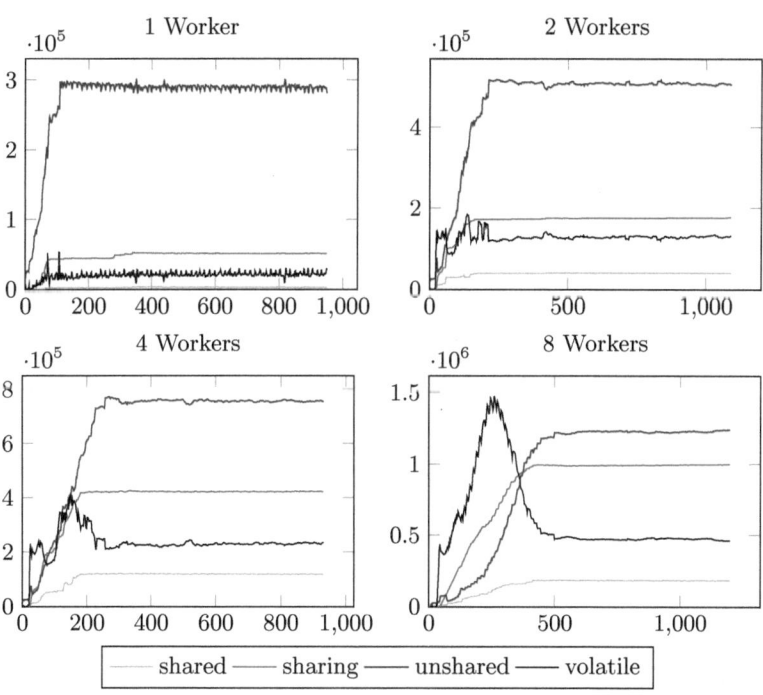

Fig. 3. Monitoring KSM-parameters within an analysis job (y-axis: number of pages - x-axis: time in [s])

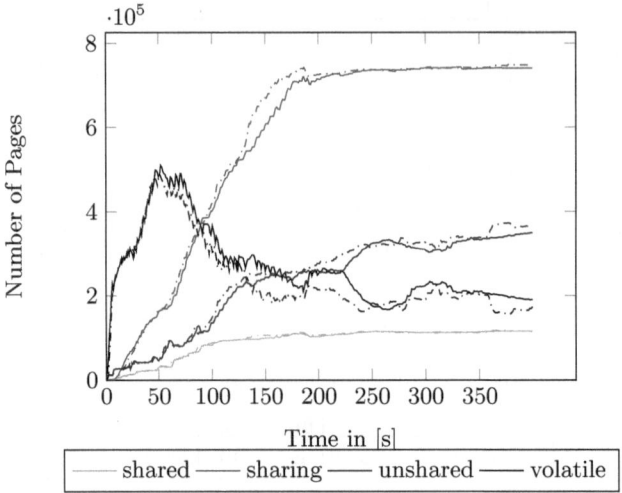

Fig. 4. Comparison of the different merging rates 585 MB/s (continous line) and 190 GB/s (dotted line)

Table 1 presents the overall gain in memory reached with KSM in the different applications. For the evaluation, the test cases have been executed with and without KSM and their memory consumption has been monitored. Initialisation and finalisation of the test cases have been neglected and the average difference has been calculated during the period KSM had a stable value. The first value in table 1 indicates the absolute difference and the second value shows the corresponding percentage. About 183 MB can already be merged in a single instance which is possibly due to file buffers, which usually contain a huge amount of zeros. This value can then be reached in every single instance which means that it is accounted n times for n processes.

Table 1. Memory reduction reached with KSM in the different applications

	serial mode	2 workers	4 workers	8 workers
Gauss	183 MB (22 %)	623 MB (33 %)	1275 MB (42 %)	2659 MB (48 %)
Brunel	100 MB (8 %)	448 MB (21%)	990 MB (27 %)	2297 MB (33 %)
DaVinci	165 MB (13 %)	890 MB (26 %)	1841 MB (29 %)	3864 MB (32 %)

5   Evaluation of Results

The results are evaluated with respect to two main considerations. First it is investigated what the gain in memory is compared to the additional CPU-consumption and furthermore a theoretical value for memory sharing must be calculated. For the theoretical model the heap of the applications was profiled in order to see the memory consumption per object and to evaluate which of them are not modified during event processing.

5.1 Simulation - Gauss

Analysing the heap profile of the simulation test case, a theoretical value of about 230 MB could be evaluated, which corresponds to the sum of all non modified objects during the event processing. Typically objects like database contents can be shared, as these are normally used in read only mode. Furthermore a simulation uses event tables for generating random numbers which can be also used by all processes. Overall it means that $(n - 1) \cdot 230$ MB must be shared as minimum within n worker processes. Comparing with table 1 it appears that KSM can even reach a higher value than calculated, since it can gain for example 623 MB within 2 worker processes. As KSM can also reduce the memory in single processes, that value is accounted n times for n processes. Thus it is likely that in 2 worker processes $2 \cdot 183$ MB are accounted for the memory reduction per process and $623\text{MB} - (2 \cdot 183\text{MB}) = 257$ MB for the sharing of objects between the processes.

5.2 Reconstruction - Brunel

The objects that can be potentially shared in the reconstruction application are nearly the same as in the simulation test case. Those are the database contents and represent in fact the description of the detector and all its conditions and parameter settings. The heap profiling accounts about 210 MB as a sum of these objects. KSM can also reach a better value in that example as shown in table 1. Extrapolating that for 8 worker processes means that $7 \cdot 210$ MB must be shared as minimum, which is also reached by KSM.

5.3 Analysis - DaVinci

Between analysis processes the same objects can be shared as explained in the last paragraph. Those datasets are also accounted with about 210 MB, which is obviously reached again by KSM in all test cases with several number of worker processes.

5.4 Additional CPU-Consumption and Cost Evaluation

An evaluation of the additional CPU-consumption has been done in order to quantify the impact of memory reduction with respect to CPU-resources regarding the given test cases. In order to do so, the average processing cost for a test case running with and without KSM has been calculated. Assuming a reconstruction job with 8 worker processes and 8000 events in total, an average processing time of 1450s for the first case and 1393s for the latter case has been determined. That is an additional CPU-consumption of 4.09%. Given a lifetime of 4 years on average for a worker node, a cost of 16 Euros per HEP-SPEC06[1]

---

[1] HEP-wide benchmark for measuring CPU performance.

can be assumed including usage and maintenance of 4 years. Since a single AMD job slot can provide a performance of 7.5 HEP-SPEC06, according to [3], it results in a total cost of 120 Euros. As the performance of Intel cores are better due to hyperthreading and as that function was switched off on the Intel Xeon test machine, an AMD job slot with 7.5 HEP-SPEC06 was assumed. The price for memory does not usually scale linearly, however for reasons of simplification a price of 10 Euros for each additional GB including usage and maintenance of 4 years has been assumed. In the test case with 8 worker processes about 2 GB can be saved with KSM, which concludes to a reduction of 20 Euros. In a first step the processing costs x an y are determined for both cases, where x represents the processing costs per second for one core and y represents the processing costs per second for one core with 2 GB extension[2]. Since eight job slots are used the total costs are in the first case $8 \cdot x \cdot 1450s$ and in the second one, due to the additional 2 GB of memory, $(7 \cdot x + y) \cdot 1393s$. A difference of 1.96% of costs have been evaluated, which leads to the fact that KSM increases processing time and costs. It must be respected in that conclusion that a test case was used, which runs under normal conditions without reaching the memory limit of the system. If jobs run out of memory and fail or start paging, then even higher cost will be caused. This will be illustrated by the following example.

For testing purposes a modified testcase of the parallel analysis job has been used, which reaches nearly 3 GB as maximum. However, it represents the standard analysis case used by LHCb for the year 2012. Assuming a test environment with 2 GB per core which represents the average memory per core provided by WLCG, the testcase will run out of memory. An analysis job with 8 workers, processing 10000 events, takes about 898.7 seconds in average as long as no memory limit is set. If it is set to 2 GB per core the jobs have taken 1327.24 seconds in average due to paging. Using KSM instead can reduce the amount of memory which has to be swapped out or can even avoid paging. A time of 944.08 seconds could be evaluated in that test case, which is 5.05 % slower than the case without memory limit and 28.87 % faster than the case in which paging occured. Assuming paging is not supported will conclude that the given test case can only run with 5 processes in parallel instead of 8. That increases the CPU-time, but also the costs as 3 cores remain idle due to the fact that the memory limit of the system is reached.

It must be respected that those values are very specific and will differ on other systems and in other software, of course. But as generalization it can be concluded that KSM will decrease costs as soon as an aplication reaches the memory limit of the system.

6   Caveats

Recent Linux kernels provide a lot of functionalities for a better handling of memory, which has to be considered in the context of KSM. It appears that some

---

[2] $x = \frac{120 Euros}{4 years} = 9.51 \cdot 10^{-7} \frac{Euro}{s}$ and $y = \frac{140 Euros}{4 years} = 1.11 \cdot 10^{-6} \frac{Euro}{s}$.

of them can be problematic for sharing memory between processes. As KSM can only work on 4 kB pages, hugepages [10] are problematic, which are used by several distributions like Red Hat 6.2. However in Red Hat 6.2 KSM already register the pages before they are considered to be merged in a hugepage. But there might be cases in which hugepages can cause a problem. Another problem can occur with Address Space Layout Randomization (*ASLR*), which is a security mechansim that scrambles the memory content of pages, as explained detailed in [13]. It influences the page alignment and decreases the probability of having pages with the same content. In order to gain the best value for memory sharing this functionality must be deactivated. This is of course a trade off between better resource utilization and higher security. Switching off the functionality of ASLR gives an attacker the chance to identify pages more easily. In [15] it is furthermore shown, that it is possible to identify, whether a page was copied from shared memory and though which page was shared with other processes. Therefore the time, which was needed to write to a page, was simply measured. This presents a problem of security especially in the context of cloud computing, as presented in [13] and [15].

7   Related Work

Memory deduplication plays an important role in cloud computing. An automatic way via Content-Based Page Sharing and Transparent Page Sharing, as described in [8] and [17], seems to be the most promising solution. Detailed studies and evaluations on Content-Based Page Sharing via KSM can be found in [9]. Those concepts can be also applied inside one single instance of an operating system as described and evaluated in [16]. The possibility of *mergeable* cache in the context of multi core programming is investigated in [7] and results of memory deduplication within several benchmarks from domains like visualization and machine learning are presented. The idea of using automatic tools came also up in other CERN experiments several years ago, as it is mentioned in [4], but the results for memory deduplication of these tests have not been evaluated to the cost of additional CPU-consumption and such tests have never been evaluated for different applications of the LHCb framework.

8   Conclusion

KSM is an easy ad-hoc solution to share memory in an automatic way. However the efficiency of KSM cannot be predicted very easily as that depends on the data layout with which memory is allcoated and modified by a software. General conditions in that context which might influence the efficiency of KSM are for example, parallel processes using similar datasets and accessing them in read-only mode. Those conditions are fullfilled indeed by the parallel prototype of the LHCb framework. Furthermore, most datasets are allocated during initialization and are not modified during the main loop of the application, which allows KSM to reach a stable value. It can be critical as soon as processes also write to pages or delete them, as KSM has to rebuild the stable and unstable tree then. Another critical parameter is the memory alignment, which is influenced by security tools but also by the way how parallel processes have been created. The worker processes in the parallel prototype of the LHCb framework are running the same process chain and are loading, in prinicple, the same datasets, which concludes that the probability of equal aligned pages is high.

Furthermore it is typically the case that adding a shared memory model on the software framework level afterwards is difficult. Implementing a shared memory model in the software of the LHCb experiment faces several problems if it is done via forking of processes during the main loop of the application. For example, the handling of counters and histograms might be problematic, as they are already set up during initialization and must be reset after the fork. Furthermore all open files must be handled, because all processes using the same file descriptor will cause problems as soon as they write or read to it. Using shared memory regions in the software will be also very difficult as the read- and write-access to shared areas has to be coordinated in order to guarantee thread safety. Furthermore the framework of the LHCb experiment is constructed in such a way, that all configurations must be provided by the user, which concludes that those ones are individual and even own services and algorithms can be applied via the configuration. That results in a high diversity, how the application can be executed, and it causes also the problem that users might do things which are not allowed by the framework. Those problems can be handled as long as the applications run sequentially but as soon as parallel processes are forked during the event loop, many classes must be protected and certain actions must be prevented, which can be possibly done by the user. All in all a lot of test cases will occur which must be validated in parallel execution as long as sharing is not handled by automatic tools like KSM. Nevertheless applying a shared memory model in the framework has the advantage that it does not consume additional CPU resources in contrast to KSM. In order to keep CPU-consumption low, a new service was introduced in the Linux kernel which adapts automatically the merging rate of KSM. The results which have been shown in this paper, were produced by a fixed merging rate. But since the CPU-consumption could be reduced to a value of 20% - 50% the influence on computing time was small.

As a conclusion, KSM is an easy solution to reduce memory consumption as long as the memory presents the restrictive resource and the CPU-consumption is not too high. With respect to tradeoff of security and CPU-resources, a shared memory model on software framework level might be a better solution.

References

1. Linux @ cern (2012), http://linux.web.cern.ch/linux/scientific6/
2. Wlcg worldwide lhc computing grid (2012), http://wlcg.web.cern.ch/
3. Alef, M.: Cpu benchmarking at gridka (2012),
   http://indico.cern.ch/getFile.py/access?contribId=40&sessionId=2
   &resId=0&materialId=slides&confId=160737

4. Arcangeli, A., Eidus, I., Wright, C.: Increasing memory density by using KSM. In: OLS 2009: Proceedings of the Linux Symposium, pp. 19–28 (July 2009)
5. Bayer, R.: Symmetric binary b-trees: Data structure and maintenance algorithms. Acta Informatica 1, 290–306 (1972), 10.1007/BF00289509
6. Belyaev, I., Charpentier, P., Easo, S., Mato, P., Palacios, J., Pokorski, W., Ranjard, F., Van Tilburg, J.: Simulation application for the lhcb experiment. Technical Report physics/0306035, CERN, Geneva (June 2003)
7. Biswas, S., Franklin, D., Savage, A., Dixon, R., Sherwood, T., Chong, F.T.: Multi-execution: multicore caching for data-similar executions. SIGARCH Comput. Archit. News 37(3), 164–173 (2009)
8. Bugnion, E., Devine, S., Govil, K., Rosenblum, M.: Disco: running commodity operating systems on scalable multiprocessors. ACM Trans. Comput. Syst. 15(4), 412–447 (1997)
9. Chang, C.-R., Wu, J.-J., Liu, P.: An empirical study on memory sharing of virtual machines for server consolidation. In: 2011 IEEE 9th International Symposium on Parallel and Distributed Processing with Applications (ISPA), pp. 244–249 (May 2011)
10. Corbet, J.: Transparent hugepages (2009), https://lwn.net/Articles/359158/
11. Corti, G., Cattaneo, M., Charpentier, P., Frank, M., Koppenburg, P., Mato, P., Ranjard, F., Roiser, S., Belyaev, I., Barrand, G.: Software for the lhcb experiment. IEEE Transactions on Nuclear Science 53(3), 1323–1328 (2006)
12. Kerrisk, M.: Linux programmer's manual (2012), http://man7.org/linux/man-pages/man2/madvise.2.html
13. Yagi, T., Artho, C., Suzaki, K., Iijima, K.: Effects of memory randomization, sanitization and page cache on memory deduplication. In: European Workshop on System Security, EuroSec 2012 (2012)
14. Schneider, O.: Overview of the lhcb experiment. Nuclear Instruments and Methods in Physics Research Section A: Accelerators, Spectrometers, Detectors and Associated Equipment 446(1-2), 213–221 (2000)
15. Suzaki, K., Iijima, K., Yagi, T., Artho, C.: Memory deduplication as a threat to the guest os. In: Proceedings of the Fourth European Workshop on System Security, EUROSEC 2011, pp. 1:1–1:6. ACM, New York (2011)
16. Suzaki, K., Yagi, T., Iijima, K., Quynh, N.A., Artho, C., Watanebe, Y.: Moving from logical sharing of guest os to physical sharing of deduplication on virtual machine. In: Proceedings of the 5th USENIX Conference on Hot Topics in Security, HotSec 2010, pp. 1–7. USENIX Association, Berkeley (2010)
17. Waldspurger, C.A.: Memory resource management in vmware esx server. SIGOPS Oper. Syst. Rev. 36(SI), 181–194 (2002)

Recalibrating Fine-Grained Locking in Parallel Bucket Hash Tables

Ákos Dudás, Sándor Juhász, and Sándor Kolumbán

Department of Automation and Applied Informatics,
Budapest University of Technology and Economics,
1117 Budapest, Magyar Tudósok krt. 2 QB207
{akos.dudas,juhasz.sandor,kolumban.sandor}@aut.bme.hu

Abstract. Mutual exclusion protects data structures in parallel environments in order to preserve data integrity. A lock being held effectively blocks the execution of all other threads wanting to access the same shared resource until the lock is released. This blocking behavior reduces the level of parallelism causing performance loss. Fine grained locking reduces the contention for the locks resulting in better throughput, however, the granularity, i.e. how many locks to use, is not straightforward. In large bucket hash tables, the best approach is to divide the table into blocks, each containing one or more buckets, and locking these blocks independently. The size of the block, for optimal performance, depends on the time spent within the critical sections, which depends on the table's internal properties, and the arrival intensity of the queries. A queuing model is presented capturing this behavior, and an adaptive algorithm is presented fine-tuning the granularity of locking (the block size) to adapt to the execution environment.

1 Introduction

In parallel environments, shared resources, such as data structures, must be protected from concurrent accesses [20]. Blocking synchronization mechanisms are the de-facto solution for avoiding race conditions and guaranteeing thread-safety. Critical sections protect parts of the data structure assuring that at all times at most one thread is allowed to access and modify critical parts of the internal structure.

Critical sections are most often realized by placing locks within the data structure itself. These locks are basic building blocks of parallel algorithms. They are supported by most operating systems, runtime environments, and for performance reasons, also by modern hardware. Mutual exclusion can be realized using software only, but hardware support, such as the compare-and-exchange and test-and-set instructions, make them cheaper.

Locks are often criticized in the literature for their disadvantageous properties. Main concerns include that threads using mutual exclusion affect each others performance by limiting the level of parallelism, while deadlock situations and erroneous thread behavior (not releasing locks) can cause program errors. Still,

R. Keller et al. (Eds.): Facing the Multicore-Challenge III 2012, LNCS 7686, pp. 60–71, 2013.

locks are favored by programmers for they are easy to use, and more importantly, they are expressed by the programming language or environment in a fashion which is familiar to the programmer.

As for performance, the most important question is the placement of the locks. A single lock, protecting the entire data structure, can limit the attainable performance as it basically serializes all access to the data structure and it makes little use of the multithreading capabilities of modern hardware. The solution to this problem is to use not a single lock but to partition the data structure into disjoint blocks and protect different blocks with different locks. The only requirement is that any operation may only access data within the block or blocks it has acquired the dedicated locks for. This partitioning allows threads to act in parallel as long as they access different blocks of the data structure.

A bucket hash table stores items arranged according to an identifying element, the *key*. Each item is unambiguously mapped to a virtual "bucket", and any operation (insert, find, delete) needs to access this single bucket. This allows a trivial partitioning of the data set for fine grained locking: each bucket can be a separate block protected by a dedicated lock. While this delivers best theoretical performance it is undesirable for it may require too much memory. In case of large hash tables with millions of buckets it is not practical to have millions of locks. A simple queue-type lock [15] requires two integer values per lock; millions of these would require megabytes of valuable memory in the CPU caches.

To overcome this difficulty, but at the same time provide good throughput, the table should be partitioned into disjoint blocks where a block contains multiple buckets. The exact number of the blocks should be chosen to assure good performance, but at the same time, the number of locks should be minimal. The number of blocks is determined by multiple factors, most of them can also change during the lifetime of the hash table. These factors include the amount of time spent within the critical sections, the frequency of the hash table accesses, and the number of concurrent threads.

In this paper, we show that the performance of a hash table is in fact largely affected by the granularity of locking. There is a threshold in the number of locks above which increasing the granularity of locking has little effect on the performance. We show that the parallel bucket hash table can be best described by a queuing network, which helps modeling its behavior. We propose an adaptive algorithm which allows the reconfiguration of the table in runtime changing the granularity of locking based on external and internal circumstances. We show that this algorithm can determine an estimated number of locks the table should use based on solely internal properties it measures during operation.

The rest of the paper is organized as follows. Section 2 cites the related literature of hash tables and their parallel implementations. The concurrent bucket hash table is modeled by a queuing network presented in Section 3, which allows further analysis and derivation of an adaptive locking strategy detailed in Section 4. The adaptive algorithm is evaluated in Section 5 followed by the conclusions in Section 6.

2   Related Work

Hash tables [10] store and retrieve items identified by a unique key. A hash table is basically a fixed-size reference table, where the position of an item is determined by a hash function. Each position in this table is a virtual "bucket", a collection of items, most often realized by a linked list or an array. Each item mapped to this location is placed in the array/list in no particular order. Inserting an item or finding one by its *key* requires mapping the *key* to a bucket and searching through the entire bucket.

Large hash tables are often used in applications and algorithms in various fields, such as model checking [1, 11], web servers [14, 21] and even in genome research [17].

There is an extensive body of research connected to parallel hash tables and data structures. The main areas are blocking and non-blocking solutions. Non-blocking methods [3, 16, 18], instead of mutual exclusion, use atomic CPU operations to maintain data integrity. While these solutions are just as good as locking methods, in this paper we focus solely on mutual exclusion.

Larson et al. in [12] used two lock levels: a global table lock and a separate lightweight lock (a flag) for each bucket. The global table lock is held just as long as the appropriate bucket's lock is acquired. They describe that for fast access spinlocks are used instead of Windows critical sections. It was shown by Michael [16] that in case of non-extensible hash tables simple reader-writer locks can provide a good performance in shared memory multiprocessor systems.

More efficient implementation like [13] use a more sophisticated locking scheme with a smaller number of higher level locks (allocated for hash table blocks including multiple buckets) allowing concurrent searching and resizing of the table. More complicated locking scenarios are also available, such as a hierarchical lock system with dynamic lock granularity escalation, as presented by Klots and Bamford [9].

Hopscotch hashing [6] is an open-address hashing scheme, which provides good cache locality, supporting parallel access. The drawback of open-address hashing is the need for resizing the table.

A commercially available library by Intel, the Thread Building Blocks has a parallel hash container called *concurrent_hash_map*. This implementation is a bucket hash table. It uses locks on various levels, including the items themselves [8].

Our bucket hash table [7] is a closed-address hashing scheme, which combines the best property of open-address hashing, namely good cache locality [6] without the need to resize the table.

The main contributions of this work are the following. First we show that the performance of bucket hash tables increases with the number of locks, but only up to a point. To find this optimal number, a queuing model is presented, which is used to show an adaptive algorithm recalibrating the hash table in runtime. We know of no such re-calibrating parallel hash table in the literature.

3   Modeling the Parallel Hash Table

This section presents empirical measurements capturing the effect of the granularity of locking in a bucket hash table. In large hash tables, the number of locks the hash table should use is significantly less than the number of buckets within the table. To find a good estimate for this number, a parallel bucket hash table is modeled with a queuing network allowing further analysis.

3.1   Scalability with Increasing Granularity

By implementing a highly optimized custom bucket hash table in C++ the physical performance of the hash table is evaluated by executing insert and find operations. The mutual exclusion was realized using the so called *ticket lock* by Mellor-Crummey and Scott [15]. Figure 1 plots the scalability of the hash table with an increasing number of locks used internally by the table. Both the complete execution time and the number of clashes (i.e. the number of lock acquisitions that resulted in waiting due to a busy lock) was measured.

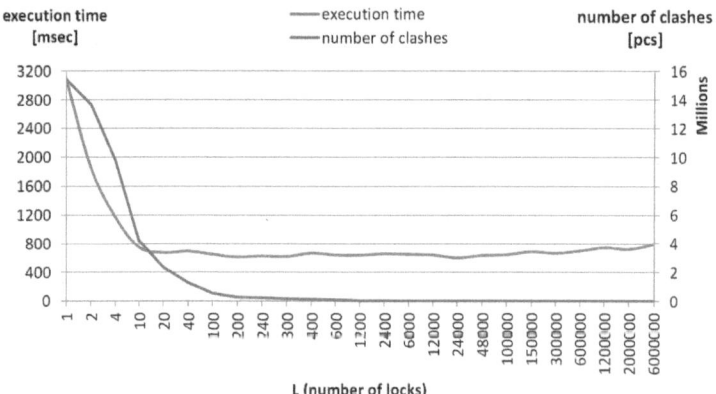

Fig. 1. The execution time and the number of clashed during lock acquisitions of 8 million inserts and 8 million find operations in a bucket hash table having 12 million buckets with an increasing number of locks used by the table internally

Using a single lock in the table is indeed a bottleneck. Increasing the number of locks up to the range of 10-100 an over 3.5 speedup is observed. Further increasing the number of locks, there is a minor increase (up to 10%), but this is insignificant compared to the performance gain with only a few dozen locks. The number of times the threads had to wait due to a lock being busy also plummets to near zero at this threshold. Above a certain limit, at approximately 50000 locks, the performance even starts to decrease due to the overhead of the locks themselves. The granularity of locking is a major factor in the throughput of a parallel hash table, but there is no point in increasing it over all limits. Our goal is finding a range in which the performance is near its peak with the lowest number of locks required.

3.2   The Queuing Model

In order to characterize the behavior of the locks, more precisely the length of blocking a thread, the system is modeled with a queuing network (see Fig. 2), similar to the one presented by Gilbert [4]. In our model there is not a fixed number of threads, but rather an infinite number of threads. This models a system in which the hash table is part of a service (i.e. a webserver) and requests come from an outside source, that is, the number of threads changes. This is not a limitation, rather a generalization of the model, with the following assumptions.

1. There are L locks in the system with infinite buffers. Selection of a lock is uniform meaning that every lock is selected independently from every other random phenomena in the system with probability $1/L$. This can be guaranteed by a good hash function that maps a particular request to a lock, supposing that items are chosen from the universe uniformly.
2. The time spent within the critical section is exponentially distributed with parameter μ. The expected timespan a thread spends in a critical section is $1/\mu$. This is common for all threads and all queries.
3. The time between two queries to the hash table is also exponentially distributed with parameter γ.

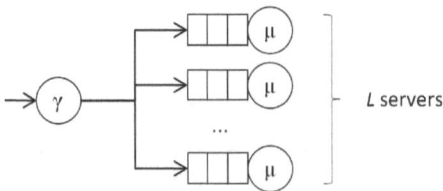

Fig. 2. The queuing network modeling the parallel bucket hash table partitioned into L blocks

When a thread is trying to acquire a lock, which is already held by another thread, "spinning" is performed. This means that the execution of the thread is not suspended; the thread remains active and constantly polls the lock. Spinning is advantageous for short critical sections [2,4]. The queue-lock allow entry into the critical section in the same order the threads have first requested it, therefore the serving discipline is first-come-first-served (FCFS) - which also guarantees starvation freedom.

This system can be simplified further as L parallel queuing networks. Every lock is (in Kendall's notation) an $M/M/1/\infty/\infty/FCFS$ queue with arrival intensity $\lambda = \frac{\gamma}{L}$, service intensity μ (see Fig. 3).

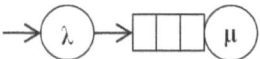

Fig. 3. The queuing network modeling a single lock in the parallel bucket hash table

4   Recalibrating Locking

The throughput of the system depends on factors, which are out of the control of the hash table, such as the arrival intensity (i.e. how often requests arrive). During the lifetime of the hash table, other circumstances may change as well, such as the required time to serve a request (service rate) can increase as the hash table is saturated. Therefore we propose an adaptive, recalibrating algorithm which periodically revises the locking strategy.

4.1   Estimating the Parameters of the System

To determine a good locking strategy, the time threads have to wait before they are allowed to enter a lock has to be minimized. To do this, the waiting time needs to be characterized, which requires the parameters of the queuing network. These parameters are listed in Table 1.

Table 1. Parameters of the queuing network

L	number of locks
$1/\mu$	average time of hashing
γ	global arrival intensity
$1 - \rho$	parameter of the geometric distribution of the queue lengths

An insert or find operation in a well designed hash table is an $O(1)$ operation which executes very few instructions and has only a few memory references. If parameters μ and γ are to be measured, all queries to the hash table should be timed, which is an expensive operation. It is not only the costly to query high resolution timers, but also recording the values (in a thread safe manner) is unreasonably costly. Initial measurements showed that a naive implementation can even double the execution time of any query.

Using a queue-type lock, every thread is able to calculate the length of the queue it joins when the lock is busy. Calculating this value is much cheaper than measuring the elapsed time within the hash table. The ticket lock by Mellor-Crummey and Scott [15] keeps two integer values for every lock: the *currently served* ticket's number and the *next available* ticket. Every threads takes a unique number by (atomically) increasing the next available counter. Comparing this number to the currently served number every thread gets how many other threads are in front of it in the queue. After calculating this value, it is recorded by the hash table. Not only is this relatively cheap, but at the same time, is is also performed only when the lock is seen in a busy state, hence the thread joining the queue would not perform any valuable work for some time anyway. To calculate and record the length of the queue only when the lock is seen busy does not reduce the throughput of the hash table. This is the only parameter recorded during normal operation.

When the hash table should revise the lock strategy being used (see Section 4.3), the process re-evaluates the number of locks used by the table by estimating the parameters of the system and finding a new optimal lock number. The update consist of the following steps.

1. Estimate parameter $1 - \rho$ using the recorded queue lengths.
2. Measure average time spent within the hash table to calculate parameter μ.
3. Calculate arrival intensity λ.

The length of the queue the waiting processes join is geometrically distributed with parameter $1-\rho$. From the measured queue lengths the average is calculated, which equals the expected value $\bar{x} = \frac{\rho}{1-\rho}$, from which (and knowing $\rho = \frac{\lambda}{\mu}$) $\lambda = \frac{\bar{x}*\mu}{1+\bar{x}}$.

μ is the parameter of the exponential distribution of the time spent within the critical section (the hash table). By executing 1000 find operations in the hash table the average of the times is approximated giving us $\frac{1}{\mu}$.

From the calculations above, all parameters of the system are estimated solely by measuring the length of the queue waiting threads join. This is a cheap operation during runtime without significant overhead. It is interesting to note that parameter λ depends only on the context the hash table is used in, yet from the internal behavior of the table it can be approximated.

Having the parameters of the system the next section describes how they are used to find a new estimate for L for which the hash table has good throughput.

4.2   Estimating the Number of Locks

When two threads are racing for the same shared resource the second thread attributes to better performance as long as there is some action it can perform while the first one is in the critical section protecting the shared resource. If the time, the second thread needs to wait for the lock, is comparable to the time the two threads act in parallel, there is no overall performance enhancement (see Fig. 4). Whenever a new thread is added to the system, it generates performance increase if the waiting time w for a lock is less then the useful time of a single thread: $w < \frac{1}{\mu}$.

From the utilization of the lock, ρ, the probability that the length of the queue (the number of threads waiting for service at the specific lock) is k is $(1 - \rho)\rho^k$ [5]. We call this state, when a specific lock has a non-empty queue, a busy lock. Clashing occurs if a thread is trying to acquire a lock which is being used, meaning that its queue is not empty. This is calculated as follows

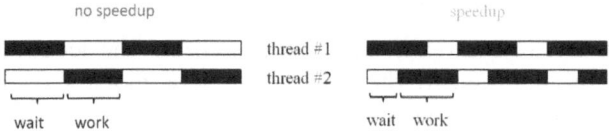

Fig. 4. Two threads acting in parallel: characterizing waiting time

$$\mathbb{P}(\text{clash}) = \sum_{k=0}^{L} \mathbb{P}(\text{busy lock is chosen}|k \text{ locks are busy})\mathbb{P}(k \text{ locks are busy})$$

$$= \sum_{k=0}^{L} \frac{k}{L}\binom{L}{k}\rho^k(1-\rho)^{L-k}$$

The first part $\mathbb{P}(\text{busy lock is chosen}|k \text{ locks are busy})$ is $\frac{k}{L}$ as any of the chosen k locks are busy. The second part, $\mathbb{P}(k \text{ locks are busy})$ is calculated by choosing exactly k locks out of L (which is $\binom{L}{k}$) and multiplying with the probability that these k locks are busy (ρ^k) and the other $L-k$ are not $((1-\rho)^{L-k})$. Further simplifying the equation we get

$$\mathbb{P}(\text{clash}) = \sum_{k=0}^{L} \frac{k}{L}\binom{L}{k}\rho^k(1-\rho)^{L-k} = \frac{1}{L}\sum_{k=0}^{L} k\binom{L}{k}\rho^k(1-\rho)^{L-k}$$

where the last sum is the expectation of a binomial distribution with parameters L and ρ, hence the final form is simply

$$\mathbb{P}(\text{clash}) = \frac{1}{L}L\rho = \rho \tag{1}$$

We calculate the following probability for describing that a thread will have to wait less than the specified threshold t

$$\mathbb{P}(w < t) = \mathbb{P}(w = 0) + \mathbb{P}(w < t)\mathbb{P}(w > 0)$$
$$= (1 - \mathbb{P}(clash)) + \mathbb{P}(clash)\mathbb{P}(w < t) \tag{2}$$

For an M/M/1 queue it is known that the distribution of the waiting time in the queue is $1 - e^{-(\mu-\lambda)t}$ [19]. Using this, knowing that $\lambda = \frac{\gamma}{L}$, and from Equations 1 and 2 we finally get

$$\mathbb{P}(w < \frac{1}{\mu}) = (1-\rho) + \rho(1 - e^{-(\mu-\frac{\gamma}{L})\frac{1}{\mu}}) \tag{3}$$

The number of locks the system should use is then the smallest L that the probability in Eq. 3 is significant (more than 0.95).

4.3 Periodic Recalibration

The last question to answer is when to recalibrate the locks. Our approach is a periodic recalibration. If the performance was monitored constantly, the recalibration could be performed when the performance decreases; this, however, due to the expensive nature of constant performance monitoring (as described in Section 4.1), is out of the question. Instead, a periodic update policy is applied.

A dedicated thread is dispatched by the hash table, which, from time to time, checks the state of the hash table. When the periodic recalibration starts, first, the hash table is "frozen." This is performed by "hijacking" the locks. The ticket lock used in this setup has a *currently served* counter to indicate which thread is next. This counter is changed to a large number effectively not allowing any new threads to acquire the locks. After waiting for the current threads to exit the critical sections (by monitoring the *currently served* number, which threads increase upon exit), a bool flag is raised indicating a *resize in progress* halting all other operations. After the recalibration has determined the new number of locks, the new locks are initialized, and the *resize in progress* flag is set to false allowing requests to proceed. The calibrator thread then goes to sleep.

The resize, apart from blocking all threads for a while, is a cheap operation. Changing the number of locks is effectively reserving a new array of integers for the locks.

The calibrator thread, of course, requires resources, and takes the CPU periodically. Not to mention that the recalibration blocks all accesses to the table for a short time. These could be though as wasteful, however, this approach turned out to be satisfying in performance.

5 Evaluating the Algorithm

This section evaluates the proposed method for recalibrating the number of locks in a parallel bucket hash table. The adaptive locking strategy is initialized with two locks, and then it is left up to the recalibration process to find an optimal number. The performance of the custom implementation is compared to the performance of the parallel hash table in Intel's Thread Building Blocks library.

The number of buckets the hash table uses is also an important parameter. The hash table (filled with 8 million items) uses 2, 4, 6 and 12 million buckets in the test cases. The number of buckets does not affect the locking granularity, but it changes the probe length within the hash table and its internal performance.

The experiments were executed on an Intel Core i7-2600K CPU at 3.4 GHz with 4 physical cores and HyperThreading capabilities running Windows 7. The data inserted into the hash table and searched consequently comes from a real-life dataset. Both the distribution of the items among the buckets (and therefore among the locks) and the access pattern of the items is determined by this real-life use-case.

The physical performance of the custom hash table is shown on Fig. 5. The results below are an average of 5 executions. Both hash tables were filled with 8 million items and another 8 million find queries were executed.

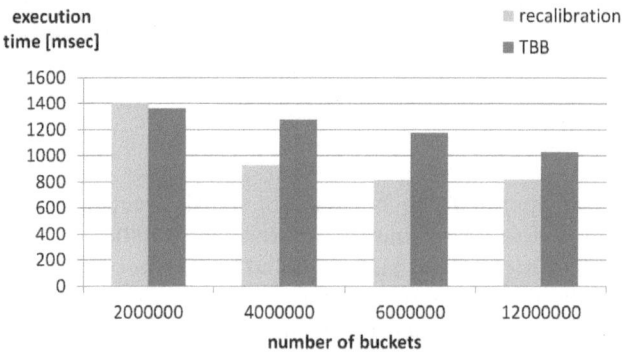

Fig. 5. The performance of the custom adaptive hash table with the estimated optimal number of locks compared to the performance of *concurrent_hash_map* of Intel's TBB for 8 million insert and 8 million lookup operations with 8 concurrent threads

The performance of the custom hash table is in almost all cases better than that of TBB. The difference is between 20 and 30%, and a slight decrease of 3% with the lowest number of buckets. The final estimated number of locks of 31 given by the algorithm is a good estimate, given that the initial tests shown in Section 3.1 indicated this order of magnitude of locks too.

Another question is if the recalibration algorithm does indeed adopts to the external circumstances. With various numbers of concurrent threads the performance of both hash tables were measured, and the final number of locks is reported on Fig. 6.

Our hash table constantly outperforms TBB by 15-40%. It is also noteworthy that our hash table has best performance at 8 threads, which means that the periodic recalibrator thread does not present itself as an overhead (8 is the number of virtual cores of the CPU). The recalibration works, as it delivers good performance, and it does indeed change the number of locks based on the

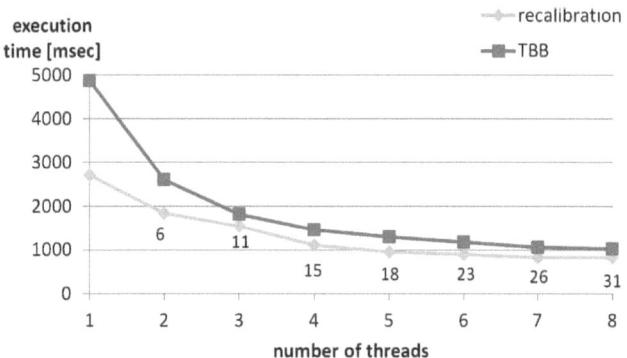

Fig. 6. The performance of the custom adaptive hash table with the estimated optimal number of locks compared to the performance of *concurrent_hash_map* of Intel's TBB with various number of concurrent threads accessing the hash tables

circumstances. The higher the number of concurrent threads is, the higher the number of locks inside the hash table get, resulting in better throughput.

6   Conclusions

In this paper, we analyzed the behavior of multithread-capable bucket hash tables. Our goal was to determine the appropriate number of locks to be used by the hash table internally. Using a global table-level lock has unfavorable consequences while using bucket level locks is undesired due to vast amount of locks that would be required, and their overhead.

Partitioning the buckets of the table into disjoint blocks and using a lock for each of these blocks is a good compromise, but leaves the question of choosing the block size open. We presented a queuing model that describes the behavior of the locks and the threads in the parallel hash table.

We proposed a heuristic argument, which describes when is fine grained locking beneficial for a data structure with respect to the bottleneck that comes with mutual exclusion. This argument and the queuing model was used to estimate the order of magnitude of locks that provides reasonable performance at the lowest cost.

By implementing the bucket hash table and examining its performance under real-life circumstances we verified that the estimate given by the proposed algorithm is in the same order of magnitude that our initial exhaustive search predicted.

With the adaptive technique presented in this paper the performance of the hash table finds an optimal number of locking granularity. With this locking scheme the performance of the hash table is about 25% better than the performance of a commercially available parallel hash table.

References

1. Barnat, J., Ročkai, P.: Shared Hash Tables in Parallel Model Checking. Electronic Notes in Theoretical Computer Science 198(1), 79–91 (2008)
2. Brandenburg, B., Calandrino, J.M., Block, A., Leontyev, H., Anderson, J.H.: Real-Time Synchronization on Multiprocessors: To Block or Not to Block, to Suspend or Spin? In: 2008 IEEE Real-Time and Embedded Technology and Applications Symposium, pp. 342–353. IEEE Computer Society Press, St. Louis (2008)
3. Gao, H., Groote, J.F., Hesselink, W.H.: Lock-free dynamic hash tables with open addressing. Distributed Computing 18(1), 21–42 (2005)
4. Gilbert, D.C.: Modeling spin locks with queuing networks. ACM SIGOPS Operating Systems Review 12(1), 29–42 (1978)
5. Harrison, P., Patel, N.M.: Performance Modelling of Communication Networks and Computer Architectures. Addison-Wesley (1992)
6. Herlihy, M., Shavit, N., Tzafrir, M.: Hopscotch Hashing. In: Taubenfeld, G. (ed.) DISC 2008. LNCS, vol. 5218, pp. 350–364. Springer, Heidelberg (2008)

7. Juhász, S., Dudás, A.: Adapting hash table design to real-life datasets. In: Proc. of the IADIS European Conference on Informatics 2009, Part of the IADIS Multi-conference of Computer Science and Information Systems 2009, Algarve, Portugal, pp. 3–10 (June 2009)
8. Kim, W., Voss, M.: Multicore Desktop Programming with Intel Threading Building Blocks. IEEE Software 28(1), 23–31 (2011)
9. Klots, B., Bamford, R.J.: Method and apparatus for dynamic lock granularity escalation and de-escalation in a computer system (1998)
10. Knuth, D.E.: The art of computer programming, vol 3. Addison-Wesley (November 1973)
11. Laarman, A., van de Pol, J., Weber, M.: Boosting Multi-Core Reachability Performance with Shared Hash Tables. In: 10th International Conference on Formal Methods in Computer-Aided Design (April 2010)
12. Larson, P.A., Krishnan, M.R., Reilly, G.V.: Scaleable hash table for shared-memory multiprocessor system (April 2003)
13. Lea, D.: Hash table util.concurrent.ConcurrentHashMap, revision 1.3, in JSR-166, the proposed Java Concurrency Package (2003)
14. Li, Q., Moon, B.: Distributed cooperative Apache web server. In: Proceedings of the Tenth International Conference on World Wide Web, WWW 2001, pp. 555–564. ACM Press, New York (2001)
15. Mellor-Crummey, J.M., Scott, M.L.: Algorithms for scalable synchronization on shared-memory multiprocessors. ACM Transactions on Computer Systems 9(1), 21–65 (1991)
16. Michael, M.M.: High performance dynamic lock-free hash tables and list-based sets. In: ACM Symposium on Parallel Algorithms and Architectures, pp. 73–82 (2002)
17. Ning, Z., Cox, A.J., Mullikin, J.C.: SSAHA: a fast search method for large DNA databases. Genome Research 11(10), 1725–1729 (2001)
18. Purcell, C., Harris, T.: Non-blocking Hashtables with Open Addressing. In: Fraigniaud, P. (ed.) DISC 2005. LNCS, vol. 3724, pp. 108–121. Springer, Heidelberg (2005)
19. Stewart, W.J.: Probability, Markov chains, queues, and simulation: the mathematical basis of performance modeling. Princeton University Press (2009)
20. Treiber, R.K.: Systems Programming: Coping with Parallelism (Research Report RJ 5118). Tech. rep., IBM Almaden Research Center (1986)
21. Veal, B., Foong, A.: Performance scalability of a multi-core web server. In: Proceedings of the 3rd ACM/IEEE Symposium on Architecture for Networking and Communications Systems, ANCS 2007, p. 57. ACM Press, New York (2007)

Impact of Variable Privatization
on Extracting Synchronization-Free Slices
for Multi-core Computers

Marek Palkowski

Faculty of Computer Science, West Pomeranian University of Technology,
70210, Zolnierska 49, Szczecin, Poland
mpalkowski@wi.zut.edu.pl
http://kio.wi.zut.edu.pl/

Abstract. Variable Privatization is an important technique that has
been used by compilers to parallelize loops by eliminating storage-related
dependences. In this paper, we present an approach that combines extracting synchronization-free slices available in program loops with variable privatization. This permits us to reduce the number of dependence
relations and as a consequence to reduce the time complexity of algorithms aimed at extracting synchronization-free slices. This leads to en-
larging the scope of the applicability of those algorithms and reducing
the time required to parallelize loops. The scope of the applicability of
the approach is illustrated by means of the NAS Parallel Benchmark
suite. Results of a performance analysis for parallelized loops executed
on a multi-core computer are presented. Received results are compared
with those obtained by other loop parallelization techniques. The future
work is outlined.

Keywords: iteration space slicing, scalar and array variable privatization, automatic loop parallelizer, NAS Parallel Benchmark.

1 Introduction

The lack of automated tools permitting for exposing parallelism decreases the
productivity of programmers and increases the time and cost of producing parallel programs. Because for many applications most computations are contained
in program loops, automatic extraction of parallelism available in loops is ex-
tremely important for multi-core systems, allowing us to produce parallel code
from existing sequential applications and to create multiple threads that can be
easily scheduled to achieve high program performance.

One of effective techniques aimed at exposing parallelism available in program
loops is the Iteration Space Slicing (ISS) framework [1]. ISS was introduced by
Pugh and Rosser in the paper [2] as an extension of program slicing proposed by
Weiser [3]. It takes loop dependence information as input to find all statement
instances that must be executed to produce the correct values for the specified array elements. Coarse-grained code is represented with synchronization-free slices
or with slices requiring occasional synchronization.

R. Keller et al. (Eds.): Facing the Multicore-Challenge III 2012, LNCS 7686, pp. 72–83, 2013.

An (iteration-space) slice is defined as follows: given a dependence graph defined by a set of dependence relations, a slice S is a weakly connected component of this graph, i.e., a maximal subgraph such that for each pair of vertices in the subgraph there exists a directed or undirected path.

Iteration Space Slicing requires an exact representation of loop-carried dependences and consequently an exact dependence analysis which detects a dependence if and only if it actually exists. For our work, the dependence analysis proposed by Pugh and Wonnacott [8], where dependences are represented by dependence relations in the Presburger arithmetic, was chosen.

Presburger arithmetic PA is the first-order theory of the integers in the language L having 0, 1 as constants, +,- as binary operations, and equality =, order $<$ and congruences $\equiv_n$ modulo all integers n$\geq$1 as binary relations. The language of PA is rich enough to express many important application problems, such as solvability of (parametric) systems of linear Diophantine equations, integer feasibility of systems of (parametric) linear constraints, integer programming, and certain problems in program description and verification.

ISS to extract synchronization-free slices relies on the transitive closure of an affine dependence relation describing all dependences in a loop. Algorithms aimed at calculating transitive closure are presented in [10,11,12]. Their time and memory complexities depend on the number of dependence relations representing all dependences in the loop. For different NAS benchmarks [7], the number of dependence relations returned by the Omega dependence analyser (Petit) [15] varies from several relations to several thousands ones. In many cases when the number of dependence relations is more than several hundreds, known implementations [10,11,12] fails to produce transitive closure due to limited resources of computers or because the time required for calculating transitive closure is not acceptable in practice (from several hours to several days). That is why reducing the number of dependence relations is very important prior to calculate transitive closure.

In this paper, we present a technique that automatically defines loop variables that can be safely privatizated, then techniques extracting synchronization-free slices are applied to parallelize the program loop.

The impact of variable privatization on reducing the number of dependence relations and loop parallelization is demonstrated by means of NAS benchmarks [7].

2 Background

In this paper, we deal with affine loop nests where, for given loop indices, lower and upper bounds as well as array subscripts and conditionals are affine functions of surrounding loop indices and possibly of structure parameters, and the loop steps are known constants.

A dependence analysis is required for correct loop parallelization. Two statement instances I and J are *dependent* if both access the same memory location and if at least one access is a write. I and J are called the *source* and *destination* of a dependence, respectively, provided that I is lexicographically smaller than J ($I \prec J$, i.e., I is executed before J).

There are three types of data dependence: *flow dependence* - data dependence from an assignment to a use of a variable; *anti dependence* - data dependence from use of a variable to a later reassignment of that variable; *output dependence* - data dependence from an assignment of a variable to a later reassignment of that variable [5,6].

Let us remind basics of the ISS framework [1]. A dependence relation is a tuple relation of the form [*input list*]→[*output list*]: *formula*, where *input list* and *output list* are the lists of variables and/or expressions used to describe input and output tuples and *formula* describes the constraints imposed upon *input list* and *output list* and it is a Presburger formula built of constraints represented with algebraic expressions and using logical and existential operators.

We use standard operations on relations and sets, such as intersection ($\cap$), union ($\cup$), difference (-), domain (dom R), range (ran R), relation application ($S' = R(S)$: $e' \in S'$ iff exists e s.t. $e \rightarrow e' \in R, e \in S$), positive transitive closure of relation R, $R+ = \{[e] \rightarrow [e'] : e \rightarrow e' \in R \lor \exists\ e\ '', e \rightarrow e'' \in R \land e'' \rightarrow e' \in R+\}$, transitive closure $R^* = R+ \cup I'$, where I' is an identity relation. In detail, the description of these operations is presented in [8,9].

Definition 1. An ultimate dependence source is a source that is not the destination of another dependence. Ultimate dependence sources and destinations represented by relation R can be found by means of the following calculations: domain(R) - range(R).

Definition 2. The set of ultimate dependence sources of a slice forms the set of its sources.

Definition 3. The representative source of a slice is its lexicographically minimal source.

Extracting synchronization-free slices consists of two steps. First, representatives of slices are found in such a manner that each slice is represented with its lexicographically minimal statement instance. Next, slices are reconstructed from their representatives and code scanning these slices is generated.

Given a dependence relation R describing all dependences in a loop, we can find a set of statement instances, S_{UDS}, describing all ultimate dependence sources of slices as S_{UDS}=domain(R)-range(R). In order to find elements of S_{UDS} that are representatives of slices, we build a relation, R_{USC}, that describes all pairs of the ultimate dependence sources that are transitively connected in a slice, as follows: $R_{USC} = \{[e] \rightarrow [e'] : e, e' \in S_{UDS}, e \prec e', (R^*(e) \cap R^*(e')) \neq \varnothing\}$.

The condition ($e \prec e'$) in the constraints of relation R_{USC} means that e is lexicographically smaller than e'. Such a condition guarantees that the lexicographically smallest source of a slice will always appear in the input tuple, i.e., the lexicographically smallest source of a slice (its representative source) can never appear in the output tuple. The intersection $(R^*(e) \cap R^*(e')) \neq \varnothing$ in the constraints of R_{USC} guarantees that elements e and e' are transitively connected, i.e., they are the sources of the same slice.

Set S_{repr} containing representatives of each slice is found as $S_{repr}=S_{UDS}$-range(R_{USC}). Each element e of set S_{repr} is the lexicographically minimal statement instance of a synchronization-free slice. If e is the representative of a slice with multiple sources, then the remaining sources of this slice can be found applying relation $(R_{USC})^*$ to e, i.e., $(R_{USC})^*(e)$. If a slice has only the one source, then $(R_{USC})^*(e)=e$. The elements of a slice represented with e can be found applying relation R^* to the set of sources of this slice: $S_{slice}=R^*((R_{USC})^*(e))$ [1].

Variable privatization consists in discovering variables whose values are local to a particular scope, usually a loop iteration. This technique allows each concurrent thread to allocate a variable in its private storage such that each thread accesses a distinct instance of a variable.

Definition 4. A scalar variable x defined within a loop is said to be privatizable with respect to that loop if and only if every path from the beginning of the loop body to a use of x within that body must pass through a definition of x before reaching that use [4,5].

Let us consider the following example.

```
for(i=1; i<=N; i++)
{
s1:   t = A[i];
s2:   A[i] = B[i];
s3:   B[i] = t;
}
```

Classes of dependences and statements being involved in dependences are as follows.

```
flow      s1: t   -->     s3: t
output    s1: t   -->     s1: t
anti      s3: t   -->     s1: t
```

Because of loop-carried dependences, the loop above is not parallelizable. Fortunately, all of the carried dependences are due to assignments and uses of the scalar variable t. All of them go away if each thread has its own copy of the variable t.

3   Applying Privatization to Extract Slices

The idea of the algorithm presented in this section is the following. Privatization can be applied to scalars or arrays. The first step of the algorithm is to search for scalar or array variables for privatization taking into account the following condition. Variable X can be privatized if the lexicographically first statement in the loop body referring X does not read a value of X, this guarantees that the same thread produces and consumes values of X [5]. Otherwise dependences involving X cannot be eliminated because a thread can read a value of X that is produced by some other thread.

Next, we split dependence relations, describing all the dependences in the loop, into two sets such that the first one comprises those relations that describe dependences where variables defined to be parallelized are involved, the second one consists of the remaining relations. If the second set is empty, this means that the privatization of variables contained in the first set eliminates all the dependences in the loop, thus its parallelization is trivial. Otherwise, for each variable X contained in the first set, we privatize X and identify inner loop nests such that they comprise all statements referring to X. Then we modify correspondent dependence relations to eliminate those dependences involving X that are carried by these inner nests. This is correct because after variable privatization, parallel threads will have the own copy of variable X and dependences among the statements involving X are eliminated. Using a set of modified dependence relations describing only those dependences that cannot be eliminated by privatization, we can apply any technique presented in [1] to extract synchronization-free slices. Reducing the number of dependences reduces the time complexity of algorithms presented in [1]. If applying a parallelization technique results in a single slice, we try to apply this technique to inner loop nests making the outermost nest to be serial.

Below, we present the algorithm that implements the idea above in a formal way.

Algorithm 1. Extracting synchronization-free-slices applying variable privatization

Input : Set of relations $S=\{R_i\}$, $1\le i\le n$, describing all dependences in a loop

Output : Code representing synchronization-free slices with privatization of variables

1 Put each scalar/array variable X, originating dependences, into set *Priv-Cand* if the lexicographically first statement, referring to X, does not read a value of X.

2 Put each relation R_i describing dependences involving variable X, $X \in$ *PrivCand*, into set *PC*.

3 Put each relation R_i describing dependences involving variable Y, $Y \notin$ *PrivCand*, into set S_{slice}

4 **If** $S_{slice} = \varnothing$, **then** privatize all variables in set *PrivCand* and make the outermost loop to be parallel. **Exit.**

5 **For each** variable X in set *PrivCand* **do**

5.1 $z =$ the minimal number of those inner loops that include all statements with X

5.2 $SET\_X = \varnothing$.

5.3 **For each** relation R_q, $1\le q\le m$, $m\le n$, from set *PC* **do**
Form new relation P_q in the following way:

$$P_q=\{[e_1, e_2, ..., e_k] \rightarrow [e'_1, e'_2, ..., e'_k] : constraints(R_q) \bigwedge_{j=1}^{z} (e_j = e'_j)\}$$

where $e_1, e_2, ..., e_k$ and $e'_1, e'_2, ..., e'_k$ are the variables of the input and output tuples of R_q respectively; k is the number of loop indices; $constraints(R_q)$ are the constraints of relation R_q.

// the constraint $\bigwedge\limits_{j=1}^{z} (e_j = e'_j)$ means that relation P_q does not describe
// dependences carried by z inner loop nests.

$SET\_X = SET\_X \cup P_q$

5.4 $S_{slice} = S_{slice} \cup SET\_X$;

6 Apply any technique presented in [1] to set S_{slice} to extract synchronization-free slices. If this results in a single slice, then make the outermost loop to be serial and repeat the presented algorithm to the rest of loop nests of the input loop.

Let us illustrate the presented algorithm by means of the following loop:

Example:

```
1: for(i=1; i<=n; i++){
2:   c = 0;
3:   for(j=1; j<=n; j++){
4:     a[i][j] = a[i][j-1] + c;
5:   }
6: }
```

The set of dependence relations for this loop includes the following relations.

$R1 = \{[i,\text{-}1,2] \to [i,j',4] : 1 \le i \le n \,\&\&\, 1 \le j' \le n\}$
$R2 = \{[i,\text{-}1,2] \to [i',j',4] : 1 \le i < i' \le n \,\&\&\, 1 \le j' \le n\}$
$R3 = \{[i,\text{-}1,2] \to [i',\text{-}1,2] : 1 \le i < i' \le n\}$
$R4 = \{[i,j,4] \to [i',\text{-}1,2] : 1 \le i < i' \le n \,\&\&\, 1 \le j \le n\}$
$R5 = \{[i,j,4] \to [i,j+1,4] : 1 \le i \le n \,\&\&\, 1 \le j < n\}$

where relations R1, R2, R3, R4 describe dependences involving variable c, relation R5 involves variable a. Applying the algorithm, we get.

1 PrivCand = $\{c\}$.
2 PC = $\{R1, R2, R3, R4\}$. PC = PC$\{c\}$.
3 $S_{slice} = \{R5\}$.
4 $S_{slice} \ne \varnothing$
5 **For** variable c **do**
  5.1 $z = 1$
  5.2 SET$\_X = \varnothing$;
  5.3 PC$\{c\} = \{R1, R2, R3, R4\}$.
      P1 = R1; P2=P3=P4=$\varnothing$;
      SET$\_X = \{P1\}$;
  5.4 $S_{slice} = \{R1, R5\}$. R = R1 $\cup$ R5.
  end for

6 $S_{repr}(R) = \{[i,-1,13]: 1 \leq i \leq n \;\&\&\; 2 \leq n\};$

Applying algorithm **Gen_affine** presented in [1] we get n synchronization-free slices represented with the following code :

```
if (n >= 2) {
 par for(t1 = 1; t1 <= n; t1++) private(c)
 {
    c = 0;   // s1(t1,-1,2);
    if (n >= t1 && t1 >= 1) {
       for(t2 = 1; t2 <= n; t2++) {
          a[t1][t2] = a[t1][t2-1] + c; // s1(t1,t2,4);
}}}}
```

4   Experiment Results

The presented algorithm was implemented by us in a tool by means of the Omega library. It generates C-like pseudo-code scanning synchronization-free slices with defining variables to be privatized. The implementation of the algorithm is available at the website http://sourceforge.net/projects/issf/. Using this tool, we have experimented with loops of the NAS 3.2 benchmark suite [7].

NAS Parallel Benchmarks (NPB) have been developed at the NASA Ames Research Centre to study performance of parallel supercomputers. The benchmarks, which are derived from computational fluid dynamics (CFD) applications, consist of five kernels and three pseudo-applications [7].

From 431 loops of the NAS benchmark suite, Petit is able to analyse 257 loops, and dependences were found in 134 loops (the rest 123 loops do not expose any dependence). For these loops, the presented approach is able to extract parallel threads for 116 (86,5%) loops. Table 1 presents the transformations used. 40 loops were parallelized by algorithms of extracting slices [1]. For 39 loops, variable privatization eliminates all dependences, hence loop parallelization is trivial. 15 loops were transformed to parallel code representing slices with variable privatization. For 22 loops, parallelism was found only in inner nests (the outermost loop is serial). The presented approach allows us to parallelize additionally 76 loops in comparison with those extracted by algorithms presented in paper [1]. The last column of the table presents steps of the algorithm producing parallel code.

To study the impact of variable privatization on reducing dependences and the time of extracting slices, the following criteria were taken into account for choosing NAS loops: (i) a loop must be computatively heavy (there are many NAS benchmarks with constant upper bounds of loop indices, hence their parallelization is not justified), (ii) code produced by the algorithm must be parallel (there are NAS loops that cannot be parallelized), (iii) structures of chosen loops must be different (there are many NAS loops of a similar structure). Applying these criteria, the following five NAS loops: *BT_error_5*, *BT_rhs_1*, *LU_erhs_3*, *SP_rhs_4* and *UA_transfer_11* have been selected. Results of experiments are presented in Table 2, where N1, N2, N3 represent loop index upper bounds.

Table 1. Loop parallelization

Technique	Number of loops	Step of the algorithm
Slicing only (S)	40	Step 6, $PrivCand = \varnothing$
Privatization only (P)	39	Step 4, $S_{slice} = \varnothing$
Slicing with privatization (P+S)	15	Step 6, $PrivCand \neq \varnothing$, $S_{slice} \neq \varnothing$
Only privatization of inner loop (P inner)	22	Step 6, card(S_{repr}) = 1; Step 4 for an inner loop
All techniques		116

From Table 2, we can see that variable privatization reduces considerably the numbers of dependence relations (see columns 4 and 5). It also reduces the time of transitive closure calculation. Without variable privatization, the calculation of transitive closure can take several hours, while the presented algorithm allows us to compute it in a fraction of a second. The parallelization of the two loops, LU_erhs_3 and SP_rhs_4, does not require transitive closure calculation because variable privatization eliminates all dependences in these loops.

Table 2. Impact of variable privatization on slices extracting

Loop	No. of statements	Technique of algorithm	No. of dependences		Time of R* calculation [sec]		No. of slices	Time of algorithm execution [sec]
			without priv.	with priv.	without priv.	with priv.		
BT_error_5	2	P+S	32	4	> 60	0.34	5	2.853
BT_rhs_1	7	P+S	46	6	> 60	0.21	N1*N2*N3	1.722
LU_erhs_3	30	P	640	0	> 60	0.00	N4*(N3-N2)*(N1-1)	0.640
SP_rhs_4	16	P inner	507	0	> 60	0.00	N3+5*(N4+N5+N8+N9+(N6-3)*N7)	0.265
UA_transfer_11	3	P+S	10	4	0.25	0.06	N1*N2	0.589

To check the performance of parallel code, speed-up and efficiency were studied for the five loops above. Speed-up is a ratio of sequential time and parallel time, $S = T(1)/T(P)$, where P is the number of processors. Efficiency, $E = S/P$, tells us about usage of available processors while parallel code is executed. Table 3 shows time (in seconds), speed-up, and efficiency for 2, 4, and 8 processors.

The experiments were carried on a workstation Intel Xeon Quad Core, 1.6 Ghz, 8 CPU (2 quad core CPU with cache 4 MB), 2 GB RAM, Fedora Linux. Parallel programs were written in the OpenMP standard [16]. Analysing data in Table 3, we may conclude that for all parallel loops, positive speed-up is achieved. Efficiency depends on the problem size defined by index loop upper bounds and the number of CPUs used for parallel program execution. For most cases, efficiency increases with increasing the problem size. Figure 1 illustrates the positive speed-up presented in Table 3 in a graphical way.

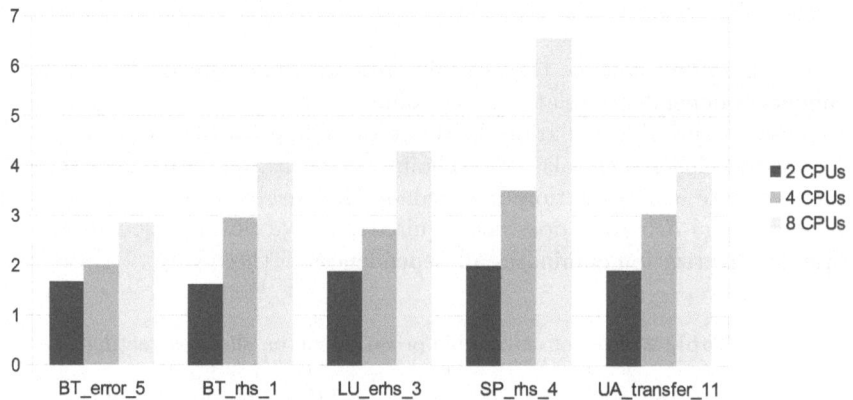

Fig. 1. Speed-up of the loops using 2, 4, and 8 CPU cores

5   Related Work

Iteration Space Slicing (ISS) was introduced by Pugh and Rosser in paper [2]. However, they did not propose how to find synchronization-free slices. They did not consider also the impact of variable privatization on extracting synchronization-free slices.

The affine transformation framework (ATF), considered in papers [13,14] unifies a large number of previously proposed loop transformations. The comparison of ATF and ISS was introduced in the paper [1]. ATF is implemented in the project Pluto [17,18]. It is an automatic parallelization tool based on the polyhedral model. The core transformation framework [13,14], mainly works to find affine transformations for efficient tiling and fusion, but not limited to those. Unfortunately, Pluto does not offer any mechanism of automatic variable privatization. This limitation did not allow us to study fully the impact of variable privatization on extracting threads by means of the Pluto tool. From 134 NAS benchmarks qualified for our experiments, Pluto is able to parallelize 46 loops only, while the presented approach parallelizes 116 ones.

Table 3. Time, speed-up, and efficiency

Loop	Parameters	1 CPU time	2 CPUs time	S	E	4 CPUs time	S	E	8 CPUs time	S	E
BT_error.f2p_5	N1=N2=N3=100	0.409	0.232	1.763	0.881	0.182	1.275	0.319	0.166	1.398	0.175
	N1=N2=N3=150	1.508	1.021	1.477	0.738	0.908	1.661	0.415	0.822	1.835	0.229
	N1=N2=N3=200	3.528	2.108	1.674	0.837	1.753	2.013	0.503	1.236	2.854	0.357
BT_rhs.f2p_1	N1=N2=N3=100	0.682	0.425	1.605	0.802	0.214	3.187	0.797	0.149	4.577	0.572
	N1=N2=N3=200	5.596	3.475	1.610	0.805	1.895	2.953	0.738	1.111	5.037	0.630
	N1=N2=N3=300	17.870	11.025	1.621	0.810	6.062	2.948	0.737	4.401	4.060	0.508
LU_erhs.f2p_3	N1,N3=32; N4,N6,N8,N10,N11=1000; N2,N5,N7,N9=1	2.231	1.333	1.674	0.837	0.987	2.260	0.565	0.936	2.384	0.298
	N1,N3=48; N4,N6,N8,N10,N11=2000; N2,N5,N7,N9=1	15.053	7.722	1.949	0.975	4.204	3.581	0.895	3.621	4.157	0.520
	N1,N3=64; N4,N6,N8,N10,N11=3000; N2,N5,N7,N9=1	79.114	42.002	1.884	0.942	29.009	2.727	0.682	18.410	4.297	0.537
SP_rhs.f2p_4	N1,N2,N3,N4,N5, N6,N7,N8,N9=75	1.648	0.833	1.978	0.989	0.478	3.448	0.862	0.330	4.994	0.624
	N1,N2,N3,N4,N5, N6,N7,N8,N9=100	3.417	1.788	1.911	0.956	0.860	3.973	0.993	0.486	7.031	0.879
	N1,N2,N3,N4,N5, N6,N7,N8,N9=125	7.790	3.901	1.997	0.998	2.216	3.515	0.879	1.186	6.568	0.821
UA_transfer.f2p_11	N1=N2=N3=100	0.018	0.012	1.529	0.765	0.009	2.044	0.511	0.09	1.976	0.247
	N1=N2=N3=200	0.610	0.378	1.614	0.807	0.194	3.144	0.786	0.178	3.427	0.428
	N1=N2=N3=300	2.347	1.231	1.907	0.953	0.772	3.040	0.760	0.603	3.892	0.487

The variable privatization is available by means of other loop parallelizers: PIPS [21,22] and Cetus [23]. PIPS provides different privatization functions [21]. The quick privatization is restricted to loop indices and is included in the dependence graph computation. The array privatization is much more expensive and is still mainly experimental [21].

Cetus is a source-to-source compiler and the successor to Polaris at Purdue University [23]. The tool privatizes variables and traverses a loop nest from the innermost to the outermost loop. At each level, it first collects definitions (write references) and uses (read references) in the loop body. Cetus aggregates all these array sections over the loop iteration space. This technique is a slightly simpler version of the one used in the Polaris parallelizing compiler for Fortran77 programs [23]. However, the both parallelizers Cetus and PIPS do not implement Iteration Space Slicing.

6   Conclusion

The proposed approach extends the spectrum of loops which can be parallelized by the Iteration Space Slicing framework [1]. The algorithm reduces the number of loop dependences and as a consequence the time of transitive closure calculation for dependence relations. The time of loop parallelization is also reduced. The technique is able to transform loops with a large number of statements and dependence relations in short time.

The paper presents the approach for privatizing scalar and array variables [19] in the context of ISS framework. In the future work, we intend to consider a combination of ISS with more advanced techniques, such as presented in [20], to find better tradeoffs between parallelism, locality, communication and memory usage. We are going also to analyse other techniques eliminating loop dependences and define most effective ones to be integrated with the ISS framework to reduce its time complexity and enlarge its scope of applicability.

References

1. Beletska, A., Bielecki, W., Cohen, A., Palkowski, M., Siedlecki, K.: Coarse-grained loop parallelization: Iteration space slicing vs affine transformations. Parallel Computing 37, 479–497 (2011)
2. Pugh, W., Rosser, E.: Iteration space slicing and its application to communication optimization. In: International Conference on Supercomputing, pp. 221–228 (1997)
3. Weiser, M.: Program slicing. IEEE Transactions on Software Engineering, 352–357 (1984)
4. Gupta, M.: On Privatization of Variables for Data-Parallel Execution. In: Proceedings of the 11th International Parallel Processing Symposium, pp. 533–541 (1997)
5. Allen, R., Kennedy, K.: Optimizing compilers for modern architectures: A Dependence based Approach. Morgan Kaufmann Publish., Inc. (2001)
6. Moldovan, D.: Parallel Processing: From Applications to Systems. Morgan Kaufmann Publishers, Inc. (1993)
7. The NAS benchmark suite, http://www.nas.nasa.gov

8. Pugh, W., Wonnacott, D.: An Exact Method for Analysis of Value-Based Array Data Dependences. In: Banerjee, U., Gelernter, D., Nicolau, A., Padua, D.A. (eds.) LCPC 1993. LNCS, vol. 768, pp. 546–566. Springer, Heidelberg (1994)

9. Kelly, W., Maslov, V., Pugh, W., Rosser, E., Shpeisman, T., Wonnacott, D.: The omega library interface guide. Technical report, College Park, MD, USA (1994)

10. Kelly, W., Pugh, W., Rosser, E., Shpeisman, T.: Transitive cloasure of infinite graphs and its applications. In: Languages and Compilers for Parallel Computing (1995)

11. Verdoolaege, S.: Integer Set Library - Manual (2011),
`http://www.kotnet.org/~skimo//isl/manual.pdf`

12. Wlodzimierz, B., Tomasz, K., Marek, P., Beletska, A.: An Iterative Algorithm of Computing the Transitive Closure of a Union of Parameterized Affine Integer Tuple Relations. In: Wu, W., Daescu, O. (eds.) COCOA 2010, Part I. LNCS, vol. 6508, pp. 104–113. Springer, Heidelberg (2010)

13. Lim, A., Lam, M., Cheong, G.: An affine partitioning algorithm to maximize parallelism and minimize communication. In: ICS 1999, pp. 228–237. ACM Press (1999)

14. Feautrier, P.: Some efficient solutions to the affine scheduling problem, part I and II, one and multidimensional time. International Journal of Parallel Programming 21, 313–348, 389–420 (1992)

15. Kelly, W., Pugh, W., Rosser, E., Maslov, V., Shpeisman, T., Wonnacott, D.: New User Interface for Petit and Other Extensions. User Guide (1996)

16. OpenMP API, `http://www.openmp.org`

17. PLUTO - An automatic parallelizer and locality optimizer for multicores (2012),
`http://pluto-compiler.sourceforge.net`

18. Bondhugula, U., Hartono, A., Ramanujan, J., Sadayappan, P.: A practical automatic polyhedral parallelizer and locality optimizer. In: ACM SIGPLAN Programming Languages Design and Implementation (PLDI 2008), pp. 101–1123 (2008)

19. Marek, P.: Automatic Privatization for Parallel Execution of Loops. In: Rutkowski, L., Korytkowski, M., Scherer, R., Tadeusiewicz, R., Zadeh, L.A., Zurada, J.M. (eds.) ICAISC 2012, Part II. LNCS, vol. 7268, pp. 395–403. Springer, Heidelberg (2012)

20. Vasilache, N., et al.: Trading Off Memory For Parallelism Quality. In: Proceedings of IMPACT 2012 (2012), `http://impact.gforge.inria.fr/impact2012/workshop_IMPACT/vasilache_memopt.pdf`

21. Amini, M., Ancourt, C., et al.: PIPS Documentation (2012),
`http://pips4u.org/doc`

22. Amini, M., et al.: PIPS Is not (just) Polyhedral Software. In: First International Workshop on Polyhedral Compilation Techniques (IMPACT 2011), Chamonix, France (April 2011)

23. Chirag, D., et al.: Cetus: A Source-to-Source Compiler Infrastructure for Multicores. IEEE Computer, 36–42 (2009)

Parallel Collision Queries on the GPU
A Comparative Study of Different CUDA Implementations

Rainer Erbes[1], Anja Mantel[1], Elmar Schömer[2], and Nicola Wolpert[1]

[1] Hochschule für Technik Stuttgart
{rainer.erbes,anja.mantel,nicola.wolpert}@hft-stuttgart.de
[2] Johannes Gutenberg-Universität Mainz
schoemer@uni-mainz.de

Abstract. We present parallel algorithms to accelerate collision tests of rigid body objects for a high number of independent transformations as they occur in sampling-based motion planning and path validation problems. We compare various GPU approaches with a different level of parallelism against each other and against a parallel CPU implementation. Our algorithms require no sophisticated load balancing schemes. They make no assumption on the distribution of the input transformations and require no pre-processing. Yet, we can perform up to 1 million collision tests per second with our best GPU implementation in our benchmarks. This is about 2.5X faster than our reference multi-core CPU implementation and more than 18X faster than current single-core implementations.

1 Introduction

Bounding volume hierarchies (BVHs) are widely used to accelerate proximity tests between two objects that can be given as triangle soups. Other applications include ray tracing, visibility culling and nearest neighbor queries.

The leaf nodes of a BVH contain the triangles of the objects and inner nodes of the hierarchy are bounding volumes such as spheres, axis-aligned bounding boxes (AABBs), oriented bounding boxes (OBBs), etc. BVHs aim at culling distant portions of the triangle sets to accelerate the collision queries. They help to give a hierarchical approximation of the objects and to localize of the near portions to perform intersection tests of the corresponding triangles [22].

For queries between rigid bodies, the hierarchies can be precomputed once and traversed at runtime. For example, this is the case when performing collision queries in the fields of motion planning and path validation in CAD. These problems can be generalized as having two geometric objects, given as triangle sets, and a number of rigid body transformations that describe the relative position of the objects. We then want to detect the collision status of the objects for every relative placement.

We want to investigate how a high number of BVH-based collision tests can be efficiently performed in parallel on the GPU. Our goal is to improve the performance of high level algorithms for sampling-based motion planning and

R. Keller et al. (Eds.): Facing the Multicore-Challenge III 2012, LNCS 7686, pp. 84–95, 2013.
© Springer-Verlag Berlin Heidelberg 2013

path validation, where collision testing consumes a significant amount of the overall running time. We have used CUDA to implement and compare several different alternatives to distribute the work to the parallel GPU threads. As a reference, we have used OpenMP to parallelize the collision queries on the CPU.

2   Related Work

Bounding volume hierarchies are widely used to accelerate proximity queries. Most prominent bounding volume types include spheres, AABBs, OBBs, RSS and k-DOPs [18,5,11,9]. Some recent work aimed to improve the performance of proximity queries by the use of more sophisticated culling techniques and traversal schemes [2,20] or hierarchy memory layout [23].

There has also been substantial work on how to exploit the parallel compute capabilities of the GPU to improve collision tests and other proximity queries. Historically, many GPU-based collision checkers use the rasterization capabilities of the graphics device and perform image space tests based on depth buffer or stencil buffer tests and distance field computation [15,1,10,7,6,19,14].

More recent work has focused on parallel BVH construction [12] and traversal [3,16,13] on the GPU and multi-core CPUs [8,21]. Lauterbach et al. [13] describe a proximity query framework that is applicable to (continuous) collision detection, distance computation and self intersection. They treat a bounding volume intersection test a basic task and describe a load balancing scheme to distribute these tasks evenly amongst all GPU cores. The authors in [17] aim at performing a high number of collision tests in parallel in the field of sampling-based motion planning. They intent to cluster similar transformations of the queried objects (that lead to similar BVH traversal) to achieve a performance gain.

Compared to previous work, our goal is to execute a high number of independent collision tests in parallel. Instead of using a sophisticated load balancing scheme or pre-processing of the input transformations, we rely on the high number of tests to evenly utilize the GPU cores while keeping the implementation complexity at a minimum. We attempt to parallelize the problem at different granularities and analyze how the achieved collision test throughput varies with the total number of tests per parallel collision query.

3   Problem Formulation

Let $\mathfrak{A}, \mathfrak{B} \subset \mathbb{R}^3$ be two objects given as triangle sets and $Bvh_{\mathfrak{A}}$ and $Bvh_{\mathfrak{B}}$ two bounding volume hierarchies that are constructed on these triangle sets. We are going to use OBB bounding volumes for our benchmarks, as they have shown to work well in the context of collision testing [5], but any other type of bounding volume could be used instead. Individual bounding volumes are being denoted as $A \in Bvh_{\mathfrak{A}}$ and $B \in Bvh_{\mathfrak{B}}$, respectively.

We assume that $\mathfrak{B}$ is static whereas we want to apply an arbitrary rigid body transformation $q \in \mathbb{R}^3 \times SO(3)$ to $\mathfrak{A}$ and obtain a transformed set of triangles $\mathfrak{A}(q)$. In the following section, we use the term *parallel collision query* for a single call to our parallel algorithms that perform a high number of individual *collision tests*. Every collision test applies a different transformation to $\mathfrak{A}$ and executes numerous *intersection tests* of bounding volume pairs or triangle pairs. Thus, the algorithm operates on a vector of different transformations $Q = (q_0, q_1, \ldots, q_n)$, with $q_i \in \mathbb{R}^3 \times SO(3)$ and delivers a result vector $R = (r_0, r_1, \ldots, r_n)$, with $r_i \in \{0, 1\}$. We want to interpret the result such that $r_i = 1 :\Leftrightarrow \mathfrak{A}(q_i) \cap \mathfrak{B} \neq \emptyset$.

4   A Basic BVH Collision Test

A basic bounding volume hierarchy collision test traverses both BVHs in tandem. It manages a *traversal stack* S of bounding volume pairs (A, B). All pairs on the stack remain to be tested for intersection. At every iteration, the algorithm pops a pair (A, B) of bounding volumes from the stack and performs an intersection test. If $A(q)$ and B do not intersect, it can proceed with the next iteration. If they do intersect, the algorithm determines the child volumes of A and B from the hierarchies and pushes all pairs of child volumes to the stack. In the case of two intersecting leaf nodes, we can perform exact collision tests with the triangles that are bounded by the nodes. If we detect one colliding triangle pair, we report that $\mathfrak{A}$ and $\mathfrak{B}$ collide and abort further BVH traversal.

Parallelization: Given a single-core implementation for BVH traversal, we can easily obtain a parallel version by using OpenMP to parallelize the main loop that iterates over the individual transformations of the collision query. We are going to use a quad-core CPU with hyper-threading so we split the total number of collision tests into 8 evenly sized pieces and assign every piece to an individual CPU thread. We want to use this CPU version as a reference for our CUDA implementations.

5   Parallel Collision Queries on the GPU

When implementing a bounding volume hierarchy traversal with CUDA, there are three major problems to be addressed:

Memory Access. There are two problems with memory access as far as BVH traversal is concerned. First, memory transactions between the GPU and video memory can only happen in chunks of 128 or 32 bytes. And second, it can be problematic to use cached memory accesses together with a random memory access pattern. Modern Nvidia GPUs use a two level caching mechanism. If we represent a bounding volume hierarchy as an array of bounding volume nodes, it is not possible to determine the order in which these volumes will be accessed. Even if we try to fit multiple bounding volumes into one cache line (e.g. we could attempt to store child nodes near its parents) it is likely that the cache line has already been evicted when we need the children, because L1 cache is a scarce GPU resource. We therefore want to access main memory through L2 only and disable L1 caching. This leads to a load granularity of only 32 byte memory segments. OBBs are an ideal candidate bounding volume to fit into 32 byte memory chunks. We took special care to represent an OBB with 15 float values. With one extra value for padding, this is exactly 64 bytes.

Code divergence. Every 32 threads of one warp always share the same instruction. However, it is possible that different threads take different execution paths at conditional instructions when the condition depends on the thread id. Whenever this happens, execution has to be serialized and the whole warp takes both execution paths, having part of the threads masked idle. It is therefore strongly recommended to avoid divergent branching as much as possible.

Workload balance. A topic that is closely related to code divergence is workload balance. In the parallelization process, we have to break down the problem into small parallel sub-problems. In our case, we solve separate collision tests for a high number of different transformations and use one thread to execute one test. It is possible that different sub-problems take a different amount of time causing the threads of one warp to run for a different amount of time. But the warp cannot stop its execution until all threads are ready. This can cause a large number of threads to stall. By trying to balance the workload amongst all threads of a common warp, this effect can be minimized.

6   Implementation Details

We have implemented different BVH traversal schemes. The schemes differ mostly in the way the work is divided into parallel sub-tasks and how these tasks are mapped to the GPU threads. To mask out the effect that the triangle tests have and to isolate the BVH traversal scheme, we first want to discuss a simplified collision test that does not perform intersection tests for the triangles contained in the leaf nodes. In this context, we classify the proximity status of two objects solely based on bounding volume tests.

6.1   One Thread Performs One Test

In our first implementation, we want one thread to perform one collision test. The kernel gets two bounding volume hierarchies, $Bvh_{\mathfrak{A}}$ and $Bvh_{\mathfrak{B}}$ and an array of transformations Q (cf. Alg. 1). Every thread manages its own traversal stack in a dedicated piece of a large global memory array. In an initialization phase, it uses its thread-id to identify the right transformation and an offset to its private region of stack memory. The main loop is very CPU-like: In every iteration, we pop a stack entry before we load, transform and intersect the corresponding bounding volumes. All pairs of child volumes are pushed to the stack until we find a pair of intersecting leaf-nodes or the stack runs empty. Eventually, the thread reports its result to a dedicated place in a result array.

6.2   One Thread Performs Some Tests

Algorithm A has no concept for workload balancing. The GPU schedules and executes groups of 32 threads (*warps*) in a SIMD fashion. This means that if

Algorithm 1

```
#define INITIALIZE
    q = Q[qIdx];
    S = { (0,0) };
    col = false;
#endif

void kernelA( Configs Q, BVH bvh_A, BVH bvh_B ) {
    qIdx = blockDim × blockIdx + threadIdx;
    S.start = globalStackArray + qIdx × STACK_SIZE;

    INITIALIZE;
    while( !S.empty() && !col ) {

        (A, B) = S.pop();

        if( intersect(A(q),B) ) {
            if( A.isLeaf() && B.isLeaf() )
                col = true;
            else
                S.push( children(A,B) );
        }
    }
    result[qIdx] = col;
}
```

Algorithm 2

```
void kernelB( Configs Q, BVH bvh_A, BVH bvh_B ) {
    qIdx = blockDim × blockIdx + threadIdx;
    nuOfThreads = blockDim × gridDim;
    S.start = globalStackArray + qIdx × STACK_SIZE;

    INITIALIZE;
    while( true ) {
        if( S.empty() || col ) {
            result[qIdx] = col;

            qIdx += nuOfThreads;
            if( qIdx ≥ Q.size() ) return;

            INITIALIZE;
        }

        (A, B) = S.pop();

        if( intersect(A(q), B) ) {
            if( A.isLeaf() && B.isLeaf() )
                col = true;
            else
                S.push( children(A,B) );
        }
    } // end of while
}
```

the first 31 threads of a warp exit the main loop right away because their root bounding volumes have shown to be disjoint, they would still have to wait for the last thread to finish the main loop before they could write their result. Until this happens they become idle and waste GPU resources.

This effect is softened if all threads of the same warp consume approximately the same computation time. To achieve this, our basic idea is to let every thread perform more than just one collision test and to read transformations and write results from inside the main loop (cf. Alg. 2). This has the advantage that if one thread has finished a collision test, it does not have to wait for the other threads in the same warp but it can launch the next test. We use a static mapping of the collision tests to the threads where every thread performs the same number of collision tests. The drawback of this method is that we need more collision tests than in case of kernel A to have the GPU fully utilized. So is not promising to let one thread perform a too high number of tests either (cf. Sec. 7).

6.3 Some Threads Perform One Test

In our third implementation, we want a group of threads to work on the same collision test. Letting one thread perform one collision test performs poorly when the traversal stack runs almost empty. So we want to use a group of threads to perform a single BV intersection test. A natural group size for current Nvidia GPUs would be a multiple of one warp (i.e. 32 threads). In the context of collision tests, this is already a quite large group size.

We use OBB hierarchies and we use a separating axis test like in [5] to decide if two oriented bounding boxes are disjoint. The separating axis test is an ideal candidate for parallelization, as we can independently test all 15 candidate axes.

These considerations led to the following choices in our implementation (cf. Alg 3): We use groups that are composed of a fixed number of 16 threads. There is a dedicated master thread, that manages the traversal stack and pops a new stack entry at every iteration of the main loop. As we represent an OBB with 15 floating point values, we use the first 15 threads of the group to load the two corresponding bounding volumes A and B from memory with coalesced reads of 15 floats. The master thread transforms A according to the transformation that belongs to the collision test. After that, the first 15 threads perform a projection of A and B on one of the 15 different separating axes. The threads share the result of the OBB intersection test through a shared memory variable.

The reader may have noticed that we only use the first 15 threads of every group. The 16th thread is always idle! This means that we waste 1/16th or about 6% of our computational resources in the first place. However, if we mask out this one thread per group, we can achieve that the threads of every two groups sum up nicely to one warp. If we decided to enforce a group size of 15 instead, we would introduce a stride of 2 which results in a sub-optimal alignment of our logical units (groups) to the physical unit of one warp. In practice, we have observed that it is beneficial to sacrifice the 16th thread.

6.4   Some Threads Perform Some Tests

In our implementation of pattern D, we use a group of 32 threads to perform 8 collision tests. To compensate for the low thread utilization ratio in the beginning of the traversal, all threads in one group share the same traversal stack. This requires to store not only the indices of the pending bounding volume pairs on the stack but also record an index for the corresponding transformation. The pseudocode for this scheme is given in Alg. 4. First, we initialize the global stack and load eight transformations to a shared memory location In the main loop, we utilize as many threads as we have stack entries left (at most 32 threads). Every thread loads and transforms a bounding volume pair and performs an intersection test. Dependent on the result of this intersection test, some but not necessarily all threads need to write new pairs of child volumes on the stack. To improve the access pattern of the global memory writes, we first write all produced stack entries densely to a shared memory array and then copy the whole array to the global memory stack.

We have tested two different implementations for the *parallel_write* to the shared memory array. The first implementation uses a static addressing scheme to assign the entries of the output array uniquely to a thread of the group. If not all threads perform a write operation, the resulting array is sparse and has to be compacted before we copy it to the global memory stack. The second implementation uses atomic operations to increment a pointer to the shared array and to perform a dense output in the first place. We found that the second option was preferable in our test cases.

7   Benchmarks and Results

We have tested our implementations in two different scenarios. Both test cases correspond to a motion planning problem: to separate the intertwined the nails

Algorithm 3

```
void kernelC( Configs Q, BVH bvhA , BVH bvhB ) {
  groupSize = 16;
  groupsPerBlock = blockDim / groupSize;

  tIdx = threadIdx % groupSize;
  gIdx = threadIdx / groupSize;

  qIdx = groupsPerBlock × blockIdx + gIdx;
  S.start = globalStackArray + qIdx × STACK_SIZE;

  __shared__ volatile int col;
  __shared__ volatile OBB A, B;

  INITIALIZE;
  while( true ) {
    if( tIdx == 0 ) {
      if( S.empty() )
        col = true;
      else
        (idxA , idxB ) = S.pop();
    }

    if( tIdx < 15 )
      (A,B) = loadVolumes(idxA , idxB );

    if( tIdx == 0 )  A = A(q);

    __shared__ cut = 1;
    if( tIdx < 15 ) {
      n = getSepAxis( A, B, tIdx );
      if( sepAxisProject( A, B, n ) ) shCut = 0;
    }
    if( tIdx == 0 && shCut ) {
      if( A.isLeaf() && B.isLeaf() )
        col = true;
      else
        S.push( children(A,B) );
    }
  } // end of while
}
```

Algorithm 4

```
void kernelD( Configs Q, BVH bvhA , textscBvh bvhB} {
  groupSize = 32;
  groupsPerBlock = blockDim / groupSize;

  tIdx = threadIdx % groupSize;
  gIdx = threadIdx / groupSize;

  qIdx = groupsPerBlock × blockIdx + gIdx;
  S.start = globalStackArray + qIdx × STACK_SIZE;

  if( tIdx < 8 )
    q[tIdx] = Q[qIdx];

  S = { (0,0,0), (1,0,0), ..., (7,0,0) };
  while( S ≠ ∅ ) {
    if( tIdx < S.size() ) {
      (t, A, B) = S.pop( tIdx );

      if( intersect( A(q[t]),B ) ) {
        if( A.isLeaf() && B.isLeaf() )
          col[t] = true;
        else
          parallel_write( sharedArray,
                          {t} × children(A,B) );
      }
    }

    copy( S, sharedArray );
  } // end of while

  if( tIdx < 8 ) result[qIdx] = col[tIdx];
}
```

models and to remove the engine from the engine bay (cf. Fig. 1). We are using 2^{20} input transformations for the moving object as they would be tested by a sampling-based motion planning algorithm [4]. To run our GPU code, we used a Nvidia GeForce GTX480 consumer card and an Intel® Xeon® E5620 quad-core CPU at 2.4GHz for our reference CPU code. The complexities of the objects in terms of triangle counts are given in the following table.

	Nails	Engine Bay
$\mathfrak{A}$	9,282	92,671
$\mathfrak{B}$	9,282	126,820

Triangle count of the objects used in our benchmarks

Fig. 1. Objects used for the benchmarks with a number of random transformations

There are different aspects we want to discuss in this section. First of all, we want to examine how the different kernel versions described in Sec. 6 behave when performing a number of collision tests. The kernels A and B make no use of the GPU's shared memory. We want to investigate how moving the traversal stack from global to shared memory influences the performance of these algorithms. All these implementations perform no triangle-triangle intersection tests but operate solely on the bounding volume hierarchies. Thus, we examine the effect that the triangle tests have on the running time in the following paragraph. Finally, we want to test how the number of collision tests that are processed in parallel influence the GPU performance and compare the results to our reference CPU implementation.

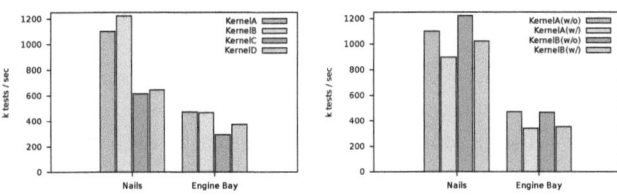

Fig. 2. Performance of different CUDA Kernels (left); performing triangle tests (right)

GPU – Kernel Version. Fig. 2 (left) shows how the different kernel versions perform in our benchmark scenarios. We can see that the kernel version A and B clearly outperform the other approaches. We were able to perform more than one million collision tests per second for the nails benchmark and around 480k tests per second for the more complex engine bay benchmark. Although version D is not too bad in the engine bay scenario, this more sophisticated traversal scheme cannot compensate for the burden of inter thread communication. The idea to let a group of threads share a common traversal stack cannot compete with the more naive versions A and B. Furthermore, our results show that it is not advantageous to use a very fine granular parallelization as was done with kernel C where we parallelized a single bounding volume test.

GPU – Shared Memory Traversal Stack. The CUDA kernels A and B make no use of the GPU's shared memory. We can therefore modify the kernels and hopefully take advantage of this GPU resource. Our first attempt is to move the traversal stack of every thread to a shared memory array to save global memory transactions. Every stack entry is a pair of two integers that identify a pair of bounding volumes. As we are using a depth first order traversal scheme, this stack cannot grow very much in size. If we are going to reserve stack space for 64 entries for every thread, we need 16KB of shared memory per warp. Because every SM only has 48KB of shared memory available, this means that a SM can only run three warps concurrently.

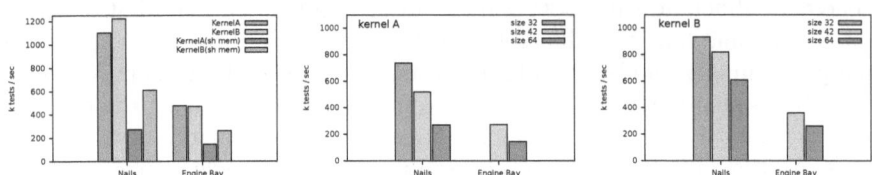

Fig. 3. Performance of kernels A and B when traversal stack resides in shared memory

The result of our experiment with a fixed stack size of 64 can be found in Fig. 3 on the left hand side. For both kernel versions, using a shared memory traversal stack has a negative effect on the performance in our tests. The high resource consumption restricts the number of threads that can run concurrently per SM. This negative effect cannot be compensated by a reduced number of global memory transactions.

One option would be to reduce the stack sizes. For a stack size of 32 entries, every SM could run up to 6 warps concurrently. However, we found that a stack size of 32 was not sufficient for all our test queries. A high triangle count causes deep hierarchies which can result in stack overflow and incorrect results. In Fig. 3, we sum up our results for different stack sizes of 64, 42 and 32 entries. The plots show how reducing the stack size can dramatically improve the algorithms performance. However, in the engine bay benchmark, the use of a 32 element stack caused stack overflow which resulted in a crash of the kernel and produced incorrect results.

If we compare these results with the diagram in Fig. 3 on the left, we can see that even the performance of the 32 element stacks is worse than the global-stack version. Overall, we could not produce any performance gain when using a shared memory stack compared to the global memory version.

GPU – Performing Triangle Tests. Fig. 2 (right) shows the effect of adding triangle-triangle intersection tests for the triangles contained in intersecting leaf nodes of the hierarchies. We show the result for kernels A and B only. Adding triangle tests causes increased computation time, extra time for loading the triangles and higher traversal time. It can also result in more divergent code as not all threads of a warp want to perform triangle tests at the same time. We found that if we perform triangle tests, the performance of our kernels drops by 30% − 35%. This is comparable to what happens when we perform the same test with the CPU version of our code.

GPU vs CPU – Saturation of the Processing Unit. Modern GPUs are capable of running hundreds of threads in parallel and even thousands of threads concurrently. The GPUs thread scheduler actively uses a high number of concurrent threads in order to hide memory latencies. Thus it is necessary to have a sufficient number of threads running to reach the peak performance of the device. In our case this means that we have to perform enough collision tests at a time. As the CPU relies on other strategies for latency hiding, like caching and branch prediction, it may not need as many jobs to fully utilize the device. However, we can expect that the CPU can also benefit from performing a sequence of tests at once. Fig. 4 shows how the number of tests influences the throughput of collision tests. We compare our CUDA implementations against our multi-core CPU approach. For kernel B we show two versions: in the first version, kernelB(8), every thread performs 8 collision tests and we perform 64 tests per thread in the second version, kernelB(64).

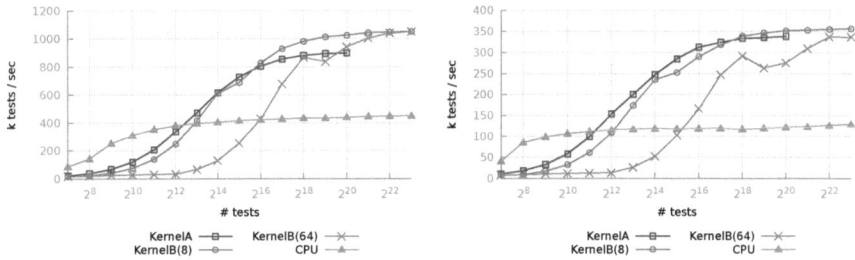

Fig. 4. Device Saturation. Nails benchmark (left) and Engine Bay benchmark (right).

Both, the CPU and the GPU, need a certain number of tests to be fully occupied. The GPU however is much more sensitive to this effect.

If we have a look at the nails benchmark, we can see that the CPU needs around 100k collision tests per query to achieve near peak performance. But we can run at 80% of peak performance already, if we only have 1024 tests per query. Kernel A needs around 2^{20} tests to fully occupy the GPU. At this point, it runs at 850k tests per second. The kernel cannot run 2^{21} tests at a time because this would require too much memory for the traversal stacks of the individual threads. This problem could be circumvented if we used a dynamic allocation of stack space. As we have predicted in Sec. 6, kernel B needs more concurrent tests to fully occupy the device. However, this kernel can achieve a higher peak performance if we run a sufficiently high number of collision tests in parallel. The cross over point depends on the number of test that one thread performs in kernel version B. Obviously, if we let one thread perform 64 tests, we need more threads to occupy the GPU. We have observed a short performance drop in kernel B when there are more than 8 active warps per streaming multiprocessor. This effect is more striking for kernelB(64) than for kernelB(8). It is independent of the collision tests being performed and it also happens if we all threads perform the exact same collision test. We assume that at this point, the kernel configuration causes a drop of the achieved memory throughput which propagates to the performance drop.

While the peak performance depends on the complexity of the input meshes, we can observe that the qualitative behavior of the different implementations is very similar for both benchmark scenarios.

8   Conclusions and Future Work

We have analyzed how we can take advantage of many-core GPUs and multi-core CPUs to accelerate the execution of a high number of collision tests. We have investigated different CUDA implementations that resulted from a different distribution of the work to the parallel threads and compared their performance against each other and against a multi-core CPU implementation. For benchmarking, we used two scenarios with different object complexity.

We could achieve a peak collision test throughput of one million tests per second for moderately complex objects and 240 thousand tests per second for highly complex models on a Nvidia GeForce GTX480 consumer card. This is about $2 - 2.5$ times as fast as our reference CPU implementation that runs on an Intel® Xeon® E5620 quad-core CPU at 2.4GHz.

The quad-core CPU implementation is preferable if there are only a few thousand collision tests per query. Furthermore, the CPU implementation is very straight forward. If a single-core version already exists, the parallelization of the main loop with OpenMP can be trivially realized. In our benchmarks, we have observed a speed-up factor of 7.5 of the multi-core version over the single-core version (the CPU utilizes 4 cores with hyper-threading).

In Sec. 7, we have seen that our kernels could not profit from the use of a shared memory traversal stack. So our current implementation does not use this GPU resource at all. In the future, we want to investigate if we could possibly use the shared memory differently to reorganize the global memory accesses. We feel that this could be another opportunity to further improve the performance of our CUDA kernels. We also plan to use our parallel collision query routines to implement a sampling-based motion planner. As collision checking consumes most of the time in those family of motion planners, we can expect a high performance benefit in this application. In this context, we are also planning to utilize the GPU to asynchronously perform the collision tests while the CPU is driving the planning process simultaneously.

References

1. Baciu, G., Keung Wong, W.S., Sun, H.: Recode: An image-based collision detection algorithm. In: Proceedings of Pacific Graphics 1998 (1998)
2. Curtis, S., Tamstorf, R., Manocha, D.: Fast collision detection for deformable models using representative-triangles. In: Proceedings of the 2008 Symposium on Interactive 3D Graphics and Games, I3D 2008, pp. 61–69. ACM, New York (2008)
3. Damkjær, J., Erleben, K.: Gpu accelerated tandem traversal of blocked bounding volume hierarchy collision detection for multibody dynamics. In: Prautzsch, H., Schmitt, A.A., Bender, J., Teschner, M. (eds.) VRIPHYS, pp. 115–124. Eurographics Association (2009)
4. Geraerts, R., Overmars, M.H.: A comparative study of probabilistic roadmap planners. In: Workshop on the Algorithmic Foundations of Robotics, pp. 43–57 (2002)

5. Gottschalk, S., Lin, M.C., Manocha, D.: Obbtree: a hierarchical structure for rapid interference detection. In: Proceedings of the 23rd Annual Conference on Computer Graphics and Interactive Techniques, SIGGRAPH 1996, pp. 171–180. ACM, New York (1996), http://doi.acm.org/10.1145/237170.237244
6. Govindaraju, N., Redon, S., Lin, M., Manocha, D.: CULLIDE: Interactive collision detection between complex models in large environments using graphics hardware. In: Proceedings of the ACM SIGGRAPH/EUROGRAPHICS Conference on Graphics Hardware, pp. 25–32. Eurographics Association (2003)
7. Heidelberger, B., Teschner, M.: Real-time volumetric intersections of deforming objects. Proc. of Vision, Modeling (2003)
8. Kim, D., Heo, J.P., Huh, J., Kim, J., Yoon, S.E.: HPCCD: Hybrid parallel continuous collision detection using cpus and gpus. Computer Graphics Forum (Pacific Graphics) 28(7), 1791–1800 (2009)
9. Klosowski, J.T., Held, M., Mitchell, J.S.B., Sowizral, H., Zikan, K.: Efficient collision detection using bounding volume hierarchies of k-dops. IEEE Transactions on Visualization and Computer Graphics, 21–36 (1998)
10. Knott, D., Dinesh, K.P.: CInDeR Collision and Interference Detection in Real-time using Graphics Hardware. Computer Graphics Forum (2003)
11. Larsen, E., Gottschalk, S., Lin, M.C., Manocha, D.: Fast distance queries with rectangular swept sphere volumes. In: Proc. of IEEE Int. Conference on Robotics and Automation, pp. 3719–3726 (2000)
12. Lauterbach, C., Garland, M., Sengupta, S., Manocha, D.: Fast BVH construction on GPUs. Computer Graphics 28(2), 375–384 (2009)
13. Lauterbach, C., Mo, Q.: gProximity: Hierarchical GPU-based Operations for Collision and Distance Queries. Computer Graphics Forum 29(2), 419–428 (2010)
14. Morvan, T., Reimers, M., Samset, E.: High performance GPU-based proximity queries using distance fields. Computer Graphics Forum 27(8), 2040–2052 (2008)
15. Myszkowski, K., Okunev, O.G., Kunii, T.L.: Fast collision detection between complex solids using rasterizing graphics hardware. The Visual Computer 11(9), 497–511 (1995)
16. Pabst, S., Koch, A., Straßer, W.: Fast and scalable cpu/gpu collision detection for rigid and deformable surfaces. Comput. Graph. Forum 29(5), 1605–1612 (2010)
17. Pan, J., Manocha, D.: GPU-based parallel collision detection for fast motion planning. The International Journal of Robotics (2012)
18. Quinlan, S.: Efficient distance computation between non-convex objects. In: Proceedings of International Conference on Robotics and Automation, pp. 3324–3329 (1994)
19. Sud, A., Govindaraju, N., Gayle, R., Manocha, D.: Interactive 3d distance field computation using linear factorization. In: Proc. ACM Symposium on Interactive 3D Graphics and Games, pp. 117–124 (2006)
20. Tang, M., Curtis, S., Yoon, S.E., Manocha, D.: Interactive continuous collision detection between deformable models using connectivity-based culling. In: Proceedings of the 2008 ACM Symposium on Solid and Physical Modeling, SPM 2008, pp. 25–36. ACM (2008)
21. Tang, M., Manocha, D., Tong, R.: MCCD: Multi-core collision detection between deformable models using front-based decomposition. Graphical Models (2010)
22. Veltkamp, R.: Hierarchical approximation and localization. The Visual Computer 14(10), 471–487 (1998)
23. Yoon, S., Dinesh Manocha, D.: Cache-Efficient Layouts of Bounding Volume Hierarchies. Computer Graphics Forum 25(3) (2006)

ÆminiumGPU: An Intelligent Framework for GPU Programming

Alcides Fonseca and Bruno Cabral

University of Coimbra, Portugal
{amaf,bcabral}@dei.uc.pt

Abstract. As a consequence of the immense computational power available in GPUs, the usage of these platforms for running data-intensive general purpose programs has been increasing. Since memory and processor architectures of CPUs and GPUs are substantially different, programs designed for each platform are also very different and often resort to a very distinct set of algorithms and data structures. Selecting between the CPU or GPU for a given program is not easy as there are variations in the hardware of the GPU, in the amount of data, and in several other performance factors.

ÆminiumGPU is a new data-parallel framework for developing and running parallel programs on CPUs and GPUs. ÆminiumGPU programs are written in a Java using Map-Reduce primitives and are compiled into hybrid executables which can run in either platforms. Thus, the decision of which platform is going to be used for executing a program is delayed until run-time and automatically performed by the system using Machine-Learning techniques.

Our tests show that ÆminiumGPU is able to achieve speedups up to 65x and that the average accuracy of the platform selection algorithm, in choosing the best platform for executing a program, is above 92%.

Keywords: Portability, Parallel, Heterogeneous, GPGPU.

1 Introduction

Since Graphics Processing Units (GPUs) have been user-programmable, scientists and engineers have been exploring new ways of using the processing power in GPUs to increase the performance of their programs. GPU manufacturers acknowledged this alternative fashion of using their hardware, and have since provided special drivers, tools and even models to address this small, but fast-growing niche.

GPUs are interesting to target because of their massive parallelism, which provides a higher throughput than what is available on current multi-core processors. But, one can argue that the difference in architectures also makes programming for the GPU more complex than for the CPU. GPU programming is not easy. Developers that do not understand the programming model and the hardware architecture of a GPU will not be able to extract all its processing power. And, even after a program has been specially designed for the GPU, its

R. Keller et al. (Eds.): Facing the Multicore-Challenge III 2012, LNCS 7686, pp. 96–107, 2013.

performance might still be worse than on the CPU. For instance, the usage of GPUs incurs on a penalty caused by memory copies between the main memory and the GPU-specific memory.

In many situations, it may not be feasible to know beforehand if a program will perform better in a GPU or in a CPU without actually executing it. And, for programs that are not repeatedly executed or that execute for a very long time it may not be useful to do so. Moreover, the performance of a program will commonly be influenced by the size of the input data, the actual GPU hardware and the structure of the program itself.

```
Double integral = new Range(RESOLUTION).map(new LambdaMapper<
    Integer, Double>() {
  public Double map(Integer input) {
    double n = RESOLUTION;
    double b = Math.pow(Math.E, Math.sin(input / n));
    double B = Math.pow(Math.E, Math.sin((input+1) / n));
    return ((b+B) / 2 ) * (1/n);
  }
}).reduce(new LambdaReducer<Double>(){
  public Double combine(Double input, Double other) {
    return input + other;
  }
});
```

Listing 1.1. Example of Map-Reduce to Calculate the Integral of a Function using the trapezoid method

integral program – CPU vs GPU on ÆminiumGPU

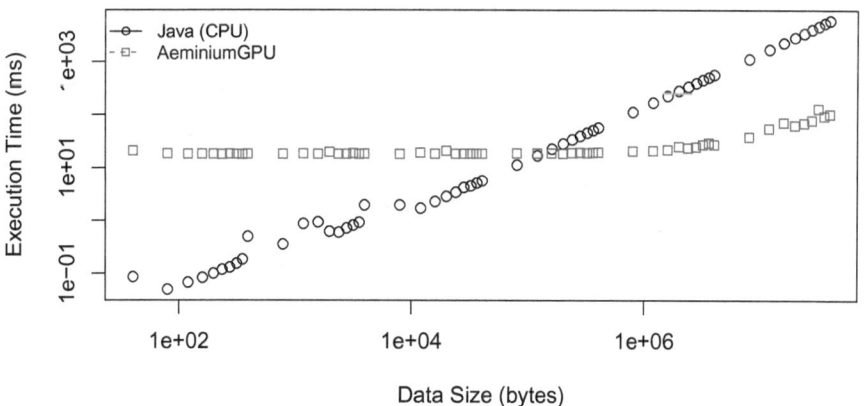

Fig. 1. Performance of the Integral program on CPU and GPU

Listing 1.1 is an example of programs that can execute on the GPU and calculates the integral of $f(x) = e^{sin(x)}$. This is an embarrassingly parallel problem, which is expressed using a data-parallel approach by means of map and reduce operations. Figure 1 shows the execution time of the program in both CPU and GPU for different data sizes. The GPU version is faster after a certain data size and it is able to achieve up to 64 times of speedup. But, note that the threshold from which the GPU performance starts to gain on the CPU is not always the same. The actual threshold value depends of the program logic and even with the hardware being used. Thus the decision whether to run a program on the GPU or CPU is not an easy one.

The goal of this work is to present a new framework which simplifies the task of writing data-parallel programs for transparently executing in GPUs, with improved performance. Our approach drives inspiration from Functional Programming and puts the power of GPUs in the hands of developers without forcing them to understand the particularities of GPU programming. While programs are written in a mainstream programming language using a Map-Reduce approach for now, specific parts of their code are compiled to OpenCL and executed on the GPU. In order to minimize the impact of well known bottlenecks in GPU programming and maximize the speedup obtained by the usage of GPUs, the framework performs several optimizations on the generated code. Such optimizations include the generation of data on the GPU in opposition to its copy from main memory, among others. Furthermore, in ÆminiumGPU, programs are compiled into "hybrid" executables that can run in either GPU and CPU platforms. Since the final purpose of ÆminiumGPU is to execute programs as fast as possible, independently of the platform being used, hybrid executables allow us to delay the decision of which platform is best for executing a specific program until run-time, when much more information is available to fundament a choice. ÆminiumGPU, by means of Machine-Learning techniques, is able to make this decision autonomously with high accuracy.

The contributions of this work are:

- A new and state-of-the-art framework for GPGPU programming, which hides GPU architectural details and execution model from developers;
- A translation library that is able to automatically generate optimized OpenCL code from code written in a mainstream general purpose programming language;
- A machine-learning solution for predicting the efficiency of programs in both CPUs and GPUs;
- And, to the best of our knowledge, the first runtime system using machine-learning techniques for autonomously deciding either to execute programs in the CPU or GPU.

2   Approach

In this section we will depict the architecture and design of the ÆminiumGPU framework. We will use the Map-Reduce algorithm as an example in this section since it is a suitable representative of data-parallel algorithms in general.

2.1   Architecture

The ÆminiumGPU framework was designed for supporting Æminium[1] and Java programming languages. Since Æminium compiles to Java, this paper will present the architecture from the point of view of Java. The Java language is not supported by GPUs. Thus it is necessary to translate Java into OpenCL functions. Translation is performed at compile-time by the ÆminiumGPU Compiler. The OpenCL functions are then executed by the ÆminiumGPU Runtime during execution. The general architecture can be seen in Figure 2.

ÆminiumGPU Compiler.
The ÆminiumGPU Compiler is a source-to-source compiler from Java-to-Java, in which the final Java code has some extra OpenCL code. The OpenCL code is based on lambda functions present in the source code. For each lambda in the original code,

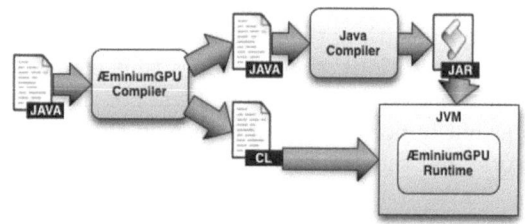

Fig. 2. Architecture of ÆminiumGPU

the compiler creates an OpenCL version. This version is later used to generate a kernel which will execute on the GPU.

The compiler was implemented using Spoon, a Java-to-Java compiler framework[2]. Spoon parses and generates the AST and generates the Java code from the AST. The ÆminiumGPU compiler introduces new phases that produce the OpenCL version of existent lambdas. The compiler looks for methods with a special signature, such as map or reduce. The AST of lambdas passed as arguments are then analyzed and a visitor tries to compile Java code to OpenCL as soon as it descends the AST.

It is important to notice that not all Java code can be translated to OpenCL. The ÆminiumGPU compiler does not support all method calls, non-local variables, for-each loops, object instantiation and exceptions. It does support a common subset between Java and C99 with some extra features like static accesses, calls to methods and references to fields of the Math object.

ÆminiumGPU Runtime. The ÆminiumGPU Runtime is a Java library responsible for providing Æminium Programs with parallel-ready lists that implement the GPU methods, such as map and reduce methods. Each list can be associated with a GPU, thus supporting several GPUs on the same machine. Whenever a GPU operation is summoned, the following phases occur: firstly the compiler-generated OpenCL function is inserted in a predefined template (specific for each operation, such as reduce) and the resulting kernel is compiled to the GPU; afterwards, the input data, if required, is copied to the GPU memory; next the kernel execution is scheduled with a suitable workgroups and workitems arrangement for the data size and operation in question; finally the output data is copied back to the host device and every GPU resource is manually released.

The templates used for Map and Reduce, since we are focusing in these operations for this work, are really straightforward. The map kernel only applies a function to an element of the input array and writes it to the output array. The reduce kernel is a generic version of NVIDIA's implementation[3], allowing for more data-types than the four originally supported.

For these operations in particular, one optimization already implemented is the fusion of maps with maps, and maps with reduces. This optimization is done by considering the Map operation a lazy operation that is only actually performed when the results are needed. This laziness allows for merging together several operations, saving time in unnecessary memory copies and kernel calls. Because of this optimization, the final kernel is only known and compiled at runtime.

All operations, even the ones that cannot be translated to the GPU, have a sequential version written in Java. For the original purposes of this framework, it was not important to parallelize on the CPU, but it will be considered in future work, and the same technique can be used.

2.2 GPU-CPU Decision

ÆminiumGPU uses Machine Learning techniques to automatically decide if a given operation should be executed on either the GPU or CPU. The problem can be described as two-classed because each program execution can be classified as either *Best on GPU* or *Best on CPU*. Supervised learning will be used, since it is important to associate certain features of programs to the two platforms.

Since decisions are hardware dependent (CPU and GPU combination), we considered two ways for tackling the problem: training the classifier in each machine; or considering CPU and GPU specifications as features in a general classifier. The former was selected for this work, although it can be extended to the later in the future. Using a large number of features would increase classification time and it would be a very hard to train a general classifier with a large set of CPU and GPUs. This means that when installing ÆminiumGPU, it is necessary to execute a standard benchmark for collecting training data.

The critical aspect for having a good classification is choosing the right features to represent programs. For instance, it is not feasible to consider the full program in ASCII, since the length would be variable and the abstraction level ill-suited for classification techniques. Table 1 lists all the features used in the classification process.

```
a(); // Level 1
for (int i=0; i<10; i++) {
    b(); // Level 2
    while ( j < 20)
        c(); // Level 3
}
```

Listing 1.2. Examples of Level categorization

Features can be extracted either during compilation or during runtime. This means that a given program will always hold the same values for the first features, while the last three features may be different, depending on the conditions of execution. Features marked with a size of 3 have three values, one for each depth of loop scopes. Listing 1.2 shows an example in which three functions are considered in 3 different loop levels. This distinction is important since operations in inner levels are executed more times than ones in the outer levels.

The choice of some selected features was inspired by other applications of Machine Learning in this area ([4], [5] and [6]). Memory accesses were considered a feature as they are one of the main reasons why GPU programs are not as fast as one would expect. As such, there are features for all three main kinds of memories in GPUs (global and slow, local and fast, global read-only and fast). Note that some GPU models may not have one of them, but it is still required for other models.

Table 1. List of features

Name	Size	Collected during	Description
OuterAccess	3	Compilation	Global GPU memory read.
InnerAccess	3	Compilation	Local (thread-group) memory read. This area of the memory is faster than the global one.
ConstantAccess	3	Compilation	Constant (read-only) memory read. This memory is faster on some GPU models.
OuterWrite	3	Compilation	Write in global memory.
InnerWrite	3	Compilation	Write in local memory, which is also faster than in global.
BasicOps	3	Compilation	Simplest and fastest instructions. Include arithmetic, logical and binary operators.
TrigFuns	3	Compilation	Trigonometric functions, including *sin, cos, tan, asin, acos* and *atan*.
PowFuns	3	Compilation	*pow, log* and *sqrt* functions
CmpFuns	3	Compilation	*max* and *min* functions
Branches	3	Compilation	Number of possible branching instructions such as *for, if* and *whiles*
DataTo	1	Runtime	Size of input data transferred to the GPU in bytes.
DataFrom	1	Runtime	Size of output data transferred from the GPU in bytes.
ProgType	1	Runtime	One of the following values: Map, Reduce, PartialReduce or MapReduce, which are the different types of operations supported by ÆminiumGPU.

In terms of operations, we performed micro-benchmarks to assess their execution cost. For instance, 4 or 5 *plus* operator calls execute much faster than one single *sin* call. As such, OpenCL functions were grouped according to the relative cost they have on execution time.

Besides these features, each benchmark also collected the execution time in both CPU and GPU, and the class to each execution belongs to. This is used for training and also evaluation.

3   Evaluation and Classifier Selection

In this section we will describe the experiments performed for verifying and validating our approach and to select a classifier to use in the implementation.

3.1   Dataset

Our workload for generating the training and testing dataset is composed by the following 8 programs:

1. A map operation that adds 1 to each element of the input array;
2. A map operation that applies the *sin* function to each element of the input array;
3. A map operation that applies the *sin* and *cosine* functions to each element of the input array and sums the values;
4. A map operation that calculates the factorial for each element of the input array;
5. A map-reduce operation that calculates the integral from 0 to the size of the array for $f(x) = e^{sin(x)}$;
6. A map-reduce operation that calculates the minimum value from 0 to the size of the array for $f(x) = 10x^6 + x^5 + 2x^4 + 3x^3 + \frac{2}{5}x^2 + \pi x$;
7. A map-reduce operation that calculates the sum of all natural numbers up to a given value that are divisible by 7;
8. A map-reduce operation that calculates the sum of all elements of the input array that are divisible by 7.

Each one of these programs was executed several times with varying amounts of input data. The size of input data varies from 10 to 10^7 elements, executing with 10 values for each power of 10, and in each level multiplied by all natural numbers until 9. Thus, the first sizes would be 10,20,30,40,50,... and the last sizes would be $50^6, 60^6, 70^6, 80^6, 90^6, 10^7$. Overall, the dataset has 440 instances of different program executions, from 8 individual programs, each executed with the 55 different data sizes.

3.2   Experimental Setup

These are the specifications of the hardware and software used for the experiments: Intel Core2 Duo E8200 at 2.66GHz; 4GB of RAM memory; NVIDIA GeForce GTX 285, with 240 CUDA cores and 1GB of memory; OS Ubuntu Linux 64bits with the NVIDIA CUDA SDK 5.0 preview 2 with OpenCL 1.1 and OpenJDK 1.7. The results presented here are specific to this particular hardware and software and can not represent all possible combinations.

3.3   Feature Analysis

To evaluate features we used two feature ranking techniques: Information Gain and Gain Ratio. Both techniques were applied to the whole dataset. The ranking obtained was different for each method, but both returned 3 groups of features: A first group of high-ranked features, a group of low-ranked features and a third group of unused or unrepresentative features. This later group exists because the dataset programs do not cover all possibilities. But, this does not mean that such features should be ignored, on the contrary, they should be studied for particular examples which are out of the scope of this work. Table 2 shows the two other groups ranked using the Information Gain method.

Table 2. Features rank using Information gain

Rank	Feature	Rank	Feature
0.2606	DataTo	0.172	OutterAccess1
0.2517	DataFrom	0.0637	Branches1
0.1988	BasicOps2	0.0516	InnerAccess1
0.1978	BasicOps1	0.0425	TrigFuns1
0.1978	ProgType	0.0397	InnerWrite2
0.1978	OutterWrite1	0.0397	InnerAccess2

Notice that features related with data sizes are high ranked, which is supported by the high penalty caused by memory transfers. Basic Operations are also very representative, since they are very common, specially in loop conditions (*BasicOps2*). The program type is also important because maps and reduces have a different internal structure. Maps happen in parallel, while parallel reduces are executed with much more synchronization in each reduction level.

Looking at the lower ranked features, it is important to consider that memory accesses also impact the decision. It is also expected that branching conditions would have an impact on the performance of programs. Finally, trigonometric functions do not have such an high impact as basic operations, but they are still relevant for the decision.

3.4 Classifier Comparison

In order to achieve the best accuracy, it is important to choose an adequate classifier. For this task, several off-the-shelf classifiers from Weka[7] were evaluated, and some custom classifiers were also developed. The used classifiers include: a **Random** classifier that randomly assigns either class to a particular instance; **AlwaysCPU** and **AlwaysGPU** that classifies all instances as *Best on CPU* and *Best on GPU*; a **NaiveBayes** Classifier; a Support Vector Machine (**SVM**) obtained from a Sequential Minimal Optimization algorithm with $c = 1$, $\epsilon = 10^{-12}$ and a Polynomial Kernel; a Multi-Layer Perceptron (**MLP**); a **DecisionTable** classifier; and a Cost-Sensitive version of the DecisionTable(**CSDT**) that uses 0.4 as the cost for 0.4 for misclassified *Best on CPU* programs and 0.6 for *Best on GPU* programs.

Besides these classifiers, we also experimented with a regression-based approach using additional metrics such as: *CPUTime* and *GPUTime*. The main idea was to use regression techniques to predict values of *CPUTime* and

GPUTime for each instance and then select the smallest value. However, regressions have shown to have a poor quality with correlation coefficients between 70 and 80%. The final classifier behaved very similarly with the Random classifier. Thus, we decided to not pursue this line of research further.

Classifiers were evaluated using both 7 and 8 fold cross validation. Data was not randomized and was ordered by program. Since the number of folds is lower than or equal to the number of programs, some programs are not present in all the training sets. This simulates the real-world scenario of classifying programs that were not previously seen. The results with 7 and 8 folds were very similar, as well as the results with randomized data. The results presented from here on are with 7 folds and without randomization.

Figure 3 shows the accuracy distribution of the evaluated classifiers. AlwaysCPU and AlwaysGPU do not have 0.5 of accuracy because programs that are faster on the GPU are larger number on the dataset. This was not balanced on purpose, to reflect the actual distribution of CPU and GPU execution times for the tested programs. The DecisionTable classifier achieved a very high accuracy, only second to its Cost-Sensitive version which had a slightly higher accuracy with a more condensed distribution.

In this problem, the distinction between False Positives and Negatives is not relevant. This may seem to contradict the usage of a Cost-Sensitive Classifier, but the cost of misclassification does not only depend on the class, but also on the size of the data in that execution, according to Figure 1. In order to represent the impact of taking the wrong decision, a measure of cost was introduced to replace the traditional confusion matrix. The cost of a misclassification is the absolute difference between the real GPU and GPU execution times previously measured during the feature extraction.

Figure 4 shows the distribution of the total cost of the classification for each cross-validation execution with a logarithmic scale on the Cost (yy axis). The lowest the cost is, the better. A perfect classifier would have a cost of 0. The random classifier has an average cost of 9.8×10^9, which can be considered as a ceiling for this dataset.

The measure of cost is important because we can see that some classifiers such as NaiveBayes and SVM have a better accuracy but have an higher penalty on performance than the classifier that executes everything on the GPU. The two versions of the DecisionTable classifier were also the ones with the lowest cost. Another evaluation metric was classification time, since it could not be representative in execution time. Except for the NaiveBayes classifiers, all others classified instances in less than 20 microseconds, which is acceptable for this task. The classifier training time was not considered for this study as it is not relevant since it is only performed once per machine.

Looking at all the metrics, the Cost Sensitive version of the DecisionTable classifier was the best, achieving 92% of average accuracy and the lowest misclassification cost.

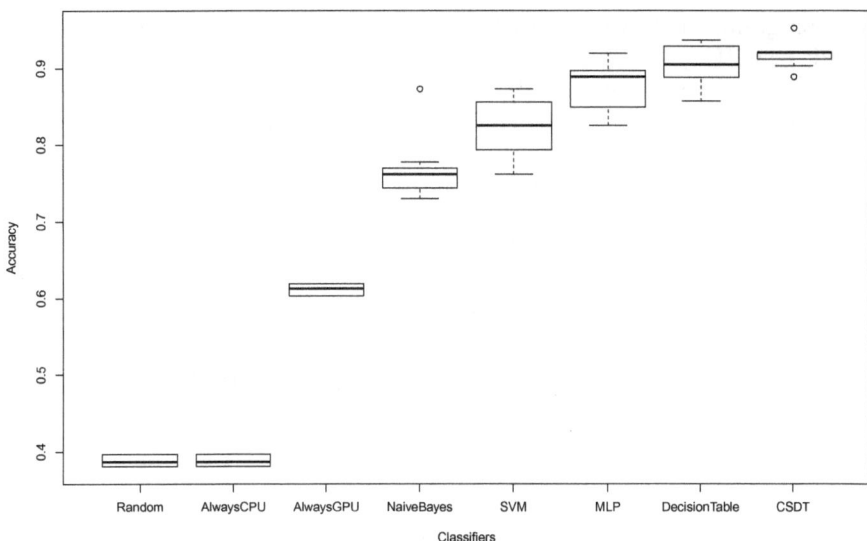

Fig. 3. Box plot of the distributions of accuracy of several classifiers

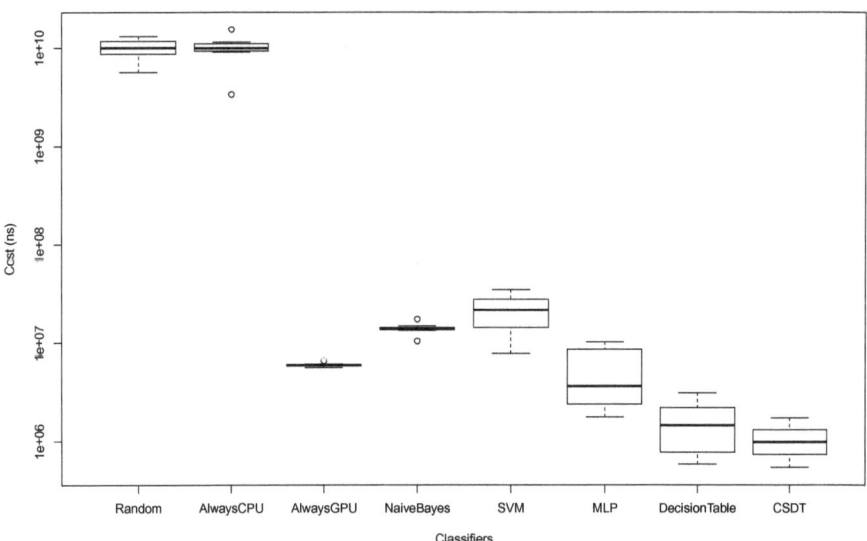

Fig. 4. Box plot of the distributions of costs of several classifiers

4   Related Work

There have been several works which can be compared with the ÆminiumGPU framework. There are also approaches that allow to write the kernel code in higher-level languages such as Aparapi[8] (for Java), Copperhead[9] (for Python) and ScalaCL[10] (for Scala) and in X10[11]. ÆminiumGPU is different from these approaches since it provides an interface at an even higher level, as it does not require programmers to write kernels, or know about which code can execute in the GPU or CPU.

Accelerate[12] has a more similar approach in which it also executes higher-level functions over arrays on the GPU. The purity of Haskell makes this some-how easier than in Java. Due to the monadic approach, programmers must type annotate all the code that can execute on the GPU, making GPU Programming less transparent than in ÆminiumGPU.

Both the second version of ScalaCL and JikesVM[13] can convert for loops to OpenCL code and execute it on the GPU. The former uses reflection while the later uses bytecode instrumentation. ÆminimumGPU uses a different approach, using a Source-to-Source compiler to generate the OpenCL code.

MARS[14] and MapCG[15] are two map-reduce frameworks for the GPU and, in the case of the latter, CPU as well with a low-level C API. Both these plat-forms follow the distributed key-value approach to map-reduce. The overhead of copying both keys and values is significant on the GPU, where every memory transfer counts, in cases where the values are not aggregated by key.

Qilin[16] is a C++ framework that has adaptive mapping in which it tries to record executes of the same program to build a cost model for future execu-tions of the program with different data sizes. ÆminiumGPU also uses previous program executions to build information for future decisions, but it does not require executions of the same program. For programs that only execute a few times in each machine, the approach used in Qilin is not feasible. There are also approaches for real-time systems[17]. However this work is limited to operations inside a ever-running loop, in which each iteration is schedule to the CPU or GPU according to estimated time, based on previous runs.

5   Conclusions and Future Work

The Æminium framework tries, as much as possible, to optimize the generated code and to schedule operations to the GPU. In many situations, performance increases as soon as the size of the input data goes above a certain threshold. But, since this value is program-dependent, ÆminiumGPU uses a Machine-Learning approach to decide which platform offers more guarantees of providing the best performance. Our tests show that ÆminiumGPU is able to achieve a 92% average accuracy with a low misclassification penalty.

The approach presented is language independent and can be applied to typical HPC languages like C and Fortran, even without using the Map-Reduce pattern. The approach can also work with other accelerators like FPGAs, and improved with specific features for those processors.

Concluding, ÆminiumGPU allows programmers to write data-parallel pro-grams whose performance can, if possible, be improved automatically by using the GPU.

Acknowledgments. This work was partially supported by the Portuguese Research Agency FCT, through CISUC (R&D Unit 326/97) and the CMU|Portugal program (R&D Project Aeminium CMU-PT/SE/0038/2008).

References

1. Stork, S., Marques, P., Aldrich, J.: Concurrency by default: using permissions to express dataflow in stateful programs. In: OOPSLA Companion, pp. 933–940 (2009)
2. Pawlak, R., Noguera, C., Petitprez, N.: Spoon: Program analysis and transformation in java (2006)
3. Harris, M.: Optimizing parallel reduction in cuda (2010)
4. Russell, T., Malik, A.M., Chase, M., van Beek, P.: Learning basic block scheduling heuristics from optimal data. In: Proceedings of the 2005 Conference of the Centre for Advanced Studies on Collaborative Research, CASCON 2005. IBM Press (2005)
5. Cavazos, J., Moss, J.E.B.: Inducing heuristics to decide whether to schedule. SIGPLAN Not. 39(6), 183–194 (2004)
6. Wang, Z., O'Boyle, M.F.: Mapping parallelism to multi-cores: a machine learning based approach. In: Proceedings of the 14th ACM SIGPLAN Symposium on Principles and Practice of Parallel Programming, PPoPP 2009, pp. 75–84. ACM, New York (2009)
7. Holmes, G., Donkin, A., Witten, I.: Weka: A machine learning workbench. In: Proceedings of the 1994 Second Australian and New Zealand Conference on Intelligent Information Systems 1994, pp. 357–361. IEEE (1994)
8. Frost, G.: Aparapi (2011), http://code.google.com/p/aparapi/
9. Catanzaro, B., Garland, M., Keutzer, K.: Copperhead: Compiling an embedded data parallel language. In: Principles and Practices of Parallel Programming (PPoPP), pp. 47–56 (2011)
10. Chafik, O.: Scalacl (2011), http://code.google.com/p/scalacl/
11. Cunningham, D., Bordawekar, R., Saraswat, V.: Gpu programming in a high level language: compiling x10 to cuda. In: Proceedings of the 2011 ACM SIGPLAN X10 Workshop, X10 2011, pp. 8:1–8:10. ACM, New York (2011)
12. Chakravarty, M., Keller, G., Lee, S., McDonell, T., Grover, V.: Accelerating haskell array codes with multicore gpus. In: Proceedings of the Sixth Workshop on Declarative Aspects of Multicore Programming, pp. 3–14. ACM (2011)
13. Leung, A., Lhoták, O., Lashari, G.: Automatic parallelization for graphics processing units. In: Proceedings of the 7th International Conference on Principles and Practice of Programming in Java, pp. 91–100. ACM (2009)
14. He, B., Fang, W., Luo, Q., Govindaraju, N.K., Wang, T.: Mars: a mapreduce framework on graphics processors. In: Proceedings of the 17th International Conference on Parallel Architectures and Compilation Techniques, PACT 2008, pp. 260–269. ACM, New York (2008)
15. Hong, C., Chen, D., Chen, W., Zheng, W., Lin, H.: Mapcg: writing parallel program portable between cpu and gpu. In: Proceedings of the 19th International Conference on Parallel Architectures and Compilation Techniques, PACT 2010, pp. 217–226. ACM, New York (2010)
16. Luk, C.K., Hong, S., Kim, H.: Qilin: exploiting parallelism on heterogeneous multiprocessors with adaptive mapping. In: Proceedings of the 42nd Annual IEEE/ACM International Symposium on Microarchitecture, MICRO, vol. 42, pp. 45–55. ACM, New York (2009)
17. Joselli, M., Zamith, M., Clua, E., Montenegro, A., Conci, A., Leal-Toledo, R., Valente, L., Feijó, B., d'Ornellas, M., Pozzer, C.: Automatic dynamic task distribution between cpu and gpu for real-time systems. In: 11th IEEE International Conference on Computational Science and Engineering, CSE 2008. IEEE (2008)

Parallel k-Means Image Segmentation Using Sort, Scan and Connected Components on a GPU

Michael Backer, Jan Tünnermann, and Bärbel Mertsching

GET Lab, University of Paderborn, Pohlweg 47-49, 33098 Paderborn, Germany
{backer,tuennermann,mertsching}@get.upb.de
http://getwww.upb.de

Abstract. Image segmentation is required to run fast and without supervision to speed up subsequent processes such as object recognition or other high level tasks. General purpose computing on the GPU is a powerful tool to perform efficient image processing and has been applied to the image segmentation problem. However, state-of-the-art approaches still perform parts of the computations on the CPU requiring costly data exchange with the main memory. In this paper we suggest a fully unsupervised color image segmentation that runs completely on the GPU including the calculation of region features. We compare our results to a popular CPU-based and a recent GPU-based method and report a computation time advantage.

1 Introduction

Computer vision algorithms for autonomous systems are expected to work unsupervised and image segmentation is often used as an initial step to reduce and abstract data for the subsequent processes, such as object detection or tracking. This grouping and filtering of information can be established with a biologically inspired concept of selective visual attention where relevant image portions are determined by data-driven conspicuity measures and task relevance [3,23]. Independent of such explicit notion of visual attention, image segmentation as an initial step must be as efficient as possible.

With the increasing prevalence of GPUs (Graphics Processing Units) in general purpose processing, methods of image processing have been adapted to run in parallel on the GPU. The SIMD (Single Instruction Multiple Data) paradigm [13], which is present in GPUs and CPU extensions, requires the avoidance of many different conditional branches driven by the input data handled by one SIMD-unit. Additionally in GPUs, developers have to explicitly take care of exploiting the fast but limited shared memory of a compute unit to obtain maximum efficiency.

For a review of image segmentation approaches we refer to the survey in [7]; in the following, we focus on approaches that utilize GPUs. *Level Set* and *Active Contours* algorithms have been accelerated utilizing the GPU [6,17]. These algorithms are typically used in medical image processing. Due to their many free

R. Keller et al. (Eds.): Facing the Multicore-Challenge III 2012, LNCS 7686, pp. 108–120, 2013.

parameters they require user interaction and are thus not suitable for automated machine vision. Clustering-based methods have been suggested for unsupervised segmentation on GPU. In [14] the *Quick Shift* algorithm [24] was applied to image segmentation. Abramov et al. [2] implemented a segmentation based on a clustering model from physics. *K-means* clustering, which can be applied to the image segmentation problem, has been accelerated with the GPU. The approach in [19] made use of the graphic rendering pipeline, but with the introduction of general purpose programming models like CUDA [1] and OpenCL [21] algorithms can be implemented in a more abstract way, decoupled from the rendering pipeline. Such approaches have been proposed in [11], [15] and [25]; however, the updating of the cluster centroids (see section 2.1) is at least partially done on the CPU, requiring multiple expensive data transfers between the GPU and main memory. To obtain disjunct spatially coherent regions from clusters, an additional labeling step has to be performed. This can be done by interpreting the image as a graph (mesh) and extracting connected components. In the basic *k-means* clustering approaches [11,15,25] the labeling step is not included. Only local connectivity is established in the *Quick Shift* variant from [14], resulting in superpixels (over-segmentation). Labeling is done globally in [2], but the calculation remains on the CPU. From the domain of graph theory, parallelized algorithms for connected components are available [16,20] but target general graphs.

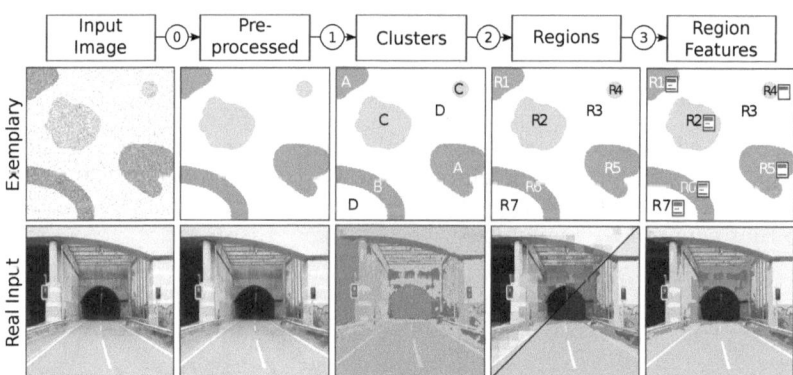

Fig. 1. Stages of the proposed method: ⓪ The bilateral filter smoothens homogeneous areas (optional). ① K-means clustering groups image points with similar colors (false color visualization). ② Local/global connected components are determined. ③ Region features – such as average color – are calculated (optional).

In this paper, we suggest a color image segmentation based on a *k-means* clustering stage and a subsequent determination of connected components for meshes; both are performed in a fully parallel fashion (Fig. 1 outlines the sequence of stages). No data exchange with the host is required during the segmentation.

The proposed method outranks sequential segmentation on the CPU and other current GPU approaches on parallel image segmentation. Furthermore, we outline how these methods can be applied to calculate certain region properties within this framework on the GPU. We analyze the time complexity of the algorithms and evaluate the execution time empirically.

2   Algorithms and Data Structures

Before we describe the completely GPU-based image segmentation pipeline outlined in Fig 1, we briefly summarize the *k-means* clustering in section 2.1, as it is the underlying concept we parallelize and use for grouping color space information in *Stage 1* (see Fig. 1 ① and section 3.2). Furthermore, in this section we explain the building blocks that are repeatedly used in the different stages to implement the procedure on the GPU. The parallel sorting network *Bitonic Sort* and the *Segmented Scan* operation are used in combination whenever certain occurrences – such as the number of pixels of each color in the *k-means* initialization – are needed to be counted, or in the process of updating the cluster centroids by summing the color space position components of the member pixels. These basic operations are also used in *Stage 3* (see Fig. 1 ③ and section 3.4) to obtain features of the regions, such as their average color. *Bitonic Sort* is described in section 2.2 and *Segmended Scan* in section 2.3. The *Union Find* structure is explained in section 2.4 and is used in *Stage 2* (see Fig. 1 ② and section 3.3) to reorganize the clusters into spatially coherent regions.

2.1   K-Means Clustering

In general, the heuristic *k-means* algorithm [5] can be used to solve the clustering problem of data points in Euclidean space. Given a number of clusters k, the goal is to assign (denoted by $r_{i,c}$) the n data points x_i to clusters c with centroids μ_c, so that equation 1 is minimized:

$$\sum_{i=1}^{n}\sum_{c=1}^{k} r_{i,c} \left\| x_i - \mu_c \right\|^2 \quad \text{where} \quad r_{i,c} = \begin{cases} 1 & : \ c = \operatorname*{arg\,min}_{1 \leq j \leq k} \left\| x_i - \mu_j \right\|^2 \\ 0 & : \ \text{else} \end{cases} \tag{1}$$

In the *k-means* algorithm (Algorithm 1), data points are assigned to the clusters and then the cluster centroids are updated. Every data point is assigned to the closest cluster and the new centroid is the (possibly weighted) average of the member data points. This *k-means* iteration is repeated until there are no more changes in the cluster centroid positions, i.e. until convergence occurs.

K-means can be applied to the image segmentation problem [8]. Due to the fact that the assignments of data points to clusters are independent from one another, it is well suited for parallelization [11,25]. In this paper, we also parallelize the re-computation of the cluster centroids on the GPU (see section 3.2).

Algorithm 1. *K-means* algorithm

// Convergence criterion; μ_c denoting the current and $\hat{\mu}_c$ the previous centroid of cluster c
until $\mu_c = \hat{\mu}_c \; \forall c \in \{1,..k\}$ **do**
    $\hat{\mu}_c \leftarrow \mu_c \; \forall c \in \{1,..k\}$
    // Phase 1: Assign data points to clusters
    for each data point x_i **do**
        cluster$[x_i] \leftarrow \underset{1 \leq j \leq k}{\arg\min} \; \|x_i - \mu_j\|^2$
    // Phase 2: Update cluster centroids
    for each cluster centroid μ_c **do**
        compute $\frac{1}{|M|} \sum_{x \in M} x$ with $M = \{x_i \; : \; \text{cluster}[x_i]{=}c\}$

2.2 Bitonic Sort

Bitonic Sort [4] is a sorting method of complexity $\mathcal{O}(n \cdot log^2 n)$ in a sequential execution which is rather slow compared to other comparison-based algorithms, such as *Merge Sort* ($\mathcal{O}(n \cdot log \; n)$). However, in contrast to these, *Bitonic Sort* is well suited for parallel execution on the GPU's SIMD architecture, as the algorithm performs comparisons in an order independent from input values. Only $\mathcal{O}(log^2 n)$ steps are necessary in a parallel execution with n processing units.

2.3 Segmented Scan

The *Scan* operation can be understood as a generalization of the *Prefix Sum* operation performed on an array. The *Prefix Sum* turns an array $A = [a_1, a_2, \ldots, a_n]$ into an array $B = [b_1, b_2, \ldots b_n]$ with $b_i = \sum_{j=0}^{i} a_j$. After this, the right most element contains the sum of all elements in the initial array. The *Scan* operation executes arbitrary binary associative operators $\oplus$ in this fashion. *Segmented Scan* performs *Scan* operations conditionally considering a head flag that identifies a segment of the data, for example all values that belong to the same cluster. *Segmented Scan* is illustrated in Fig. 2. We use a *Blockwise Segmented Scan* as suggested in [18], which is tailored for the GPU architecture and utilizes the fast shared local memory. $\mathcal{O}(n)$ sequential steps are required which can be performed in $\mathcal{O}(log \; n)$ in parallel.

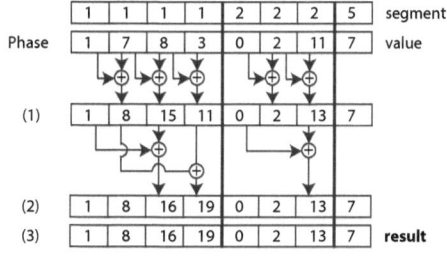

Fig. 2. Illustration of a *Prefix Sum* calculated with *Segmented Scan*

2.4   Union Find

The *Union Find* data structure [9] is used to represent disjunct sets as trees, organized as an indexed array and every element has a parent associated. Each set has a root, an element which can be reached tracing the parent relations from every member of the set. The root is its own parent (see Fig. 3).

Three operations are defined for the *Union Find* structure. *MakeSet(x)* produces a set that only contains a single element x; *Union(x,y)* merges the set that contains x with the set that contains y and *Find(x)* returns the root of the set containing x. The central *Find* operation can be calculated more efficiently when the path to the root is compressed, which leads to an average runtime of $\mathcal{O}(log\ n)$ for this operation.

These operations can be used to determine the connected components in a graph representation of an image on the GPU as shown in section 3.3.

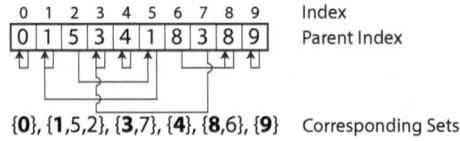

Fig. 3. Example of the *Union Find* structure, with the root of each set printed in bold

3   The Proposed Segmentation Algorithm

The proposed method consists of two main stages, *clustering* and the *connecting* (① and ② in Fig. 1). A preprocessing (Fig. 1 ⓪) can be added to improve the results and a stage trailing the main stages can calculate region features in a parallel fashion (Fig. 1 ③). Within each stage the processing is done in parallel and between the stages no transfer between the GPU program and the host program on the CPU is required. In this section we describe the stages in the order the data pass through them.

For each step, we state the time complexity dependent on the parameters given in Table 1. In Table 2, we summarize the runtimes and include a simplified overall complexity ($\mathcal{O}(\log^2 n)$) that only depends on the image size, disregarding typically small and fixed parameters (see "Common range" in Table 1).

3.1   Stage 0: Preprocessing

We implemented a bilateral filter [22] on the GPU and used it as an initial step to enhance homogeneity of areas which are only weakly textured (often due to noise) and keep the contours intact. The *CIELAB* colorspace[1] is advantageous for the filtering [22] and also for the segmentation as the magnitude of change in

---

[1] CIE: Commission Internationale de l'Eclairageis.

Table 1. Parameters considered in the formal runtime analysis. In our tests we used the parametrization given in the row "Common range" for different images sizes.

Parameter		Common range
n	Image size in pixels	-
w	Kernel size of the bilateral filter in pixels	4×4
i_{pre}	Number of iterations of the bilateral filter	5
k	Number of clusters	< 1024
i_{kM}	Number of $k\text{-means}$ iterations	3
F	Number of elements in the (reduced) color space	2^{15}

Table 2. Summary of time complexities of the different stages. "Overall (simplified)" considers the image size only, disregarding typically small and fixed parameters. For the optimal parallel execution n workers are assumed, while the complexity in practice is that of the sequential execution divided by the number of workers.

Phase	Sequential execution	Optimal parallel execution
Preprocessing	$\mathcal{O}(n \cdot w \cdot i_{pre})$	$\mathcal{O}(w \cdot i_{pre})$
k-Means initialization	$\mathcal{O}(n \cdot \log^2 n)$	$\mathcal{O}(\log^2 n)$
k-Means iterations	$\mathcal{O}(i_{kM} \cdot F \cdot (\log^2 F + k))$	$\mathcal{O}(i_{kM} \cdot \log^2 F + k)$
Connected components	$\mathcal{O}(n \cdot \log n)$	$\mathcal{O}(\log^2 n)$
Region features	$\mathcal{O}(n \cdot \log^2 n)$	$\mathcal{O}(\log^2 n)$
Overall (simplified)	$\mathcal{O}(n \cdot \log^2 n)$	$\mathcal{O}(\log^2 n)$

any direction has a similar perceptual importance which leads to a visually more pleasing result. Therefore, we perform a color space conversion to *CIELAB*, prior to the filtering on the GPU. The complexity of this stage is $\mathcal{O}(n \cdot \omega \cdot i_{pre})$ in sequential and $\mathcal{O}(\omega \cdot i_{pre})$ in maximum parallel execution.

3.2 Stage 1: GPU-Based K-Means Clustering

A *k-means* clustering as described in section 2.1 is executed in this stage. For this process, initial cluster centers are required. We determine their number and color space position based on samples drawn in equal intervals from the image. When a sample pixel has a similar color (below a certain color space distance) as an existing candidate, the exiting candidate is replaced by the weighted average of itself and the new candidate. The positions of the resulting cluster centers are updated in the *k-means* procedure.

To initialize the data for a parallel *k-means* computation we quantize the color space (this gives an additional speedup and good results with quantization exponent $Q = 5$) and compute the weight attribute $weight[x_i]$ for every point x_i in this reduced color space. This is done by performing *Bitonic Sort* with regard to the color, summing the occurrences with *Segmented Scan* and then in parallel assigning the results to the *weight*$[x_i]$ (see Algorithm 2). Fig. 4 depicts these steps. The asymptotic runtime of this initialization depends on the image size n with $\mathcal{O}(n \cdot log^2n)$ in the sequential case and $\mathcal{O}(log^2n)$ when n processing units work in parallel.

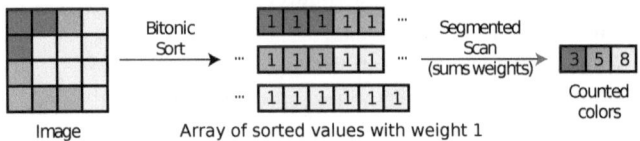

Fig. 4. Illustration of the *k-means* initialization

Algorithm 2. *K-means* initialization

// Phase 1: Color quantization with quantization exponent Q
for each pixel p in image I **do in parallel**
    $L'[p] \leftarrow L[p] \cdot 2^{-Q}$
    $a'[p] \leftarrow a[p] \cdot 2^{-Q}$
    $b'[p] \leftarrow b[p] \cdot 2^{-Q}$
// Phase 2: Compute weights of the color values
// Let SC_{color*} denote that the sorting criterion (SC) is the reduced color value
BitonicSort(I, SC_{color*})
SegmentedScan($I, SC_{color*}, O = \{weight_+\}$)
// Phase 3: Initialize reduced color space
// Let $\sum_{x_i} weight_+$ denote the resulting weight for the reduced color x_i.
for each data point x_i **do in parallel**
    weight$[x_i] \leftarrow \sum_{x_i} weight_+$

After the initialization, a fixed number of *k-means* iterations is executed. Fixing the number of iterations in advance avoids costly communication between the GPU and the host which is otherwise required to check convergence criteria. The clustering is performed on the reduced color space as listed in Algorithm 3, so this stage does not depend on the image size. Color space points are assigned in parallel to the nearest cluster centers. Then *Bitonic Sort* is performed with the cluster membership as a sorting criterion followed by *Segmented Scans* operating on L', a', b' and the weights. The updated cluster centroids are then calculated as the weighted average of the color points assigned to the cluster (see Algorithm 3).

The runtime of the *k-means* stage is given by number of iterations i_{kM}, the size of the (quantized) color space F and the number of clusters $k \ll F$ as $\mathcal{O}(i_{kM} \cdot (F \cdot k + F \cdot log^2F))$ where the $F \cdot k$ is caused by the assignment of data points to clusters and $F \cdot log^2F$ by the recalculation of the cluster centroids. In maximum parallel execution, the runtime is reduced to $\mathcal{O}(i_{kM} \cdot (k + log^2F))$.

After the *k-means* clustering similarly colored pixels are grouped; however, they are not necessarily connected in the image.

Algorithm 3. *K-means* iterations

until $\mu_c = \mu_{c'} \;\; \forall c \in \{1,..k\}$ **do** //Convergence criterion
$\quad \mu_{c'} \leftarrow \mu_c \;\; \forall c \in \{1,..k\}$
$\quad$ // Phase 1: Assign points to clusters. The x_i denote the colors in the reduced color space
$\quad$ **for each** color point x_i **do in parallel**
$\qquad$ cluster$[x_i] \leftarrow \underset{1 \leq j \leq k}{\arg\min} \; \|x_i - \mu_j\|^2$
$\quad$ // Phase 2: Update centroids. $SC_{cluster}$ indicates cluster assignment as sorting criterion (SC).
$\quad$ BitonicSort$(X, SC_{cluster})$
$\quad$ // The $array_\oplus$ denote the arrays and operators
$\quad$ SegmentedScan$(X, SC_{cluster}, O = \{L'_+, a'_+, b'_+, weight_+\})$
$\quad$ // Let $\sum_c array_+$ denote the resulting sum for an $array$ for cluster c
$\quad$ **for each** cluster centroid μ_c **do in parallel**
$\qquad$ compute $\mu_c \leftarrow \left(\sum_c L'_+, \sum_c a'_+, \sum_c b'_+ \right)^T \cdot \frac{1}{\sum_c weight_+}$

3.3 Stage 2: GPU-Based Connected Components

To determine which image points belong to spatially coherent regions, an undirected graph is constructed in which every pixel corresponds to a node with the cluster membership and the index of its parent associated. The purpose of Algorithm 4 is to merge adjacent nodes when they belong to same cluster. After executing the algorithm, all pixels of the same cluster in the spatially coherent region share the same parent which is also the root node of a *Union Find* structure (see section 2.4). Conflicts have to be avoided when the parent index is updated in parallel. Fig. 5 (a) shows a possible conflicting situation, when nodes of set A and B are to be merged with set C at the same time. For nodes from both sets, the parent of C would be set to the root of set A and to the root of set B concurrently. Our algorithm avoids this by performing the merging row- and column-wise such that each node is only involved in one column or row at the same time.

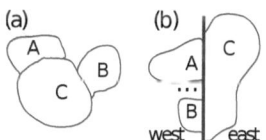

Fig. 5. Possible conflicting situations when merging in parallel

Fig. 6 illustrates the algorithm. Initially, every node is in its own set and the first column/row is used as a starting point for merging. In the first iteration, the algorithm tries to merge the nodes of every second column with their eastern neighbor in parallel. To avoid the conflict shown in Fig. 5 (b), it first tries to merge from east to west and if that fails the algorithm merges from west to east. We do not have to consider other conflicts between nodes of different columns since each node is only involved in the merging of one column and its neighboring column at the same time. The rows are handled likewise. In the next iteration, the starting point is set to the first unused column (this is one in the second iteration and three in the third) and then the offset between considered columns and rows is doubled (every fourth row in the second iteration and every eighth in the third). The algorithm terminates when all columns and rows have been considered for merging.

In our implementation, we use one kernel in a local step to process the small blocks (when i is low) that fit into the fast shared memory of the compute units. In a subsequent global step, we execute kernels for every j-l pair of the loops over the remaining rows and columns, respectively.

Non-coalesced memory accesses can happen if the processing elements of a compute unit try to merge different regions. It is then not possible to take advantage of the broadcast mechanism that usually combines the read requests to a single read operation of that memory cell. The number of non-coalesced memory accesses depends on the actual input image; it is low for images with large regions and higher for images with many small irregular regions. Moreover, by the path compression in the *Union Find* data structure (see section 2.4) and by doubling the step value i the number of accessed memory cells is kept at a low logarithmic value with regard to the image size. However, in practice this stage accounts for only about 10 % of the total run-time of our method.

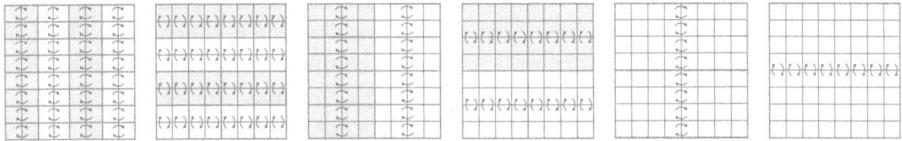

Fig. 6. Illustration of the connected components algorithm

The algorithm has a runtime of $\mathcal{O}(n \cdot \log n)$ in the sequential case and $\mathcal{O}(\log^2 n)$ in the parallel case, since a single *Find* operation costs $\mathcal{O}(\log n)$ and we have $\mathcal{O}(\log n)$ iterations of the outer loop.

3.4   Stage 3: GPU-Based Region Feature Computation

Different region features can be calculated similar to the initialization phase of the *k-means* algorithm (see section 3.2). The generic pattern is to use *Bitonic Sort* on the region membership and then perform a *Segmented Scan* with an associative binary operator working on the data required for the wanted feature. To calculate the average region color, for example (as illustrated in Fig. 1 ③), a *Segmented Scan* that sums the values in each color channel and the number of pixels in the region would follow the *Bitonic Sort*. Another example is the calculation of the region bounding boxes which can be done by executing *Segmented Scan* with maximum and minimum operators on the pixel coordinates. In our ongoing work to enhance a region-based attention system by replacing sequential with parallel segmentation, we also used this pattern for computing more complex region features such as 2D central moments. With $\mathcal{O}(n \cdot log^2 n)$

Algorithm 4. Connected Components for the image graph

$first \leftarrow 0 //$ starting point
$i \leftarrow 1 //$ step between columns and rows
while $i < \max(w, h)$ **do** $// w$ and h denote width and height of image I
    for $j \leftarrow first$ **to** h **by step** i **do in parallel**
        for $l \leftarrow 0$ **to** w **do in parallel**
            // Find root and compress path with $\mathrm{Find}(I_{(x,y)})$. $I_{(x,y)}$ is the pixel/node at position (x, y)
            rootCurrent $\leftarrow \mathrm{Find}(I_{(l,j)})$
            rootNbrEast $\leftarrow \mathrm{Find}(I_{(l+1,j)})$
            // Union both sets if pixels belong to the same cluster and sets are disjunct
            if cluster[rootCurrent]=cluster[rootNbrEast]
            and rootCurrent$\neq$ rootNbrEast **then**
                parent[rootNbrEast] $\leftarrow$ rootCurrent
                rootNbrEast $\leftarrow \mathrm{Find}(I_{(l+1,j)})$
                if rootCurrent$\neq$ rootNbrEast **then**
                    parent[rootCurrent] $\leftarrow$ rootNbrEast
        end for
    end for
    for $j \leftarrow first$ **to** w **by step** i **do in parallel**
        for $l \leftarrow 0$ **to** h **do in parallel**
        ... (analog to above)
        end for
    end for
    $i \leftarrow i \cdot 2$
    $first \leftarrow i - 1$
end while

(sequential) and $\mathcal{O}(log^2 n)$ (optimal parallel), the runtime of this stage is the same as for the *k-means* initialization.

4   Evaluation

To show the quality and characteristics of the segmentation result, we visualize it for the images in Fig. 7. A random color visualization that emphasizes the region boundaries and a visualization with region average colors is shown in Fig. 8. The results were obtained with our method, a popular graph-based CPU method [12] (as a reference for segmentation quality) and a GPU-based *Quick Shift* [14] (their implementations were available online and we used them for the empirical comparative runtime analysis described below).

When their original size differed, the images were scaled to 512×512 and we used default parameters of the algorithms' implementations. All results show over-segmentation with regard to coherent surfaces or objects, as color is the only homogeneity measure used. *Quick Shift* shows over-segmentation in very homogeneously colored areas. This can be modulated with parameters σ and ρ (see [14]), but with increasing region sizes heavy under-segmentation occurs. The graph-based algorithm and the proposed method shows small fragments in rough or textured areas and over-segmentation where strong gradients are present and around some object contours. The *Quick Shift* results could be cleaned up in a post-processing by connecting similarly colored super-pixels, whereas for the proposed method small regions can be removed or merged. In the depicted results, we kept small regions, but they can be easily filtered out on the GPU by adding a region size threshold.

Fig. 7. Input images used for evaluation. Image (a) is taken from [14], (b) to (d) from the PASCAL-2007 dataset [10].

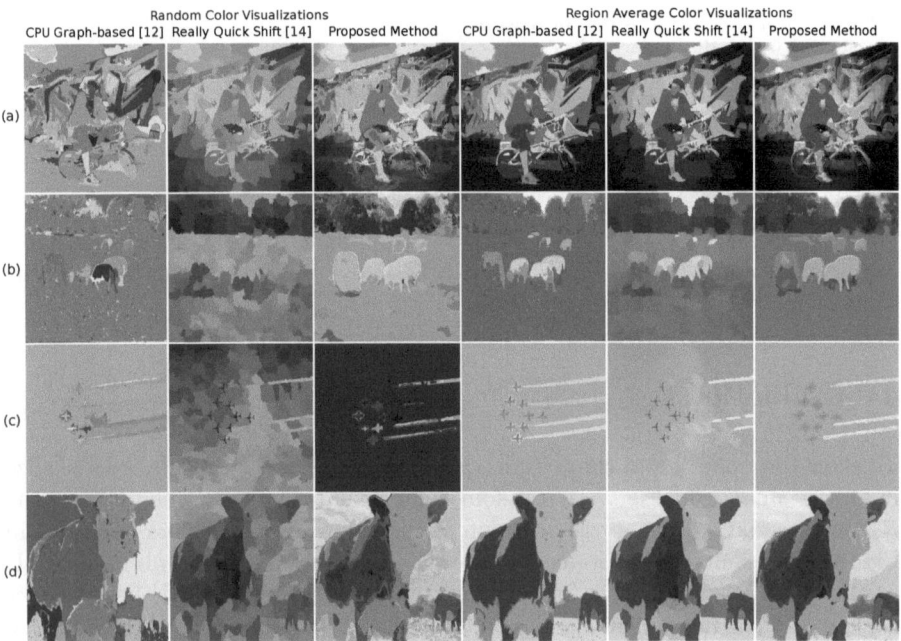

Fig. 8. Random and average color visualization of segmentation results obtained with methods from [12], [14] and our method. Input images (a) to (d) are shown in Fig. 7.

In order to evaluate the computational performance of our method, we segmented 100 images of the PASCAL-2007 database [10] at multiple resolutions with our method and the methods from [12] and [14]. For the experiments we used a PC with a four-core 2.66 GHz Intel Xeon W3520 CPU with 4GB main memory and a GeForce GTX 580 (3GB memory). We report the mean runtimes for the different resolutions in Fig. 9. Only for the lowest resolution (64×64) the sequential CPU-based method is the fastest (2.68 ms); for all other resolutions our method is the fastest. These results compare well with other state-of-the-art approaches. The proposed method appears to be almost twice as fast compared to results reported for the GPU-based approach in [2] which was tested with

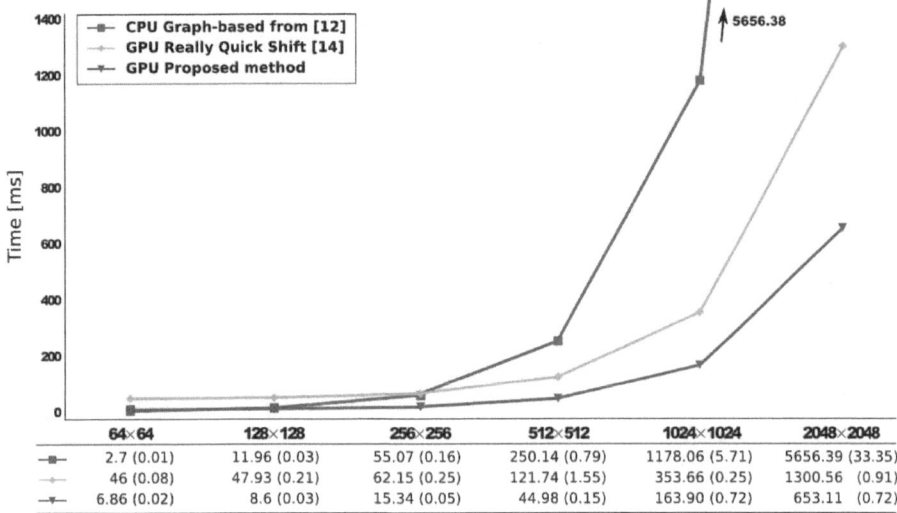

	64×64	128×128	256×256	512×512	1024×1024	2048×2048
■	2.7 (0.01)	11.96 (0.03)	55.07 (0.16)	250.14 (0.79)	1178.06 (5.71)	5656.39 (33.35)
	46 (0.08)	47.93 (0.21)	62.15 (0.25)	121.74 (1.55)	353.66 (0.25)	1300.56 (0.91)
	6.86 (0.02)	8.6 (0.03)	15.34 (0.05)	44.98 (0.15)	163.90 (0.72)	653.11 (0.72)

Resolution [pixels]

Fig. 9. Computation times of our method and the methods from [12] and [14] dependent on image size. The table below the chart gives the numerical values and the standard error of the mean (in brackets), both in milliseconds.

similar resolutions (note that they used an NVIDIA GeForce GTX 295 with an older and less efficient architecture).

5   Conclusion

We proposed a GPU-based image segmentation based on a parallel *k-means* clustering and a novel GPU approach to determine connected components in a graph representing the image. All stages of segmentation utilize the GPU and no data exchange with the CPU is required. The appearance of the result is similar to the popular graph-based method from [12]. We analyzed the runtime formally and performed empirical tests on 100 images showing that our method outperforms the state-of-the-art GPU *Quick Shift* variant. Furthermore, our framework is highly extensible as all kinds of region features can be calculated in parallel as outlined in section 3.4.

References

1. NVIDIA CUDA (Compute Unified Device Architecture) C - Programming Guide (2012), http://www.nvidia.com/content/cuda/cuda-documentation.html
2. Abramov, A., Kulvicius, T.: Real-time Image Segmentation on a GPU. In: Facing the Multicore Challenge, vol. 5, pp. 3–5 (2011)
3. Aziz, M.Z., Mertsching, B.: Fast and Robust Generation of Feature Maps for Region-based Visual Attention. IEEE Trans. on Image Proc. 17(5), 633–644 (2008)

4. Batcher, K.E.: Sorting Networks and Their Applications. In: Spring Joint Computer Conference, AFIPS 1968, New York, USA, pp. 307–314 (1968)
5. Bishop, C.M.: Pattern Recognition and Machine Learning (Information Science and Statistics), ch. 9, vol. 4, pp. 424–427. Springer (2007)
6. Cates, J.E., Lefohn, A.E., Whitaker, R.T.: GIST: An Interactive, GPU-based Level Set Segmentation Tool for 3D Medical Images. Medical Image Analysis 8(3), 217–231 (2004)
7. Cheng, H.D., Jiang, X.H., Sun, Y., Wang, J.: Color Image Segmentation: Advances and Prospects. Pattern Recognition 34(12), 2259–2281 (2001)
8. Coleman, G.B., Andrews, H.C.: Image Segmentation by Clustering. IEEE 67, 773–785 (1979)
9. Cormen, T.H., Leiserson, C.E., Rivest, R.L., Stein, C.: Introduction to Algorithms, 2nd edn., ch. 21, pp. 498–524. The MIT Press (2001)
10. Everingham, M., Van Gool, L., Williams, C.K.I., Winn, J., Zisserman, A.: The PASCAL Visual Object Classes Challenge 2007 (VOC 2007) (2007), Results, http://www.pascal-network.org/challenges/ VOC/voc2007/workshop/index.html
11. Farivar, R., Rebolledo, D., Chan, E., Campbell, R.: A Parallel Implementation of K-Means Clustering on GPUs. In: PDPTA, pp. 1–6 (2008)
12. Felzenszwalb, P.F., Huttenlocher, D.P.: Efficient Graph-Based Image Segmentation. International Journal of Computer Vision 59(2), 167–181 (2004)
13. Flynn, M.J.: Some Computer Organizations and Their Effectiveness. IEEE Transactions on Computers C-21(9), 948–960 (1972)
14. Fulkerson, B., Soatto, S.: Really Quick Shift: Image Segmentation on a GPU. In: ECCV Workshops, vol. i, pp. 8–11 (2010)
15. Hong-tao, B., Li-li, H., Dan-tong, O., Zhan-shan, L., He, L.: K-Means on Commodity GPUs with CUDA. CSIE 3, 651–655 (2009)
16. Kalentev, O., Rai, A., Kemnitz, S., Schneider, R.: Connected Component Labeling on a 2D Grid Using CUDA. Journal of Parallel and Distributed Computing 71, 615–620 (2011)
17. Roberts, M., Packer, M., Sousa, M., Mitchell, J.R.: A Work-Efficient GPU Algorithm for Level Set Segmentation. In: Conference on High Performance Graphics, HPG 2010, pp. 123–132 (2010)
18. Sengupta, S., Harris, M., Garland, M.: Efficient Parallel Scan Algorithms for GPUs. NVIDIA Technical Report NVR-2008-003 66(1), 1–17 (2008)
19. Shalom, S.A.A., Dash, M., Tue, M.: Efficient K-Means Clustering Using Accelerated Graphics Processors. In: Song, I.-Y., Eder, J., Nguyen, T.M. (eds.) DaWaK 2008. LNCS, vol. 5182, pp. 166–175. Springer, Heidelberg (2008)
20. Soman, J., Kishore, K., Narayanan, P.J.: A Fast GPU Algorithm for Graph Connectivity. In: IPDPS Workshops, pp. 1–8 (2010)
21. Stone, J.E., Gohara, D., Shi, G.: OpenCL: A Parallel Programming Standard for Heterogeneous Computing Systems. Computing in Science & Engineering 12(3), 66–73 (2010)
22. Tomasi, C., Manduchi, R.: Bilateral Filtering for Gray and Color Images. In: ICCV, pp. 839–846 (1998)
23. Tünnermann, J., Mertsching, B.: Continuous Region-based Processing of Spatiotemporal Saliency. In: VISAPP, pp. 230–239 (2012)
24. Vedaldi, A., Soatto, S.: Quick Shift and Kernel Methods for Mode Seeking. In: Forsyth, D., Torr, P., Zisserman, A. (eds.) ECCV 2008, Part IV. LNCS, vol. 5305, pp. 705–718. Springer, Heidelberg (2008)
25. Zechner, M., Granitzer, M.: Accelerating K-Means on the Graphics Processor via CUDA. In: INTENSIVE, pp. 7–15 (2009)

Solving High-Dimensional Problems on Processors with Integrated GPU

Alexander Heinecke

Technische Universität München, Boltzmannstr. 3, D-85748 Garching, Germany

1 Motivation

In the last five years GPU-computing has become a powerful means of high performance computing. This development drove instruction set extensions such as AVX for general purpose CPUs or even created new architectures, e.g. Intel's Many Integrated Core Architecture based on regular general purpose components stemming from the x86 world. GPUs and accelerators in general can be regarded as co-processors. If we go back 20 or 25 years we see a similar scenario with floating point co-processors (e.g. x87 unit). These special function units eventually merged into the general purpose processors' architectures. Since the introduction of Intel's MMX technology in 1997 we can witness a similar process for all kinds of media (signal, audio and video) processing. Since 2011 GPUs and CPUs are merging onto one die.

The goal of this poster is to present the architectures of Intel Ivy Bridge (Core i7-3770K, quad-core at 3.5 GHz) and AMD Llano (A8-3850, quad-core at 2.9 GHz) and to evaluate their performance in terms of theoretical numbers and as well for a real-world application stemming from the field of data mining. In case of this application we are exploiting the entire heterogeneous chip including the CPU cores using a highly optimized intrinsics implementation on the CPU cores and OpenCL, which was generated at runtime, on the integrated GPU (iGPU). The obtained results are compared to the performance achieved on a recent discrete GPU (NVIDIA GTX680, code-named Kepler) by using different criteria: absolute performance, platform efficiency and energy efficiency.

2 Application and Results

The targeted data mining application can be considered as a scattered data approximation problem, starting from m known observations, $S = \{(\boldsymbol{x}_i, y_i) \in \mathbb{R}^d \times \mathbb{R}\}_{i=1,\dots,m}$, with the aim to learn the functional dependency $f(\boldsymbol{x}_i) \approx y_i$ as accurately as possible. Reconstructing a smooth function f then allows an estimate $f(\boldsymbol{x})$ for new properties $\boldsymbol{x}$. We aim at representations $f = \sum_{j=1}^{N} \alpha_j \varphi_j(\boldsymbol{x})$ as a linear combination of N basis functions $\varphi_j(\boldsymbol{x})$ with coefficients α_j. We rely on *adaptive sparse grids* (see [1] for details) to mitigate the curse of dimensionality: Regular grid with equidistant meshes and k grid points in each dimension contain k^d grid points in d dimensions. When following derivations discussed elsewhere ([2]), we end up with a linear system of equations which has to be

R. Keller et al. (Eds.): Facing the Multicore-Challenge III 2012, LNCS 7686, pp. 121–122, 2013.

Mode	Energy Watts	checkerboard GFLOPS	redshift GFLOPS	Energy Watts	checkerboard GFLOPS	redshift GFLOPS
		Intel Core i7-3770K			AMD A8-3850	
CPU only	77	179	181	100	41	43
iGPU only	62	47	48	100	56	55
Hybrid	77	132	133	100	80	81
GTX680	240	1040	1020	-	-	-
GTX680+i7	280	1160	1165	-	-	-

solved: $\left(\frac{1}{m}BB^T + \lambda I\right)\alpha = By$. Since the dataset's size directly influences the dimensions of matrices B and B^T an efficient implementation of those operators is mandatory, see [2].

In the following, we use two test scenarios, both with a moderate dimensionality of $d = 5$ and distinct challenges. The first dataset with 2^{18} data points classifies a regular $3 \times \cdots \times 3$ checkerboard pattern. The second one is a real-world dataset from astrophysics, predicting spectroscopic redshifts of galaxies based on more than 430,000 photometric measurements.

From the values given in the result table we can derive that Intel's Ivy Bridge CPU clearly outperforms AMD's Llano chip: theoretical peak performances are as follows (all single precision): Intel CPU: 224 GFLOPS, Intel iGPU 294 GFLOPS, AMD CPU: 92 GFLOPS, AMD iGPU 480 GFLOPS, which ranks both CPUs at the same theoretical performance level. It is not surprising that the i7 is faster than the A8 since it features AVX. The results obtained on the iGPU and through hybrid execution are definitely more interesting: Both deliver similar performance, however the A8's peak performance is much higher, which results in a lower efficiency, most likely caused by the iGPU's VLIW instruction set. In case of hybrid execution we can recognize an interesting behavior: On the A8 we are achieving a remarkable speed up (please note that we cannot just add CPU and iGPU performance since we have to reserve one CPU core for iGPU handling) but on the i7 the performance significantly drops. Using Intel's GPA tool we were able to measure the energy consumed by CPU cores and iGPU and we uncovered that we are hitting the TDP limitation of 77W already when using only the CPU cores or the iGPU. In case of hybrid execution the CPU cores' and iGPU's clock is adjusted so that whole chip stays inside its power budget. When moving the focus from raw performance numbers to power efficiency numbers it turns out that Ivy Bridge is as twice as efficient as AMD's Llano.

References

1. Bungartz, H.-J., Griebel, M.: Sparse grids. Acta Numerica 13, 147–269 (2004)
2. Heinecke, A., Pflüger, D.: Emerging architectures enable to boost massively parallel data mining using adaptive sparse grids. International Journal of Parallel Programming, 1–43 (published online, June 2012)

Pulsar Searching with Many-Cores

Alessio Sclocco[1] and Rob V. van Nieuwpoort[2]

[1] Faculty of Sciences
Vrije Universiteit Amsterdam
Amsterdan, The Netherlands
a.sclocco@vu.nl
[2] Netherlands eScience Center
Amsterdam, The Netherlands
r.vannieuwpoort@esciencecenter.nl

Abstract. Pulsars are rapidly rotating neutron stars whose signal is received on Earth periodically. They are relatively newly discovered astronomical objects (the first was discovered only in 1967) and elusive ones: so far only two thousand of them are know. Their properties, especially their big mass and precise period, can be used to probe space and gravitation. This makes them important not only for astronomers, but for physicists and other scientists as well: the discovery of the first binary pulsar by Hulse and Taylor in 1973 [1] has been so important for proving general relativity and other aspects of gravitation that they won the 1993 Nobel prize for physics. Thus, being able to discover new pulsars is an important goal of current radio astronomy.

The process of finding a new pulsar is, however, difficult and time consuming: it involves a brute-force search over hundreds of thousands of parameter combinations. Moreover, the amount of data that needs to be searched is huge: the input of a typical observation using a radio telescope like LOFAR [2] is in the order of hundreds of terabytes. During the process petabytes of intermediate results are produced and analyzed. Thus, searching for pulsars clearly is a big data problem.

The challenges are not only limited to the amount of data that needs to be processed: the signal received from a pulsar is usually quite faint and can be completely covered by radio frequency interference and, even when there is no artificial noise, a long integration time may be necessary to properly detect its profile. There is, furthermore, the inter-stellar medium to take into account: typical effects of the interaction between the emission and the medium are dispersion, scintillation and scattering. And this is not the only interaction: if the pulsar is orbiting with a companion of some kind, the interaction between them modifies the signal and makes it even more difficult to detect from Earth.

We propose to reduce the time necessary to search for new pulsars using many-core accelerators, e.g. modern GPUs. We design and implement the whole searching pipeline, using OpenCL to build the three most important computational kernels of this application: dedispersion, folding and the signal to noise computation. An overview of our pulsar searching pipeline is presented in Figure 1. Using our prototypical tool we are able to find pulsars in test data sets generated with Duncan Lorimer's

R. Keller et al. (Eds.): Facing the Multicore-Challenge III 2012, LNCS 7686, pp. 123–124, 2013.
© Springer-Verlag Berlin Heidelberg 2013

SIGPROC. To overcome one of the main problems of using accelerators, i.e. the expensive memory transfers between device and host memory, we keep all the intermediate results in device memory. Moreover we use auto-tuning, a technique that we know to be effective with many-core architectures [3], to identify which parameters are the best suited for each specific device used to run our prototype.

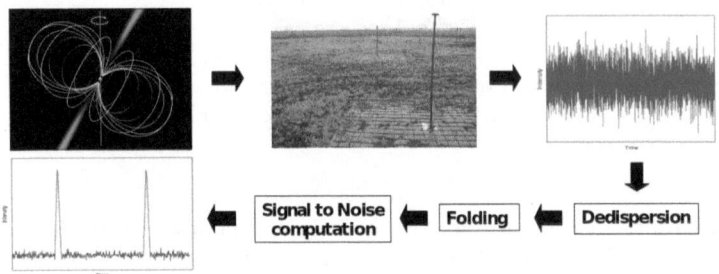

Fig. 1. Representation of the pulsar search pipeline

References

1. Hulse, R.: The discovery of the binary pulsar. Bulletin of the American Astronomical Society 26, 971–972 (1994)
2. Romein, J., Mol, J., van Nieuwpoort, R., Broekema, P.: Processing LOFAR Telescope Data in Real Time on a Blue Gene/P Supercomputer. In: URSI General Assembly and Scientific Symposium (URSI GASS 2011), Istanbul, Turkey (August 2011)
3. Sclocco, A., Varbanescu, A.L., Mol, J.D., van Nieuwpoort, R.V.: Radio astronomy beam forming on many-core architectures. Parallel and Distributed Processing Symposium, International, 1105–1116 (2012)

Scheduling Overheads for Task-Based Parallel Programming Models

Mathias Nachtmann, Jose Gracia, and Colin W. Glass

High Performance Computing Center Stuttgart (HLRS)
University of Stuttgart, 70550 Stuttgart, Germany
{nachtmann,gracia,glass}@hlrs.de

Modern supercomputer architectures offer ever more power, but rely heavily on a hierarchical organization of resources. While internode communication can easily be handled by MPI, efficient usage of multi-core CPUs requires the programmer to parallelize a given problem using shared-memory programming models. Hybrid approaches to high scalability become ever more popular and are frequently very successful. Here, we will look at scheduling overheads of three different models. Hybrid approaches to high scalability become ever more popular and are frequently very successful. Here, we will look at scheduling overheads of three different models: OpenMP, StarSs, and FastFlow. All three models supports the general concept of task-parallelism, i.e. they allow independent units of work, so-called tasks, to be executed concurrently by a collection of threads. OpenMP is not only a data-parallel model, but also supports the more general concept of task-parallelism, that means it allows independent units of work, so-called tasks, to be executed concurrently by a collection of threads. StarSs allows a more general way of describing dependencies between tasks as data- dependencies. Based on this information, the runtime will schedule the tasks dynamically, guaranteeing an efficient exploitation of available compute cores,possibly at the expense of a larger overhead compared to more simple models. FastFlow is a newly developed model that allows decomposing an application into a collection of interrelated skeletons or pattern, as for instance pipelines or task farms, thus allowing parallel execution on concurrent data items and stages. FastFlow specifically aims at the efficient execution of fine-grained tasks.

To quantify the overheads, we have run two series of benchmarks. In the first one, the task duration has been varied to sample a wide range of values. In the second series, the task duration was kept constant, but the number of tasks has been varied. Benchmark results are shown in figures 1 and 2.

Figure 1: There is a difference between the two OpenMP implementations. The task-based version has greater overhead than the version with the omp for pragma(without schedule). All programming models are scaling in the end the same way, they only differ in their scheduling overhead. Every line, except omp_for has its point from which the task duration carries the weight.

Figure 2: What we can conclude in the end: The scheduling overhead of OpenMP and StarSs with various numbers of tasks is constant. The OpenMP

R. Keller et al. (Eds.): Facing the Multicore-Challenge III 2012, LNCS 7686, pp. 125–126, 2013.
© Springer-Verlag Berlin Heidelberg 2013

overhead is lower than the overhead in StarSs. FastFlow has its problems in the region with a little number of tasks but with an increased number of tasks it scales better than StarSs.

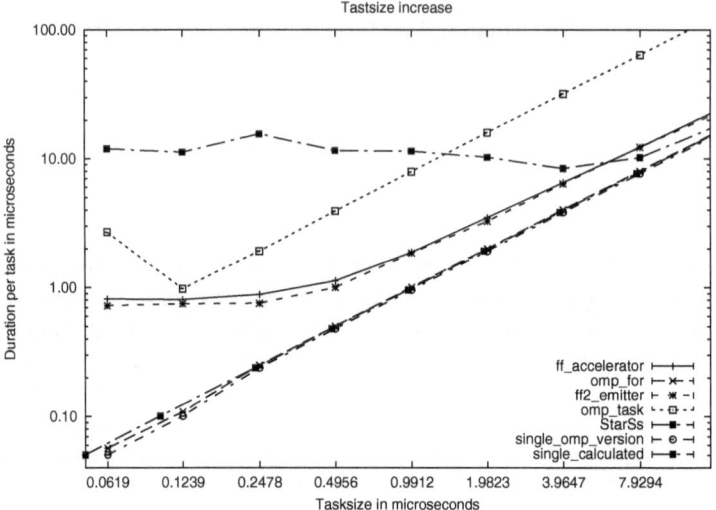

Fig. 1. Tastsize increase

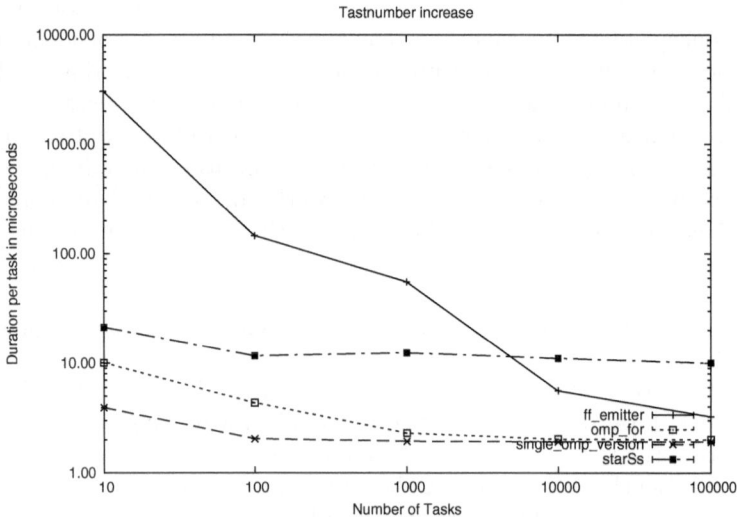

Fig. 2. Tastnumber increase

PINstruct – Efficient Memory Access to Data Structures

Rainer Keller[1] and Shiqing Fan[2]

[1] HFT Stuttgart, Schellingstrae 24, Stuttgart
rainer.keller@hft-stuttgart.de
[2] HLRS, Nobelstrasse 19, Stuttgart, Germany
fan@hlrs.de

Abstract. Modular programming requires structuring a program's data into classes, records and arrays. Access to these data structures is highly dependent on the nature of the algorithm, the programming language, it's compiler, the Application Binary Interface (ABI) defined by the OS and finally the requirements of the underlying hardware. The programming language however may not allow the compiler to reorder data structures. This is specially true for libraries, with MPI being a good example. Since the communication library's routines are comparatively seldom called, the cache may be "cold", i. e. the MPI library's memory accesses into data structures may be slow, too diverse and pollute the cache. In this paper we introduce a tool to analyse the memory access pattern of structures the Open MPI implementation. This tool shows the order in which data structures such as datatype and communicator information are accessed. It shows that previous work to re-order data structures for better padding has proven worthwhile, however further restructuring is necessary.

1 Introduction

The Message Passing Interface (MPI) is the de-facto parallel programming model for large scale. Parallel programming however adds another level of complexity in every respect. Application programmers optimizing for performance may see the MPI library as hindering scalability. Some efforts have been done to measure and compare the overhead of MPI [1] or to overcome the effects of supposedly wasteful CPU ressources, i. e. busy-waiting in receive operations. While MPI libraries over the years have continuously been amended, there still is room for improvement with regard to optimization of MPI's data structures. These cache misses within MPI are of course not visible with micro-benchmarks such as NetPipe [3] or even small-scale application-type benchmarks like NPB [4], since the data sizes and memory access patterns of the benchmark is not large enough to evict MPI's code and data.

With MemPin [2], based on Intel Pin, a new tool was build. MemPin allows tracing all memory accesses to registered memory windows. A PMPI-based wrapper was implemented to intercept point-to-point communication calls and track the memory accesses into the data structures of Open MPI's `MPI_Datatype`, `MPI_Communicator`, `MPI_Request` and the actual user buffer.

Figure 1 shows the results of the run of the unoptimized `ompi_communicator_t` data structure within an `MPI_Send`: apart from the inefficient 4 holes, first `c_flags`

R. Keller et al. (Eds.): Facing the Multicore-Challenge III 2012, LNCS 7686, pp. 127–128, 2013.
© Springer-Verlag Berlin Heidelberg 2013

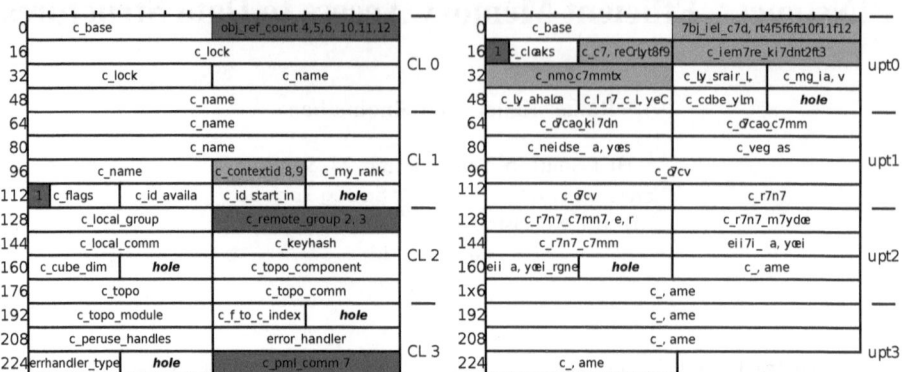

Fig. 1. The Open MPI communicator data structure unoptimized (left) and optimized (right)

in cache-line 1 is accessed, then the second cache-line, then cache-line zero, then cache-line three, each time incurring a cache-miss. Note, that no other data of the structure is touched.

Moving the c_name (which is used for debugging purposes) to the end, and reordering, there is one (likely) cache-miss for cache-line zero – all consecutive accesses are however in the same cache-line with only two holes of 4 bytes each.

References

1. Buntinas, D., Mercier, G., Gropp, W.: Implementation and evaluation of shared-memory communication and synchronization operations in MPIch2 using the Nemesis communication subsystem. Parallel Computing 33(9), 634–644 (2007)
2. Fan, S., Keller, R., Resch, M.: Advanced memory checking frameworks for MPI parallel applications in Open MPI. In: Proc. of the 5th Int. Workshop on Parallel Tools for HPC (2011) (submitted for publication)
3. Snell, Q.O., Mikler, A.R., Gustafson, J.L.: NetPIPE: A Network Protocol Independent Performance Evaluator. In: IASTED Int. Conf. on Intelligent Inf. Management and Systems (1996)
4. Van der Wijngaart, R.F.: The NAS parallel benchmarks version 2.4. Tech. rep., NASA Advanced Supercomputing (NAS) Division, NAS-02-007 (2002)

Development of a GPU-Accelerated Mike 21 Solver for Water Wave Dynamics

Peter Edward Aackermann[1], Peter Juhler Dinesen Pedersen[1],
Allan Peter Engsig-Karup[1], Thomas Clausen[2], and Jesper Grooss[2,*]

[1] Technical University of Denmark (DTU),
Department of Informatics and Mathematical Modelling, 2800 Kgs. Lyngby, Denmark
[2] DHI Group, 2970 Hoersholm, Denmark
{s093066,s093053}@student.dtu.dk

Motivation

With encouragement by the company DHI are the aim of this B.Sc. thesis[1] to investigate, whether if it is possible to accelerate the simulation speed of DHIs commercial product MIKE 21 HD, by formulating a parallel solution scheme and implementing it to be executed on a CUDA-enabled GPU (massive parallel hardware).

MIKE 21 HD is a simulation tool, which simulates water wave dynamics in lakes, bays, coastal areas and seas and it is one of DHIs most applied commercial products. For this reason a drastic improvement in simulation speed has the potential to change the type of optimization problems where MIKE 21 HD is applicable and thereby open new market segments for DHI.

Model Equations and Discretization

MIKE 21 HD simulates water wave dynamics by solving a set of hyperbolic partial differential equations called shallow water equations which are given as

$$\frac{\partial \zeta}{dt} + \frac{\partial p}{\partial x} + \frac{\partial q}{\partial y} = \frac{\partial d}{\partial t} \tag{1}$$

$$\frac{\partial p}{\partial t} + \frac{\partial}{\partial x}\left(\frac{pp}{h}\right) + \frac{\partial}{\partial y}\left(\frac{pq}{h}\right) + gh\frac{\partial \zeta}{\partial x} + \frac{gp\sqrt{p^2+q^2}}{C^2h^2} = 0 \tag{2}$$

$$\frac{\partial q}{\partial t} + \frac{\partial}{\partial y}\left(\frac{q^2}{h}\right) + \frac{\partial}{\partial x}\left(\frac{pq}{h}\right) + gh\frac{\partial \zeta}{\partial y} + \frac{gq\sqrt{p^2+q^2}}{C^2h^2} = 0 \tag{3}$$

The solution scheme used is the Alternating Direction Implicit (ADI) method, which results in many tri-diagonal matrix systems, which have to be solved efficiently for each time step.

---

[*] We want to thank Allan Peter Engsig-Karup, Thomas Clausen and Jesper Grooss for supervision and support throughout the project.
[1] B.Sc. thesis: http://www2.imm.dtu.dk/pubdb/views/publication_details.php?id=6367

R. Keller et al. (Eds.): Facing the Multicore-Challenge III 2012, LNCS 7686, pp. 129–130, 2013.
© Springer-Verlag Berlin Heidelberg 2013

Solution Approach

Two different parallel solution schemes are implemented. The first ($S1$) solves each tri-diagonal system in parallel using a single CUDA thread for each system. This approach use the same tri-diagonal solution algorithm as MIKE 21 HD, the Thomas algorithm. The other solution schemes ($S2$) adds more parallelism into the system by using several threads to solve each system in parallel. In order to do this efficient are several parallel solution algorithms investigated. The focus have been on the Parallel Cyclic Reduction (PCR) algorithm and a hybrid algorithm of Cyclic Reduction (CR) and PCR.

Results

We discover that $S2$ are beneficial for small problems, while $S1$ yields better results for larger systems. We have obtained 42x and 80x speedup in double-precision for $S1$ and $S2$ respectively, compared to a representative sequential C implementation of MIKE 21 HD. For comparison can a 3072×3072 system be solved in double-precision on the GPU twice as fast as a 512×512 system on the CPU. Furthermore, the impact of switching to perform calculation in single-precision have been investigated. This resulted in 145x and 203x speedup for $S1$ and $S2$, respectively. We furthermore achieve near linear scaling when using method $S1$ compared to a quadratic scaling on the CPU.

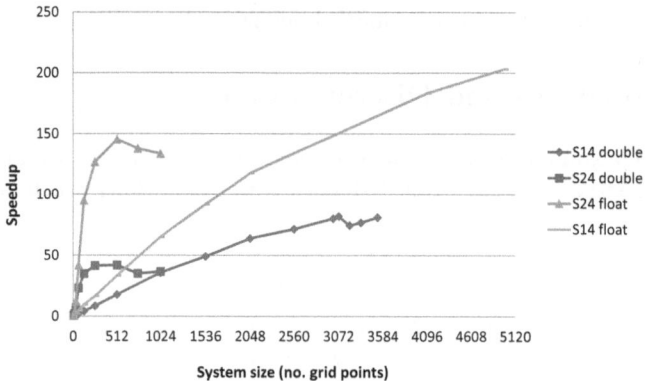

Fig. 1. Speedup of optimized S1 and S2 in single- and double-precision against an implemented CPU version. Result achieved on NVIDIA GeForce GTX 590.

Further Research

An investigating of the precision impact of switching from double- to single-precision. Especially, using mixed-precision in the core math calculation is anticipated to be beneficial without losing to much precision.

GPU-Accelerated and CPU SIMD Optimized Monte Carlo Simulation of ϕ^4 Model

Piotr Bialas, Jakub Kowal, and Adam Strzelecki

Faculty of Physics, Astronomy and Applied Computer Science
Jagiellonian University
ul. Reymonta 4, 30-059 Krakow, Poland

This contribution is concerned with an efficient implementation of the Monte-Carlo simulations of the φ^4 model[1]. The problem is defined as follows: having a vector field φ defined on a regular rectangular two or three dimensional grid we want to generate the field configurations with probability proportional to $\exp(-H(\varphi))$ where $H(\varphi)$ is some function of all the fields φ_i.

The actual generation is done by the mean of the Metropolis algorithm. This amounts to sequentially updating all the points of the lattice. The crucial feature of this algorithm is that the update is local *i.e.* the new value of the field in a given point depends only on the values of fields in the immediate neighborhood of the updated point. In our case this neighborhood is extended compared to usual nearest neighbors (see figure 1 (Right)). The update is random and requires a good source of pseudo-random numbers. We use the Tausworthe RNG[3].

While model is inherently parallelizable, grid points that lie in the same neighborhood cannot be updated together. Taking into account a larger neighborhood means that a simple checkerboard decomposition pattern cannot be used and we have devised a new grid decomposition scheme.

On GPU we adopt the hierarchical scheme from ref. [2] suitably modified to account for bigger neighborhood. We first divide the whole lattice in blocks of 32×32 points. Then we start a kernel that process every forth block (see figure 1). Each block is assigned to a block of 128 threads. First we fetch the values of the fields from global to shared memory (including border points). After that each thread updates one point from the first partition. Then after synchronization, next partition is updated and so on. After processing all eight(2D) or 16 (3D) partitions the kernel writes the shared memory back into global and new kernel is started processing next batch of blocks. Altogether in this way we managed to achieve 0.13 nanoseconds for single lattice field update on *NVIDIA GTX 470*, reaching around 430 Gflops that is 40% of 1088 Gflops peak performance of this device.

In order to provide unbiased CPU vs GPU speed up results we provide multithreaded vectorized CPU implementation. It uses OpenMP for parallel execution, SSE/AVX and compiler vector extensions for vectorization. This implementation does mimic GPU SIMT execution model. The SIMD instructions are used to process four (SSE) or eight (AVX) updates in parallel. We use partitions as on GPU but we use only one level *i.e.* we do not partition the lattice into blocks. However not all scalar *x86* instructions have vector counterparts. In particular direct *XMM*

R. Keller et al. (Eds.): Facing the Multicore-Challenge III 2012, LNCS 7686, pp. 131–132, 2013.

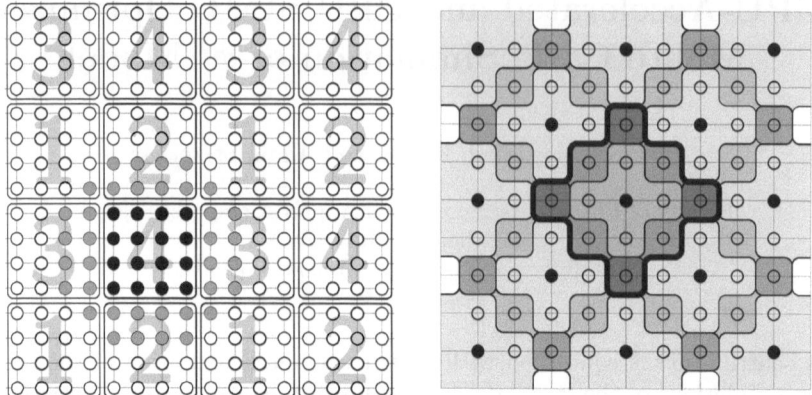

Fig. 1. (Left) The partition of the lattice into blocks. The blocks with same number are processed in parallel by different thread blocks. (Right) Partitioning of the blocks into disjoint sublattices. Thick black line denotes the neighborhood used in updating the center point. Black points are processes in parallel by different threads of the same thread block.

registers gather and scatter and vectorized integer operations for full length AVX 256-bit registers are missing, which makes impossible to port random number generator from 128-bit SSE to 256-bit AVX. Initially planned for AVX standard, these were postponed to AVX2 planned for 2013. As soon AVX2 capable CPU devices appear on the market we plan to revise our evaluation.

Our CPU *OpenMP* and *SSE/AVX* implementation compiled via GCC 4.4 or higher and running on *Intel Core i5 2.5 Ghz* quad core CPU presented 15× performance boost comparing to single threaded scalar code and 3.76 nanoseconds for single lattice field update. Which gives the 15 Gflops that is ~ 10% of the 160 Gflops peak performance of tested i5 CPU. There is no significant increase in performance while switching from SSE to AVX instructions.

This gives around 28× advantage to GPU, which is noticeably less than promised by many publications, however much higher that comes from comparison of tested i5 CPU to *GTX 470*. This can be traced back to 128-bit only *Tausworthe* random number generator implementation and inefficient vector store and load operations (gather/scatter).

References

1. Parisi, G.: Statistical Field Theory, ch. 5. Perseus Books Publishing (1998)
2. Weigel, M.: J. Comput. Phys. 231, 3064 (2012)
3. Howes, L., Thomas, D.: Efficient random number generation and application using CUDA. In: Nguyen, H. (ed.) GPU Gems 3, ch. 37. Addison Wesley (August 2007)

Protable Codes on New HPC Architectures[*]

Mhd. Amer Wafai, Colin W. Glass, and Christoph Niethammer

University of Stuttgart, HLRS,
Nobelstr. 19, 70569 Stuttgart, Germany
{wafai,glass,niethammer}@hlrs.de

1 Introduction

Due to the fast evolution of computer architectures, which tends towards many-core, software has to be constantly optimized or re-written in order to sustain performance.

To avoid re-writing and thus saving time and effort, pragma-based parallel programming models have been introduced. The idea is that developers specify the intrinsic parallelism once and the corresponding compilers take care of the underlying architecture, generating suitable binaries.

Computer architectures, nowadays, come with many cores per chip. For example, the AMD Interlagos comes with 12 cores per chip and each computing node can include multiple chips. Intel Sandy Bridge comes with 8 cores per chip. Moreover recent CPGPU come with thousands of cores, like the NVIDIA GTX 680 which has 1536 computing cores.

In this work the molecular dynamics code CMD is parallelized using different programming models and the results are compared.

2 Pragma-Based Programming Models

GPUs are an attractive choice for many problems because of their high performance and memory bandwidth. To use GPUs, software developers should have detailed knowledge of the underlying GPU architecture and the corresponding programming environment (CUDA, OpenCL ...) which are considered to be hardware-related programming languages. For each new GPU generation, codes need be optimized to achieve good performance. In order to avoid this, pragma-based programming models have been developed. What OpenMP is for the CPU, OpenACC (including HMPP and PGI accelerator) wishes to become for GPU. While pragma-based approaches are simple and powerful, there are limitations to their applicability. The following checklist is a good basis for evaluating the compatibility of a code with OpenACC:

- Profile and analyze the code regarding computationally intensive hotspots.
- If present: check if the hotspot meets the following criteria.

---

[*] This work has been supported by the German Research Foundation (DFG) funding the Sonderforschungsbereich 716 (SFB716) project D.2.

R. Keller et al. (Eds.): Facing the Multicore-Challenge III 2012, LNCS 7686, pp. 133–134, 2013.

- Data structure should not contain pointers.
- Data structure should be structures of array rather than array of structures.
- No function calls within the hotspot.
- No IOs
- No access to global and volatile variables
- The hotspot should have a fixed number of arguments.

If the code passes, chances are very good that it is well suited for porting with OpenACC.

3 Results

In this work, CMD has been parallelized with OpenMP (CPU) and CUDA, OpenACC, HMPP (GPU). OpenACC and HMPP show poor performance due to data transfers between device and host memories. The results clearly indicate that more control of data locality needs to be provided within these approaches.

The CUDA version on GPU is compared to the OpenMP version running on state-of-the-art CPUs. Figure 1 shows that NVIDIA Fermi C2050 outperforms the other hard-ware/parallelization for huge systems (more than 65000 molecules). AMD Interlagos shows a good performance for smaller systems, with degrading performance at larger system sizes, possibly due to data locality. Whereas Sandy bridge shows stable results and outperforms Interlagos at 300,000 molecules.

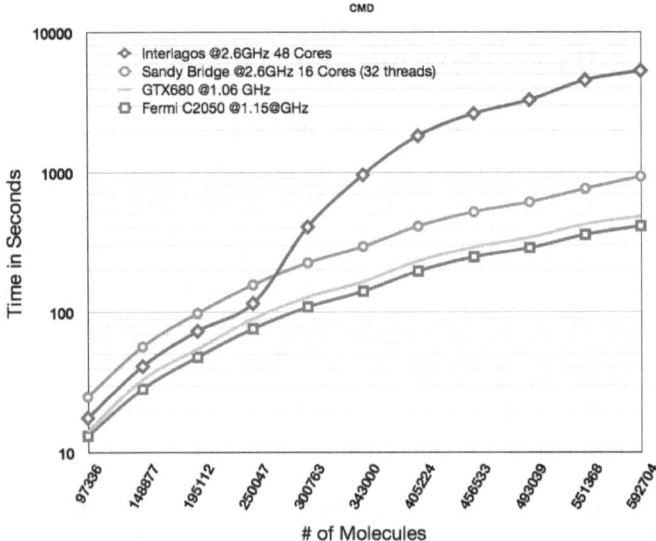

Fig. 1. Time comparison of CMD on many platforms using pragma-based programming models and CUDA

GASPI – A Partitioned Global Address Space Programming Interface

Thomas Alrutz[1], Jan Backhaus[2], Thomas Brandes[3], Vanessa End[1],
Thomas Gerhold[4], Alfred Geiger[1], Daniel Grünewald[5], Vincent Heuveline[6],
Jens Jägersküpper[4], Andreas Knüpfer[7], Olaf Krzikalla[7], Edmund Kügeler[2],
Carsten Lojewski[5], Guy Lonsdale[8], Ralph Müller-Pfefferkorn[7],
Wolfgang Nagel[7], Lena Oden[5], Franz-Josef Pfreundt[5], Mirko Rahn[5],
Michael Sattler[1], Mareike Schmidtobreick[6], Annika Schiller[9],
Christian Simmendinger[1], Thomas Soddemann[3], Godehard Sutmann[9],
Henning Weber[10], and Jan-Philipp Weiss[2]

[1] T-Systems SfR, Stuttgart & Göttingen
[2] DLR, Institut für Antriebstechnik, Köln
[3] Fraunhofer SCAI, Sankt Augustin
[4] DLR, Institut für Aerodynamik und Strömungstechnik, Braunschweig & Göttingen
[5] Fraunhofer ITWM, Kaiserslautern
[6] Engineering Math. and Comp. Lab (EMCL), Karlsruher Institut für Technologie
[7] Zentrum für Informationsdienste und Hochleistungsrechnen (ZIH), TU Dresden
[8] Scapos AG, Sankt Augustin
[9] Forschungszentrum Jülich
[10] Deutscher Wetterdienst (DWD), Offenbach

At the threshold to exascale computing, limitations of the MPI programming model become more and more pronounced. HPC programmers have to design codes that can run and scale on systems with hundreds of thousands of cores. Setting up accordingly many communication buffers, point-to-point communication links, and using bulk-synchronous communication phases is contradicting scalability in these dimensions. Moreover, the reliability of upcoming systems will worsen.

GASPI, a Global Address Space Programming Interface, provides a partitioned global address space (PGAS) API. It is currently worked out in a German BMBF-funded project[1] with partners at T-Systems SfR, Fraunhofer ITWM, Fraunhofer SCAI, KIT, TU Dresden, scapos AG, FZ Jülich, DLR and DWD – see http://www.gaspi.de. The new GASPI specification focuses on three key objectives: scalability, flexibility and fault tolerance.

GASPI offers a small, yet powerful API based on asynchronous and one-sided communication routines, synchronisation primitives, and communication collectives. These routines give fine-grained control over one-sided read and write communication primitives, global atomics, passive receives, communication groups and communication queues. All these features allow to break up

---

[1] The GASPI project is funded by the German Federal Minstry for Education and Research (BMBF) with funding code 01IH11007.

R. Keller et al. (Eds.): Facing the Multicore-Challenge III 2012, LNCS 7686, pp. 135–136, 2013.

bulk-synchronous communication and enable new algorithmic strategies and implementation approaches. By these means, GASPI aims to initiate a paradigm shift from bulk-synchronous two-sided communication patterns towards an asynchronous communication and execution model. However, this step requires a sophisticated rearrangement of the communication patterns in most of the algorithms and applications.

GASPI uses one-sided RDMA-driven communication and is implemented on top of the IB-Verbs layer and the OFED stack. This approach guarantees best performance and wide-spread portability. While its fault tolerant mechanisms offer new capabilities to deal with node failures, the concept of memory segments allows to treat heterogeneous platforms. Fault tolerance is accomplished by providing a timeout value as an argument to all non-local communication calls. The health status of each communication partner can be checked at any time. This model also allows to dynamically resize the number of active nodes. By its lean and versatile body GASPI aims at scaling towards the exascale age.

The GASPI project promotes the dissemination and visibility of the API by means of dedicated projects in performance-critical application domains ranging from basic routines in sparse and dense linear algebra and high level solvers to computational fluid dynamics, turbo-machinery, weather and climate prediction, oil and gas applications, and molecular dynamics.

This short talk and poster outlines the basic concepts of GASPI and puts light on the paradigm shift from bulk-synchronous two-sided communication patterns towards a scalable and asynchronous communication and execution model.

Parallel Fully Adaptive Tsunami Simulations

Michael Bader, Alexander Breuer, and Martin Schreiber

Department of Informatics,
Boltzmannstrasse 3, 85748 Garching, Germany
{bader,breuera,martin.schreiber}@in.tum.de
http://www5.in.tum.de/

Abstract. We present our framework for parallel simulations of hyperbolic partial differential equations on triangular grids. As a proof-of-concept, we implemented the shallow water equations using a finite volume method together with the Riemann solvers of LeVeque and George [1] and multi-resolution geoinformation datasets. The results show a parallel fully adaptive simulation applied to the 2011 Tohoku tsunami field-benchmark.

Efficient adaptivity is realized by grid-traversals which follow the Sierpiński space filling curve. A stack- and stream-based approach accounts for locality and cache efficiency by arranging the data exchange among cells. For tsunamis we used the normalized height mass exchange as adaptivity criterion in every time step. Therefore, if a certain refinement threshold is exceeded, the corresponding cells are refined by newest vertex bisection. Values falling below a coarsening threshold result in a merge of the respective triangles.

Our parallelization approach is designed to tolerate unpredictable workload per cell, caused, for example, by loading bathymetry data during refinement or flux solvers with computations depending on specific classifications of the Riemann problem. We address load balancing by

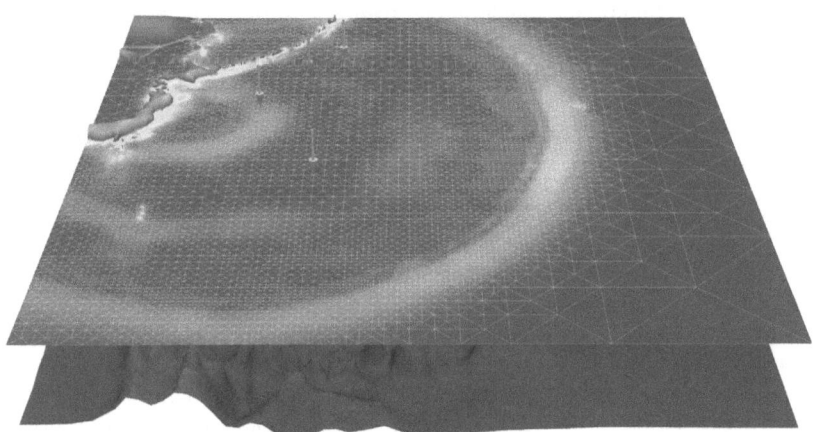

Fig. 1. Tsunami simulation state 10000 seconds after the earthquake. Bouy placements are marked with arrows.

R. Keller et al. (Eds.): Facing the Multicore-Challenge III 2012, LNCS 7686, pp. 137–138, 2013.
© Springer-Verlag Berlin Heidelberg 2013

creating by far more work units than there are cores available on shared memory systems. This approach is realized by massive tree-splittings of the mesh along the Sierpiński curve, which gives one work unit per split sub-tree. As a result the framework is able to execute these work units in an arbitrary order using OpenMP or TBB tasking constructs (See [2]).

The results show that the fully adaptive simulation provides benchmark solutions close to the ones achieved on regular grids with a substantial gain in terms of performance. An objective and detailed analysis of the error with field as well as analytical benchmarks is part of our ongoing research. Since there are many ways to implement the presented algorithm, a publication of source-code seems to be mandatory. Therefore we released the source-code at `http://www5.in.tum.de/sierpi/`.

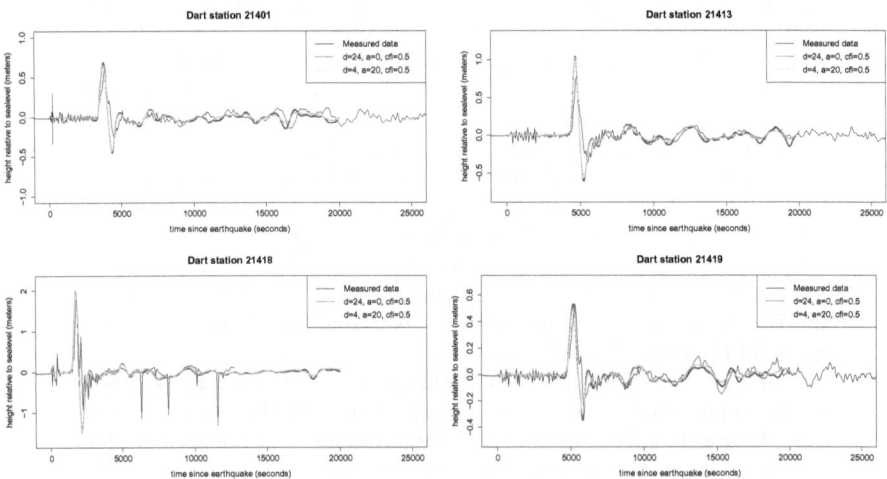

Fig. 2. Elevation of bouys for simulation on regular grid (red) and adaptive grid (blue)

Acknowledgement. This work was supported by the German Research Foundation (DFG) as part of the Transreg. Collab. Res. Centre "Invasive Computing" (SFB/TR 89).

References

1. George, D.L.: Augmented riemann solvers for the shallow water equations over variable topography with steady states and inundation. J. Comput. Phys. 227(6), 3089–3113 (2008)
2. Schreiber, M., Bungartz, H.J., Bader, M.: Shared memory parallelization of fully-adaptive simulations using a dynamic tree-split and -join approach. In: Proceedings of HiPC 2012 (2012)

Implementation of Stable Skew–Symmetric Matrix Factorization for Fermi GPUs Using CUDA

Neven Krajina

Department of Mathematics, Faculty of Science, University of Zagreb
neven.krajina@gmail.com

Although not as common as symmetric matrices, skew-symmetric matrices arise in practice in fields such as physics, biology and economy, as well as a first step in solving the skew-symmetric eigenvalue problem. It was shown in [1] that every skew-symmetric matrix A admits a stable factorization of the form $P^T A P = G J G^T$, where P is a permutation matrix, G is a lower-triangular matrix and J is a block-diagonal matrix with 2×2 matrices $J_2 = \begin{pmatrix} 0 & -1 \\ 1 & 0 \end{pmatrix}$ and zeros on the diagonal. To obtain this factorization, we proceed as follows; first, to fulfill the requirements of numerical stability, we need to find the maximal value x of A located at (r, c), and permute the rows and columns of A so that $(P^T A P)_{21} = a_{rc}$. If $a_{rc} = 0$, the algorithm runs to completion with trapezoidal G. Otherwise, we set $P = (2r)(1c)$ if $r \neq 1$ or $P = (2c)(1c)$ if $r = 1$. If A is partitioned as

$$A = \begin{pmatrix} A_{11} & -A_{21}^T \\ A_{21} & A_{22} \end{pmatrix},$$

where A_{11} is 2×2 matrix, it can be factored as

$$A = \begin{pmatrix} \sqrt{x}I & 0 \\ \sqrt{x}A_{21}A_{11}^{-1} & I \end{pmatrix} \begin{pmatrix} J_2 & 0 \\ 0 & A_{22} + A_{21}A_{11}^{-1}A_{21}^T \end{pmatrix} \begin{pmatrix} \sqrt{x}I & -\sqrt{x}A_{11}^{-1}A_{21}^T \\ 0 & I \end{pmatrix}.$$

It can be easily shown that $(A_{21}A_{11}^{-1})^T = -A_{11}^{-1}A_{21}^T$ and that $A_{22} + A_{21}A_{11}^{-1}A_{21}^T$, the so-called Schur complement, is again skew-symmetric matrix. We can thus proceed with the factorization of Schur's complement in the same manner. In the end, we have

$$A = P_1 G_1 \cdots P_k G_k J G_k^T P_k^T \cdots G_1^T P_1^T,$$

where P_i is a permutation matrix, and G_i is a lower-triangular,

$$G_i = \begin{pmatrix} I_{2i-2} & & \\ & \sqrt{x_i}I_2 & \\ & C_i & I_{n-2i} \end{pmatrix}.$$

If we want to interchange matrices G_i and P_{i+1}, we have to multiply the C_i block with the transpose of P_{i+1} from the left. Also, multiplying matrices G_i and G_{i+1} results in matrix

$$G_i G_{i+1} = \begin{pmatrix} I_{2i-2} & & & \\ & \sqrt{x_i}I_2 & & \\ & C_{1i} & \sqrt{x_{i+1}}I_2 & \\ & C_{2i} & C_{i+1} & I_{n-2i-2} \end{pmatrix}.$$

R. Keller et al. (Eds.): Facing the Multicore-Challenge III 2012, LNCS 7686, pp. 139–140, 2013.
© Springer-Verlag Berlin Heidelberg 2013

The algorithm for factorization of A is as follows.

$stride \leftarrow 0$
while $stride \leq n - 2$ **do**
    find the maximum entry x of matrix A
    if $x = 0$ **then**
        break;
    end if
    permute rows and columns of A so that $A_{21} = x$
        and permute columns of preceding G factors
    calculate the Schur complement
    calculate $\sqrt{x} A_{21} A_{11}^{-1}$
    $A \leftarrow A_{3:n,3:n}$
    $stride \leftarrow stride + 2$
end while

All of the steps mentioned can be done in parallel, but have to be done in exactly the specified order. Finding the value and indices of maximum element can be done by reduction. To permute rows and columns, we can use a kernel that does one transposition at a time. Since we only store the lower part of matrix A, we have to apply both row and column transposition at once (see Fig. 1).

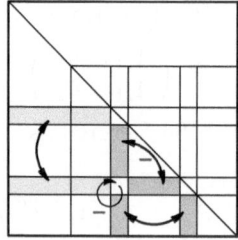

Fig. 1. Transpositions performed on rows and columns at once. Minus below the arrow indicates that elements need to have their sign changed before swapping.

Since $A_{11}^{-1} = \begin{pmatrix} 0 & x^{-1} \\ -x^{-1} & 0 \end{pmatrix}$, $A_{21} A_{11}^{-1}$ sums down to swapping columns of A_{21} and multiplying the first one with $-x^{-1}$ and the second with x^{-1}. From the definition of Schur complement, we can see that we have to calculate $A_{ij} = A_{ij} + (A_{i1}A_{j2} - A_{j1}A_{i2})/x$, where $3 \leq i < j \leq N$, which can highly benefit from data reuse. At the end, the only bottleneck of this algorithm is checking whether the maximum is equal to zero, since we have to copy its value to host, but this is something we cannot avoid.

Reference

1. Bunch, J.R.: A Note on the Stable Decomposition of Skew–Symmetric Matrices. Math. Comp. 38(158), 475–479 (1982)

The IMData Approach to Accelerate Data Intensive Workloads

Marcus Völp, Nils Asmussen, and Hermann Härtig

Technische Universität Dresden, Dresden, Germany,
{voelp,nils,haertig}@os.inf.tu-dresden.de

Abstract. Having started operational work in August 2012, the ESF young researcher group IMData seeks to develop new integrated mechanisms for accelerating data intensive workloads in heterogeneous many-core systems. This extended abstract and the accompanying poster summarizes the observations that motivate the project and the approach we are going to take.

Accelerator architectures such as GPGPUs, IBM Cell, and signal processors achieve their performance and energy advantages by offering a vast number of very simple and specialized cores. The tremendous core count of these architectures stems in part from a sacrifice of even the most fundamental hardware features that interacting applications and operating system kernels require. However, for not frequently interacting workloads, this tradeoff pays off in gigantic speedups.

Comparing different Alpha generations, Kumar et al. [2] already found that little less than five simple cores occupy the same area as a large out-of-order core motivating a combination of few big and many little cores in single-ISA heterogeneous systems. However, the chip area required to support an operating system suprised us. We configured two Tensilica Xtensa cores [1] for a 400MHz 65nm Low Power Process Technology using the Xtensa Xplorer Tools. One of it is used in the Tomahawk MPSoC accelerator for Software Defined Radio [3]. The other has all features enabled that modern general purpose operating systems require (interrupts, exceptions, MMU, ...). Adding OS support to a core (notice, we stick to the same ISA and application-level execution profile) increases the core's area by almost 100% from 0.095 mm^2 to 0.171 mm^2 (excluding caches). Therefore, just by removing hardware support for the operating system, thread parallelism could be doubled. Additionally, replacing the 32 KB tightly coupled SRAM with two 16 KB caches for instructions and data, multiplies chip area by almost another factor of two (from 0.299 mm^2 to 0.516 mm^2).

The research direction, which we derive from this obseration is therefore how to enable complex, interactive and data intensive workloads on accelerator platforms without sacrificing the benefits obtained from hardware specialization. The immediate questions that arise are: "How can we control applications without having full hardware support for running an operating system kernel beneath them?", "How can applications on different cores interact with each other?",

R. Keller et al. (Eds.): Facing the Multicore-Challenge III 2012, LNCS 7686, pp. 141–142, 2013.

"How can they synchronize on shared data and communicate results?", "How can critical parts of applications be isolated?", and finally, "How can all this be achieved without reintroducing the area-expensive hardware mechanisms of general purpose architectures?".

At the hardware level, the starting point will be the Tomahawk processor built by TU Dresden's mobile communications group. On top of it, the L4 microkernels NOVA and Fiasco.OC from TUD's operating systems group will provide efficient and light-weight communication and synchronization mechanisms to the data intensive applications, which we draw from in-memory databases and from other research fields of TUD's database and data analytics group. In addition, our probablistic model checking group will support us by looking into new techniques for investigating functional and non-functional properties of our algorithms and system components.

References

1. Tensilica, Inc., Xtensa customizable processors (2011),
   http://www.tensilica.com/products/xtensa-customizable.htm
2. Kumar, R., Farkas, K.I., Jouppi, N.P., Ranganathan, P., Tullsen, D.M.: Single-ISA Heterogeneous Multi-Core Architectures: The Potential for Processor Power Reduction. In: Proceedings of the 36th Annual IEEE/ACM International Symposium on Microarchitecture, MICRO 36, p. 81. IEEE Computer Society, Washington, DC (2003), http://dl.acm.org/citation.cfm?id=956417.956569
3. Limberg, T., Winter, M., Bimberg, M., Klemm, R., Tavares, M.B., Ahlendorf, H., Matus, E., Fettweis, G., Eisenreich, H., Ellguth, G., Schlüssler, J.: A Heterogeneous MPSoC with Hardware Supported Dynamic Task Scheduling for Software Defined Radio. In: 46th Design Automation Conference (DAC 2009), San Francisco, USA, pp. 267–317 (2009)

PRAgMaTIc – Parallel Anisotropic Adaptive Mesh Toolkit

Georgios Rokos[1] and Gerard Gorman[2]

[1] Software Performance Optimisation Group, Department of Computing,
Imperial College London, South Kensington Campus, London SW7 2AZ, UK
georgios.rokos09@imperial.ac.uk
http://www.doc.ic.ac.uk/~gr409/
[2] Applied Modelling and Computation Group,
Department of Earth Science and Engineering, Imperial College London,
South Kensington Campus, London SW7 2AZ, UK
g.gorman@imperial.ac.uk
http://www3.imperial.ac.uk/people/g.gorman

Abstract. The numerical methods used to model complex geometries required by many scientific applications often favour the use of unstructured meshes and finite element discretisation methods over structured grid alternatives. This flexibility introduces complications, such as the management of mesh quality and additional computational overheads arising from indirect addressing [5]. Using the Finite Element Method for the numerical solution of PDEs, a posteriori error estimations on the PDE solution help evaluate a quality functional [4] and determine the low-quality mesh elements. Mesh adaptivity methods ([3], [1]) provide an important means to control solution error by focusing mesh resolution in regions of the computational domain when and where it is required.

Adaptive algorithms are grouped into two main categories, h-adaptivity and r-adaptivity algorithms. The first category contains techniques which try to adapt the mesh by changing its topology. This can be done by removing existing mesh elements, a technique known as coarsening, increasing local mesh resolution by adding new elements, a procedure called refinement, or replacing a group of elements with a different group, which can be achieved through swapping. The second group of adaptive algorithms encompasses a variety of vertex smoothing techniques, all of which leave mesh topology intact and only attempt to improve quality by relocating mesh vertices. Algorithm 1 demonstrates the general procedure for the solution of a PDE on an adaptive mesh.

A problem is said to be anisotropic if its solution exhibits directional dependencies. An anisotropic mesh contains elements which have some suitable orientation. In this case, the error estimation is given in the form of a metric tensor field $M(\mathbf{x})$, i.e. a tensor which, for each point in the domain, represents the desired length and orientation of a mesh edge containing this point. Adapting a mesh so that it distributes the error uniformly over the whole mesh is equivalent to constructing a uniform mesh consisting of equilateral triangles with respect to the non-Euclidean metric $M(\mathbf{x})$.

R. Keller et al. (Eds.): Facing the Multicore-Challenge III 2012, LNCS 7686, pp. 143–144, 2013.
© Springer-Verlag Berlin Heidelberg 2013

Algorithm 1. General algorithm for the adaptive solution of PDEs

Mesh $\mathcal{M}_0 \leftarrow$ initial auto-generated mesh
solve PDE on $\mathcal{M}_0$
$\mathcal{E}_0 \leftarrow$ a posteriori estimation of solution error
while $\mathcal{E}_i \geq predefined\_tolerance$ **do**
    compute metric tensor field $\mathcal{T}_i$ from $\mathcal{E}_i$
    perform initial coarsening on $\mathcal{M}_i$
    repeat
        perform refinement on $\mathcal{M}_i$
        perform coarsening on $\mathcal{M}_i$
        perform swapping on $\mathcal{M}_i$
        $L_{max} \leftarrow$ longest mesh edge
    until (pre-defined number of iterations is reached) **or**($L_{max} - \sqrt{2.0} < 0.01$)
    perform smoothing on $\mathcal{M}_i$
    solve PDE on $\mathcal{M}_i$
    $\mathcal{E}_i \leftarrow$ a posteriori estimation of solution error

PRAgMaTIc is an open-source mesh adaptivity framework, built with large-scale multiprocessing in mind. It implements coarsening, refinement and swapping alongside an optimisation-based vertex smoothing algorithm proposed by Freitag et al. [1]. Parallel execution is based on an older parallel framework [2], improved through a novel approach which combines the idea of mesh partitioning with low-level intervention in mesh data structures in order to achieve good data locality, high performance and thread safety. PRAgMaTIc supports both NUMA (via OpenMP) and distributed-memory (via MPI) systems. Current work is on improving performance and scalability of adaptive algorithms. Support for CUDA/OpenCL is planned for the near future. PRAgMaTIc can be downloaded from Launchpad under the BSD licence: https://launchpad.net/pragmatic.

References

1. Freitag, L., Jones, M., Plassmann, P.: An efficient parallel algorithm for mesh smoothing. In: Proceedings of the 4th International Meshing Roundtable, Sandia National Laboratories, pp. 47–58. Citeseer (1995)
2. Freitag, L.F., Jones, M.T., Plassmann, P.E.: The Scalability Of Mesh Improvement Algorithms. In: IMA Volumes in Mathematics and its Applications, pp. 185–212. Springer (1998)
3. Li, X., Shephard, M., Beall, M.: 3d anisotropic mesh adaptation by mesh modification. Computer Methods in Applied Mechanics and Engineering 194(48-49), 4915–4950 (2005)
4. Vasilevskii, Y., Lipnikov, K.: An adaptive algorithm for quasioptimal mesh generation. Computational Mathematics and Mathematical Physics 39(9), 1468–1486 (1999)
5. Piggott, M.D., Farrell, P.E., Wilson, C.R., Gorman, G.J., Pain, C.C.: Anisotropic mesh adaptivity for multi-scale ocean modelling. Philosophical Transactions of the Royal Society A: Mathematical, Physical and Engineering Sciences 367(1907), 4591–4611 (1907)

Author Index